Managing Organizationa

C000102541

RIOT! Routledge Studies in Innovation, Organization and Technology

Managing Organizational Ecologies

Space, Management and Organizations

**Edited by Keith Alexander
and Ilfryn Price**

Routledge
Taylor & Francis Group

NEW YORK   LONDON

First published 2012
by Routledge
711 Third Avenue, New York, NY 10017

Simultaneously published in the UK
by Routledge
2 Park Square, Milton Park, Abingdon, Oxon OX14 4RN

First issued in paperback 2017

*Routledge is an imprint of the Taylor & Francis Group,
an informa business*

© 2012 Taylor & Francis

The right of Keith Alexander and Ilfryn Price to be identified as the
authors of the editorial material, and of the authors for their individual
chapters, has been asserted in accordance with sections 77 and 78 of the
Copyright, Designs and Patents Act 1988.

All rights reserved. No part of this book may be reprinted or reproduced or
utilised in any form or by any electronic, mechanical, or other means, now
known or hereafter invented, including photocopying and recording, or in
any information storage or retrieval system, without permission in writing
from the publishers.

Trademark Notice: Product or corporate names may be trademarks or
registered trademarks, and are used only for identification and explanation
without intent to infringe.

Library of Congress Cataloging-in-Publication Data
    Managing organizational ecologies : space, management and
organization / edited by Keith Alexander and Ilfryn Price.
        p. cm. — (Routledge studies in innovation, organization and
technology ; 22)
    Includes bibliographical references and index.
  1. Facility management—Environmental aspects.   2. Work
environment.   3. Office layout.   4. Building layout.   I. Alexander,
Keith, 1949–   II. Price, Ilfryn, 1949–
    TS177.M36 2012
    658.2—dc23
    2011048275

ISBN 13: 978-1-138-10731-1 (pbk)
ISBN 13: 978-0-415-89699-3 (hbk)

Typeset in Sabon
by IBT Global.

Contents

PART II

Social Constructs and Contradictions

PART III

Management Issues

PART IV

Applications in Practice

Figures and Tables

FIGURES

TABLES

Forewords

The book aims to reach three communities: those managing workplaces strategically and researchers or educators in both business and the built environment. A representative of each offers their contribution.

ALAN GREEN

It was whilst listening to a conference talk by If[1] Price in 2000 that I was first introduced to the power of workspace to influence the behavior and performance of individuals, of teams and of organizations and to some of the theory that underpins that power. I had had an early insight as manager of an engineering R&D team, when I saw firsthand the dramatic effect on morale of a move into a light, modern lab and office environment. But in 2000 I was leading the move of an established knowledge-based organization, a UK intelligence agency, into new accommodations. We were faced with an existential challenge at the end of the Cold War and needed to transform the whole organization in order to address the challenges of the new international paradigm. We had the opportunity, through PFI, to transform the workspace at the same time, and we chose to use that as an enabler and catalyst for transforming our structure, processes, culture and behavior. We adopted some of the modern design approaches described here by Myerson, and developed new relationships between our various operational functions and our internal and outsourced facility managers. The program was successful and allowed us to respond effectively and promptly to the unpredictable security and intelligence challenges of the twenty-first century. In so doing we engaged closely with academics and consultants, with the architects and the construction team, with the future facility operators and service providers, with IT and their suppliers, with the strategic leaders and organizational developers, with HR and with managers and, crucially, with the whole workforce to understand how our organization could function much more effectively in new ways, with new partners, in a new and very different workspace. It was an example of a vigorous organizational ecology in action, albeit a project-based, time-bounded one. And it worked.

From that experience I am confident that, both strategically and operationally, FM can enable (or constrain) and catalyze (but not determine) transformational change in behavior at the personal, group and organizational levels, and thus be a strategic factor in superior organizational performance. But it cannot do it alone: it is the conjunction of FM, information and communications technology, human resources and organizational development that delivers effect. It is a leader's role to establish that healthy organizational ecology within your organization and with its partners.

This is an important book. It develops stimulating ideas of organizational ecology, but crucially it brings together thinkers and professionals from a wide variety of disciplines in a complementary way that enhances their individual contributions. And practitioners can use those ideas to inform their understanding of the factors and dynamics of organizational performance, and to craft the agile, responsive, high-performing organizations that will be the survivors in the turbulent, unpredictable and competitive world that we all face.

HUW MORRIS

This is an excellent book for which there is a clear need for in the business and management and construction management fields of teaching and research. It brings together a number of leading researchers in the field to give their different perspectives on the challenges of conceptualizing the task of Facilities Management and the means by which built environments are constructed and managed.

The editors are leaders in their field and they have secured important contributions from Facilities Management, organization studies and business and management. The book is less managerial and structural or functional in orientation than most competitor texts and offers a more nuanced set of chapters that use descriptive analytical, social constructivist and critical perspectives to comment on Facilities Management and space use in practice.

Managing organizational ecologies seeks bridges between, on the one hand, construction and Facilities Management focused on building provision and, on the other, business and management and organization studies. In so doing it contributes greatly to our understandings of how space and the built environment are constructed and managed in policy and practice in the UK and elsewhere. This often overlooked subject is of great importance to managers and the building and construction professionals who work with them.

WIM PULLEN

When Keith and Ilfryn invited me to write a foreword there was not one moment of hesitation. First thing I want to say is that these two men are—even though very experienced in the academic thinking about FM-very open-minded. Almost all conversations I can recall at least comprised the question or the attitude of willingness to understand. While Facilities Managers are known as doers and problem solvers, both Ilfryn and Keith tried to grasp the meaning of space, services and workplaces for the end users and their managers, for their students and academic colleagues.

Second is my appreciation for their effort to bring together contributions of other like-minded authors in this volume: like-minded in the sense that although they come from different backgrounds, they all were willing to spend time to write down their observations, beliefs, theories and research outcomes. Diversity rules in this book. There is a lot to learn because of the different perspectives.

Yet, and this is my third point, I learned by browsing the different chapters that if we one day will fully understand the interaction between people, their work and their workplace environments that does not mean we will be able to manage these elements and their interaction.

Finally—Bring Your Own—is a hype. This should apply also to the readers of this book: bring your own reflections, thoughts and stories. Sharing them not only imparts richer (academic) understanding. It makes it also bearable that utopia—this aforementioned "one day"—will probably never be there.

NOTES

1. Ilfryn's usual nickname

Acknowledgments

If any one individual was a, perhaps inadvertent, catalyst for this book it is Wim Pullen of the Centre for People and Buildings in Delft. In the planning for the 2009 EuroFM Research Conference he invited a wider theoretical engagement. Others within that network, who perhaps represented a dominant, structural-functional conversation within FM, objected. Ilfryn responded with an abstract on practical postmodernism, FM and socially constructed realities, inspired by earlier contributions to a Salford, UK, symposium on theory in the built environment. Later that year, over a coffee in a listed and renovated former cotton mill in Manchester (the world's first industrial city) Keith suggested we develop the theme into a book.

Contributions come from many who have inspired us and/or worked with us over the 20-odd years we have both been academics in FM, variously in business and 'built environment' schools. Of the countless inspirational academics we have worked with we acknowledge the debt to two in particular—to Tom Markus, whose work created the foundations for considering buildings as social objects, and to Franklin Becker's insights into organizations as ecologies, which influenced the early development of FM. The book serves as a reminder of these important beginnings and an encouragement to reconsider these basic tenets in managing creative and innovative environments for the organizations of tomorrow.

It was whilst Keith was working with Tom Markus in the Building Performance Research Unit at Strathclyde University that his interest in building performance developed. The early work laid the foundations for a leading involvement in the emerging field of FM and for the creation of CFM almost 30 years ago. Franklin Becker, Frank Duffy, Mike Joroff, Ceri Davies and Bernard Williams had a major influence in those early years, but it has been the five generations of CFM research teams in Glasgow and Manchester that have enabled the contribution and recognition to grow and deserve credit.

Ilfryn's ideas on organizational ecologies and space began when he was part of the management team setting up the first Western office in Guangzhou PRC in 1983. He was introduced to FM 10 years later by Gerry Barron-Fox (ex–Herman Miller), Fari Akhlagi and Tony Thompson. His wider interests in organizational ecology have also benefitted especially from discussions over the years with David Smith, Lily Evans, Ray Shaw, Michael Lissack, Ian McCarthy, Andrew Lord, Tudor Rickards, Geetha Narayan, Jameson Gill and Rory Ridley-Duff. Finally, Kate Distin, you were kind enough to acknowledge me as an inspiration for *Organisational Evolution*. Here, for me, is what you started.

Introduction

Space, Management and Organizations

Keith Alexander and Ilfryn Price

In his influential writing, Thomas Markus (1993) argued that buildings are usually treated as art, technical or investment objects, rarely as social objects. For him, whilst form and space are permanent, function as 'the social practice of use' is inscribed into the building and can change. The implication is that buildings are in this sense shaped by their users, by occupants and visitors in the past, and by us as soon as we arrive. A building is not so much a product as a process and a constantly unfolding narrative. We know of no evidence that Tom Peters read Markus but he likewise argued (1992, p. 413):

> In fact, space management may well be the most ignored—and most powerful—tool for inducing culture change, speeding up innovation projects, and enhancing the learning process in far-flung organizations. While we fret ceaselessly about facilities issues such as office square footage allotted to various ranks, we all but ignore the key strategic issue—the parameters of intermingling.

This book was born out of our shared observation that physical space could indeed induce change, speed up innovation and enhance learning, not only in offices, but also in classrooms, hospitals and communities but only if the narratives (*sensu* Markus & Cameron, 2002) develop differently. Managers of the organizations concerned may not see the potential, but, in general, they are not given the message by those who provide and manage the space concerned. Equally space is not, in general, part of the research and educational agenda of the relevant academic groups.

In the last 30 years the function of space provision has badged itself as Facility or Facilities Management. The difference is a historical accident (Price, Ch. 7), and we will henceforth simply say FM. Despite the intentions of its pioneers, such as Fritz Steele and Franklin Becker, organizational and community results do not even loom large in FM research and education. Markus's and Peters's criticisms remain valid.

We hope this volume will build some conceptual bridges between the managers, their FMs and their respective educators. Contributors stem from three broad fields. Some are organization and management theorists giving one or both our twin themes of ecology and space their attention. Others are scholars in the broad field of the built environment where, in the main, construction is treated as physical rather than social. Last, and as inspiration rather than least, are people who, as managers, have used physical spaces as organizational enablers of strategic change. They are the exception rather than the rule. Most Facility or Facilities Managers (FMs) think more of building operations than of business results and managers/users remain unaware of the latent potential of space. Their respective narratives are as divided as those described by Donald (1994).

FM as a discipline emerged in the US in the decade before Peters wrote *Liberation Management* and claimed early successes impacting organizations. It has since become global while expanding in scope and diluting in impact. It has embraced ever-more building services as advertised by providers and commentators, yet its professional and research press shows little concern with the results for the organizations who occupy particular facilities or the communities they serve. We hope here to remind FM of its roots and remind organizations, in the broadest sense, and those who theorize concerning them of space. We asked our contributors to stimulate debate and challenge various aspects of predominant thinking. The result is our call for, and alert to the opportunities in, a fundamental reevaluation of practice.

Research in management and organizational theory generally neglects space in organizations. It is left implicit to practice as something 'limiting' without actually 'existing.' By making *the case for space* we postulate the emergence of a spatial and ecological theory of organizations that markedly breaks with the resource-based view common in organizational theory and practice. Organizational space describes the feedback between the spatial environment and the health, mind and behavior of humans in and around an organization. It is a field of research in which interdisciplinarity must be central. It draws from management, organization and architecture (Dale & Burrell, 2008); environmental psychology (Evans & Mitchell, 1998); social medicine (Macintyre, Ellaway & Cummins 2002); and spatial science (Festinger, Schachter & Back, 1950). In essence, it could be regarded as a special field of expertise of organization studies and change management applied to architecture.

However the scientific field of organizational space (Kornberger & Clegg, 2004; Clegg & Kornberger, 2006; Dale & Burrell, 2008; Tissen & Lekanne Deprez, 2008) should be distinguished from social architecture in which the development of information and communication technologies is central. Until recently organizational science regarded concepts of spatiality and space as ideas with little practical relevance, although Kornberger and Clegg did introduce the generative building locating it metaphorically at the edge of chaos (as, more literally, did Price, 2002), beyond what they saw as architecture as a discourse of order and control—a discourse the prevalence of which we acknowledge but also challenge (see Reflections). Tissen and Lekanne Deprez likewise believe that *spatial organization theory* will enable organizations and allow managers and employees to perform *beyond* existing boundaries and limits, whether perceived or real, structural or incidental, to achieve better results more easily in a complex, volatile and turbulent world (cf. Myerson, Ch. 2). They argue the theory, although emergent, is a way of bringing knowledge, people and technology together in an inherently more effective way than traditional organizational configurations, as the latter requires continuous adaptation through restructuring and change.

Traditional organizational configurations continue to exist in the minds of managers and employees responsible for leading organizational transformation to create agile, 'boundaryless organizations' (Ashkenas, Ulrich, Jick & Kerr, 2002). In practice, they often result in the opposite. The contingencies are the organizational, architectural, technological and natural conditions under which organizations function. In the end they influence the performance of an organization, but first they mix in the intermediates. In this way, humans in and around organizations will, for instance, notice these contingencies and will give them meaning (Clegg & Kornberger, 2006; Van Marrewijk & Yanow, 2010).

The contingencies also influence social contact (Becker, 1981; Steele, 1973) and the functionality of the spatial environment (Sharles, 1923). Subsequently, the intermediates influence different performances, for instance, the health, the mind and the behavior of people in and around organizations. The spatial environment can cause illness, such as with the sick building syndrome (US Environmental Protection Agency, 1991), but it can also positively influence the vitality of people or the recovery after an operation (Ulrich, 1984). The performances can provoke managerial intervention. In turn, these interventions will change the contingencies, and by doing so, change the elements, relations and properties of the conditions under which people function.

STRUCTURE

Part I: Organizational Ecologies

The part explores organizations as ecologies. The term "organizational ecology" was itself coined to capture the fact that all organizations are essentially complex systems characterized by the interdependence of the social and the physical (Becker, 1981). Changes in any one aspect of the system reverberate throughout. Organizational ecology conceptualizes the workplace as a system in which physical design factors both shape and are shaped by work processes, the organization's culture, workforce demographics and information technologies.

Price places Becker's coining of the term within the context of theories of evolution by selection, traceable to Darwin himself and developed in different directions by schools of human ecology, scholars of population ecology and a more recent resurgence in ecological interpretations of socially constructed modes of thought. Myerson explores the impact on the ecologies of large organizations that have been driven, in the last decade, to explore more adaptive physical settings. Vischer calls on organizations and their FMs to rediscover their role in facilitating the emergence of human capital. Hudson's chapter, via media representations of space, then Hoffmann, Munthe-Kaas and Elle's, via the wider movement for creative urban spaces, both argue for the introduction or reintroduction of creativity into the workplace. The latter chapter in particular explicitly positions FM within the social sciences. Beard continues the theme, suggesting greater consideration of both the ecological and spatial dynamics of learning and information processing.

Part II: Social Constructs and Contradictions

The part explores resulting contradictions that need to be addressed by those responsible for the contribution a facility makes to an organization. Price explores the history of FM's global spread, arguing that as the term has replicated both geographically and content-wise it has lost both specificity and strategic content. George Cairns, who was one of the first scholars to address the need to consider the philosophical foundations for research and practice in FM, revisits the area, arguing for *phronēsis*, or practical wisdom, and questioning the methodological orthodoxy that seeks to label organizational research as either realist/positivist/quantitative or relativist/qualitative. Lindahl, Hansen and Alexander elaborate on the need to bring both into evaluations of a building's usability; a term that, like FM 30-odd years ago, crossed from the world of information systems to that of the built environment. Coenen and von Felten suggest a truly service-oriented conception of FM, thinking of various 'customers' constructs rather than simply delivering a serviced building.

Stuart describes a practical example of such an approach, showing the greater value achievable when a workspace was truly developed with business intent. Yet again he reprises a point lost on FM as it developed. Becker, Quinn, Rappaport and Sims (1994) distinguished business- and cost-driven workspaces 15 years ago and ECHQ[1] has arguably recaptured an even older emphasis on movement and learning (cf. Beard, Ch. 6). It has also dramatically rebalanced the space allocated to 'desks' as opposed to the staff and customer experience. Finally, by reference to realist ethnographic studies, Ellison and Flowers question whether the functional and expert approach to facilities supply actually delivers successful interorganizational relationships of the kind that it falls to FM to broker.

Part III: Management Issues

The part raises management issues that arise from considering organizations as complex ecologies and addresses the implications for practicing FMs and their education. The chapters highlight the need for engagement, effective communication and relationship management—processes that require awareness of, and changes to, prevailing social constructs. Alexander introduces concepts of value co-creation and refers to recent work on creating shared value in the civic economy. He draws from case studies of values-based organizations seeking to add social value and work from business economics and service marketing to argue for FM to be considered as a value-based service system. Michell broadens the view by focusing on communities and considers FM as a social enterprise using the case of townships in Cape Town, South Africa, to argue for a socially inclusive view of FM. She proposes that engaged, community-based FM in disadvantaged neighborhoods is critical to their regeneration. Bull and Kortens consider strategies for communication by FM in a corporate setting. Specifically they contrast an example of successful workplace change with one where poor communication correlated with diminished staff loyalty. Concluding the part, Roper turns to the educational implications for FM of a social constructivist view. She proposes the changes required in education to provide a solid grounding in social construction as an important perspective in FM and suggests that the concepts of social dynamics in workplace settings are primary improvements to FM education.

Part IV: Applications in Practice

This final part provides practical examples of organizational and management concepts in commercial office environments and educational, healthcare, industrial and community settings. Haynes discusses how office space can impact on creativity, knowledge creation and transfer through enhanced interactions. He explores the relationships between office space and its occupants' behavior and shows how linkages are made between office nodes and social networks. Informal interactions form an integral component of the "connected workplace." Thomas addresses the challenges of creating effective learning environments. She identifies the key factors increasing and adapting learning environments to achieve positive outcomes, including community development.

Turning to the patient environment, Macdonald describes research on the impact of dense networks and managed dialogue. She describes research correlating exceptional standards with the leadership behavior of FMs in creating dense networks through dialogue, the management of structural holes and true strategic brokerage—in short, shifting conversations. Breslin investigates the coevolution of practices within an equipment supplier and attributes its demise and extinction to a failure to change dominant socially constructed and spatially embedded routines. The example is a cautionary tale of the importance of the issues we have raised and the risks if they are ignored.

NOTES

1. The name given to the London Head Quarters of built asset consultants E C Harris

REFERENCES

Ashkenas, R., Ulrich, D., Jick, T., & Kerr, S. (2002). *The boundaryless organization: Breaking the chains of organizational structure.* San Francisco: Jossey-Bass.

Becker, F. D. (1981). *Workspace: Creating environments in organizations.* New York: Praeger.

Becker F. D., Quinn K. L., Rappaport A. J., &. Sims W. R. (1994). *Implementing innovative workplaces—organizational implications of different strategies.* Ithaca, NY: Cornell International Workplace Studies Program

Clegg, S. R., & Kornberger, M. (Eds.). (2006). *Space, organizations and management theory.* Copenhagen: Liber and CBS Press.

Dale, K., & Burrell, G. (2008). *The spaces of organisation and the organisation of space: Power, identity and materiality at work.* London: Palgrave MacMillan.

Donald, I. (1994). Management and change in office environments. *Journal of Environmental Psychology, 14*(1), 21–30.

Evans, G. W., & Mitchell, J. (1998). When buildings don't work: The role of architecture in human health. *Journal of Environmental Psychology, 18*, 85–94.

Festinger, L., Schachter, S., & Back, K. (1950). *Social pressures in informal groups—A study of human factors in housing.* Stanford, CA: Stanford University Press.

Kornberger, M., & Clegg, S. R. (2004). Bringing space back in: Organizing the generative building. *Organization Studies, 25*(7), 1095–1114.

Macintyre, S., Ellaway, A., & Cummins, S. (2002). Place effects on health: How can we conceptualise, operationalise and measure them? *Social Science & Medicine, 55*(1), 125–139.

Markus, T. A. (1993). *Buildings and power.* London: Routledge.

Markus, T. A., & Cameron, D. (2002). *The words between the spaces: Buildings and language.* London: Routledge.

Peters, T. (1992). *Liberation management: Necessary disorganization for the nanosecond nineties.* London: Macmillan.

Price, I. (2002). The complex adaptive workplace: A theoretical link between office design and productivity. In G. T. Frizelle & H. Richards (Eds.), *Tackling industrial complexity: The ideas that make a difference.* Cambridge: Institute for Manufacturing. Retrieved August 25, 2011, from http://www.ifm.eng.cam.ac.uk/mcn/pdf_files/part5_4.pdf unpaginated

Sharles, F. F. (Ed.). (1923). *Business building—A complete guide to business for the wholesaler, retailer, manufacturer, agent, etc. Volume I.* London: Pitman.

Steele, F. (1973). *Physical settings and organization development.* Reading, MA: Addison-Wesley.

Tissen, R., & Lekanne Deprez, F. (2008). *Towards a spatial theory of organizations: Creating new organizational forms to improve business performance* (Nyenrode NL: Research Papers Series 08–04, Nyenrode Business Universiteit). Retrieved August 25, 2011, from http://ideas.repec.org/p/dgr/nijrep/2008–04.html

Ulrich, R. S. (1984). View through a window may influence recovery from surgery. *Science, 224*(4647), 420–421.

US Environmental Protection Agency. (1991). *Office of air and radiation. Indoor air facts no. 4: Sick building syndrome.* Washington, DC: Environmental Protection Agency.

Van Marrewijk, A. H., & Yanow, D. (Eds.). (2010). *Organizational spaces. Rematerializing the workaday world.* Cheltenham, UK: Edward Elgar.

Part I

Organizational Ecologies

1 Organizational Ecologies and Declared Realities

Ilfryn Price

As noted by Darwin himself (1871), and posited as core to his explanation for *The Descent of Man*, the human species has a unique ability to represent and share ideas through languages. Language for Darwin was not a true instinct. It had to be learned, but "man has an instinctive tendency to speak, as we see in the babble of our young children; whilst no child has an instinctive tendency to brew, bake, or write." Hence (p. 74; emphasis added):

> As Max Muller (69. 'Nature,' January 6th, 1870, p. 257.) has well remarked a struggle for life is constantly going on amongst the words and grammatical forms in each language. The better, the shorter, the easier forms are constantly gaining the upper hand, and they owe their success to their own inherent virtue. To these more important causes of the survival of certain words, mere novelty and fashion may be added; for there is in the mind of man a strong love for slight changes in all things. *The survival or preservation of certain favoured words in the struggle for existence is natural selection.*

When coined words, or metaphors and other parts of speech, create an ontic dump (Feldman, 1987) they bring forth or express a certain reality. A word, or phrase, expresses what previously required a more complex trope. Successful words may then find their meaning mutating with time as they are adopted within different communities. FM offers an example (Price, Ch. 7). Ecology offers another. According to the Oxford English Dictionary (OED), its original expression (Haeckel, 1866) was as "the branch of biology that deals with the relationships between living organisms and their environment also the relationships themselves, esp. those of a specified organism." Subsequently, and especially in the US, social geographers adopted social or cultural ecology as "the study of the relationships between people, social groups, and their environment; (also) the system of such relationships in an area of human settlement"; a use that waned as theories of environmental determinism became unfashionable. More recently it has come to mean "in extended use: the interrelationship between any system and its environment; the product of this." The

OED cites examples such as the ecology of British Television and even of the game of cricket! In the course of such developments the word itself has been preserved and replicated even as its specific link to naturally evolving[1] biotic systems, the domain of original Darwinian selection, diminished. Such semantic change is of course common. The proposition I develop in this chapter is that semantic drift may be considered the source of variation in the evolution of inter- and intra- organizational ecologies, the cultural equivalent of genetic mutation. First, however, we need to consider how to conceive the term itself.

ORGANIZATIONAL ECOLOGY: METAPHOR OR ONTOLOGICAL CLAIM

The E Word

As we have seen, the possibility of natural selection acting on language and culture rather than biota goes back to Darwin. Others, too numerous to mention, have since explored the idea of cultural evolution (Aldrich et al., 2008) but, as that paper by several leading current proponents of the theory acknowledged with commendable understatement, "although the idea of generalizing core Darwinian principles in the social sciences has a long history, it has not proved popular." As they conclude:

> We hypothesize that much of the resistance to the idea of generalizing Darwinism to include social evolution stems from an ingrained suspicion of social scientists to ideas from biology. Students in the social sciences are repeatedly warned against 'social Darwinism' and any idea of explaining human behavior in terms of genes. Not only are the issues more complex than the students are often told, but also the idea of generalizing Darwinism has nothing to do with standard (and often dubious) accounts by social scientists of 'social Darwinism,' 'sociobiology' or 'genetic reductionism.' (p. 592)

I hypothesize the reaction is even more deeply rooted in the process through which 'organizations' or 'schools of thought' emerge around shared ideas embodied in language. Semiotic representations, as influencers of social action, "categorize and constitute the social world in an ongoing, circular process" (Tietze, 2007). In given communities certain words carry a shared meaning. Sometimes they engender an almost automatic negative reaction; hence, for example (Price, 2009), the word 'open-plan' is generally viewed as acceptable among FM professionals but evokes immediate antagonism among many occupants of traditional offices, not least academics.[2] 'Positivism' affords another example of semantic drift or the mutation of meaning.[3] Originally derived from Comte's third or positive stage in societal development when rational science would prevail over dogma, it has become a pejorative term in many schools of organizational studies, on a par and even interchangeable with 'reductionist.' Proponents of such views tend to come from communities of research that pride themselves on epistemological, and frequently ontological, relativism. For this community words such as 'evolution' or 'ecology' provoke mental responses such as "but that is positivism" and hence almost automatic denial. Evolution, as a metaphor in organizational studies, equates to ruthless competition (Whittington, 1993; Morgan, 1986). The reaction is different in detail, but perhaps not in underlying cause, to the reaction of religious fundamentalists to the same words.

Human Ecology

In another, principally North American, use of the metaphor, 'human ecology' has been used to denote academic faculties that incorporate both social and natural sciences as well as design. From one of the major centers of the field Franklin Becker and Fritz Steele advocated their own metaphor of organizational ecology at least 30 years ago. As Becker (2007, pp. 46–47) recently put it:

> The concept of "organizational ecology" was coined to capture the fact that all organizations are essentially complex ecological systems characterized by the interdependence of social and physical systems. Changes in any one aspect of the system reverberate throughout the system. Organizational ecology conceptualizes the workplace as a system in which physical design factors both shape and are shaped by work processes, the organization's culture, workforce demographics, and information technologies.

Becker's work was one of the seminal influences that led Keith Alexander and me to suggest a volume that restated that view, with examples, but also sought to integrate it with wider considerations of ecological theory in organizational science. One of those wider considerations is the broad field labeled 'population ecology,' which does not see itself as dealing in metaphor. Somewhat surprisingly, judging from the lack of cross-references in the respective literatures, the two schools, human and population, seem to have developed independently of each other.

Population Ecology and Natural Selection in Organizational Theory

Population ecology (Hannan & Freeman, 1977; Aldrich, 1979) tends to identify its roots in Campbell's (1965) seminal chapter on *variation, selection and retention in sociocultural evolution*. Aldrich's work has been reprinted (2008) and his preface to the new edition looks back to the emergence of the field in the 1970s alongside 'new' institution theory. He wrote, and writes, about organizations as "goal-directed, boundary maintaining entities," a definition with which I take some issue (Price, 2009), but one that was very clearly and explicitly constructed so as to include not just commercial firms or government bodies, but also diverse forms such as campaigning bodies, voluntary associations or fraternities. For Aldrich such entities are founded, then struggle for members and resources in their environment. In the process certain organizational forms better adapted to that environment are retained. Others are not. He considers only a few, such as large firms or public bodies, relatively immune to such selective pressure.

The book, *Organizations and Environments*, is careful not to push the analogy too far, noting that social scientists had yet to identify "a social analogue to the rigid duplication process of the gene-chromosome system." (p. 47) There perhaps its author was being overly cautious and understanding the gene-chromosome system as more rigid than it in fact is (Hull, 1988). When Darwin was writing *The Origin of Species* an understanding of the particulate inheritance, the gene-chromosome system, population genetics, the double helix and much more also lay far in the future and the lack should not detract from the broad sweep of Aldrich's and others' ideas. They of course borrow the core Darwinian concept. More organizations are formed (individual organisms born) than the environment can support. They vary. Survival favors, over time, organizations (individuals) better adapted to their environment, hence differential selection. Biological lineages have, via genes, a means of retaining and transmitting the preferentially selected genetic recipes. As a first order, process selection operates on living entities as they interact with each other. At a second level, selection operates on the routines, the coded information that is replicated. Any number of works have explained it and argued vehemently over the details (e.g. Sammut-Bonnici & Wensley, 2002; Breslin, 2011).

Common to much of that debate is however the, usually implicit, assumption that selection operated on either individual organizations or populations of similar organizations. In parallels drawn from biology organizations were interpreted as the interactors, the individual entities that competed for resources; some of their properties, their routines and competencies or their strategies, paradigms or technologies were the replicators. Ultimately, for the population ecologists, their proposed selection process operated on rationally, or largely rationally, determined managerial designs. In terms of the, still current, debate between evolutionary science and intelligent design, population ecology granted a strong role to the latter. In essence the organization was treated as if its DNA equivalent was one large gene that was either reproduced *in toto* or was rejected by the environment; a proposition too constricting for a truly evolutionary, as opposed to a simply ecological, approach (Weeks & Galunic, 2003).

ORGANIZATIONAL EVOLUTION WITHOUT DESIGN

Science as a Process

David Hull's (1988) seminal book and the earlier work it embodied offered an alternative view of selection via "conceptual interaction." His empirical evidence base came from subgroups within the broad community of biological sciences dividing, as they did, on issues such as methods of taxonomic classification. Informal and emergent group boundaries were maintained by the social processes in groups and the broader rules of conduct, the process, of science. For Hull, science was a selection process between different paradigms or constructs. The paradigms were the replicators interacting by means of the subgroups adhering to different variations on a broad theme. Other studies have observed similar empirical processes at work; hence, Morrell (2008, p. 616), while not writing from a remotely ecological perspective, identified self-forming, narrative language (Bennett, 1989) or epistemic (Haas, 1989) communities in the field of evidence-based management. In a similar manner, without considering the linguistic turn in organizational studies, Stotz, Griffiths and Knight (2004), philosophers of science who had been influenced by Hull, identified different communities of scientists sharing different conceptions represented by the word 'gene,' another example of different variations on a common word or signifier forming part of a shared, community narrative.

Organization as Process

I drew heavily on Hull's argument (Price, 1995) in conceptualizing organizational learning as a selection process heavily mediated, and even counterbalanced, by prevailing organizational paradigms or memetic codes acting, much like genes in a large gene pool, to dampen or select out innovation unless environmental pressure punctuates an existing equilibrium (Price & Kennie, 1997). I did, however, fall into the trap of conceiving of the organization as the primary interactor, selected or not *in toto*. My argument also rested on the observation that organizational innovation appeared to be easier in small, isolated communities; the sociocultural equivalent of biology's peripheral isolates (Sammut-Bonnici & Wensley, 2002).

It has since been claimed (Griffiths, 2000) that Hull's work can be read in two ways, as a literal evolutionary theory of science or as a 'conservative (small *c*) social epistemology.' Paradoxical as it might seem to many who employ evolution as a metaphor for slow change "most of natural selection is concerned with preventing evolutionary change rather than with driving it" (Dawkins, 1986, p. 125). Evolution by natural selection has an inbuilt tendency to conserve, maintaining in the biosphere the established gene pool of a particular ecosystem and, in cultural contexts, Waddington's (1977) "conventional wisdom of the dominant group" or Csikszentmihalyi's

(1988) domain (the symbol system of the influential group). Vischer (Ch. 3) shows how FM has developed a dominant paradigm or narrative of cost, while Stuart (Ch. 11) shows a specific case of what was possible when that paradigm was interrupted.

Within organizational theory the most explicit departure from the designed ecology model was offered when Weeks and Galunic (2003, p. 1315) argued explicitly for firms as ecologies containing populations of individuals who carry particular *modes of thought* (ideas, assumptions, values, beliefs and know-how) that "when they are enacted as language and behavior and other forms of expression create the macro-level patterns of culture." In this view, it is the modes of thought that are (or are not) replicated, not through the interaction of organizations *per se*, but in the thought processes of individuals. The formal organization, or firm, is an outcome rather than an instrument of cultural evolution (ibid.) and not fundamentally different from, say, the less formal semantic communities identified by Hull (1988) or Stotz at al. (2004). In an ontic dump of their own, Weeks and Galunic adopted the collective term 'modes of thought' specifically to avoid the different semantic nuances conveyed by the components thereof. Acknowledging Dawkins's (1976) proposed name for a cultural replicator, they proffered the firm as *an intraorganizational ecology of memes*. In part their hypothesis can be interpreted as applying, to organizations, Hull's proposal and indeed Waddington's or even Darwin's earlier *Dangerous Idea* (Dennett, 1995). In so doing they explored new ground in organizational theory by getting beyond the macro view of traditional population ecologic studies and exploring the micro-level of replication processes (Shepherd & McKelvey, 2009), a field that still suffers a lack of empirical studies.[4] Can that situation be rectified?

EMPIRICAL ORGANIZATIONAL ECOLOGY

Memes and Language

In the late 1970s biologists introduced two ontic dumps to denote a hypothetical 'unit of cultural evolution,' Dawkins's (1976) 'meme' and Lumsden and Wilson's (1981) 'culturgen.' If, *qua* Darwin, there is a selection competition between favored words, 'meme' has unequivocally won even if there is still no agreement on what, if anything, a meme is, how it is transmitted or whether it has a place in organizational studies. Many who have adopted the term have restricted themselves to Dawkins's original concept of cultural artifacts such as fashions or stories spread by some form of imitation hence, for example, O'Mahoney's (2007) exploration of management fashions or examinations of prospective emotional selection in urban myths (Heath, Bell & Sternberg, 2001). Memes, in such views, are a gloss within culture rather than a deeper enabler of culture. At the opposite extreme

(Blackmore, 1999) memes, although transmitted by imitation, are the basis of culture. For her free will is an illusion generated by memes as they convert brains into minds. Many found this a claim too far, for example, Aldrich (in Murmann, Aldrich, Levinthal & Winter, 2003, p. 6; emphasis in original) referring to Blackmore:

> Let's accept the argument that, in fact, she's right, and let's take routines and competencies as the equivalent of memes. Humans, decisions, strategies, and so forth would not be our focus anymore. Those are all, again, simply ways in which routines and competencies make copies of themselves. It's a fairly radical way of thinking about selection logic. It means that if we truly focused on routines, competencies, practices, and so on, we would NOT follow people anymore in our research. Instead, we would follow how competencies spread, replicate, and insinuate themselves into organizations. People would disappear from our equations.

Alternatively, of course she's right, but routines and competencies are simply expressions of 'modes of thought' rather than the actual replicators. Weeks and Galunic avoid the question of agency, arguing that their modes of thought can be enacted either consciously or unconsciously. They do, however, question whether we should be asking why we have the firms we have or whether the firms have us: a distinction resonant of Lodge's parody of the critical turn in literary studies: "you are what you speak or rather what speaks you" (Dennett, 1991 p. 411). Here (cf. Langrish, 2004), we begin to see a resonance with Darwin's suggestions reported at the beginning of the chapter. We also see the rationale for Shepherd and McKelvey's suggestion that an empirical memetics might be grounded in an examination of speech acts between members of a group with variation occurring in what is represented and the response evoked. We approach a potentially interesting and ironical synthesis of Darwin's ontologically real proposals and social constructionism/constructivism. The postmodern denial of ontological reality because "there is nothing outside the text" is reinterpretable as a description of an ontological reality in its own right.

The boundary is, unintentionally so far as I can gather, explored in two works by an example of that now rare individual, the independent scholar (Distin, 2005, 2010). In the former she subjected the *Selfish Meme* to a critical reappraisal, arguing that what is replicated in culture, and hence what might by precedence be labeled a meme, is what she termed representations: linguistic and other symbols expressing and giving rise to what Weeks and Galunic would call modes of thought. She and I have corresponded extensively and find little or no difference between her interpretation of the philosophic concept of a representation and the semiotic concept of a signifier (a word or part of speech that conveys a message interpreted as the signified). After a diversion into learning by gifted children, she returned to *Cultural*

Evolution in 2010, offering a powerful restatement of Darwin's (1871) thesis, updated in the light of recent scholarship in linguistics and information transfer. In her model the coevolution, in our species, of verbal and manual dexterity provided the substrate for representation in firstly verbal, or natural, language and more recently in a variety of symbolic, artefactual languages that are not necessarily verbal. It enabled the human capacity to meta-represent, to think about representations, and hence free will, ability for autonomous choice. Alternative means of representing information gave us new means to think about it. She is careful to stress, bringing in arguments from evolutionary linguistics (Hurford, 2003), no claim to natural language evolving for two-way communication. Rather the innate linguistic disposition to homonyms (same sound but different meaning) over synonyms (different words carrying the same meaning) is taken as evidence of language evolving primarily for speaking rather than listening.[5]

Both semantic drift, as particular words take on different meanings, and what we might call semantic immunity syndrome, the automatic, dismissive reactions to certain terms, can be seen as natural extensions of such a tendency. Natural language transmits semantic information, but also (Kirby, 2007) information about its own construction; hence (Distin, 2010, p. 77) it is "beautifully analogous to DNA for it provides—to receivers with the innate disposition to receive it—its own means of replication." It also conditions the receivers. Distin is effectively updating Darwin's hypothesis. Language, "or strictly natural spoken language, provides a substrate for cultural evolution" (ibid.) and in so doing a medium in which it evolves itself via semiotic processes. In the process the evolutionary account of culture comes to resemble the wider field of social construction and language in organizational theory.

Evolutionary Social Construction

Distin and the linguistic scholars she draws on are not arguing that language represents some abstract thought. Rather they are asserting a position similar to that of the postmodern, or constructionist, turns in organizational studies in which language or discourse shapes what is perceived as real. Organizations, from that perspective, are systems of 'conversations' in the broad sense explored, for example, by Ford (1999). The modes of thought explored by Weeks and Galunic are the equivalent of Ford's socially or linguistically constructed realities. Distin's (2010) book is, as she notes, a development of her first yet she deliberately avoids using the word meme. The reason explained in an afterword was a perception that "though memetics has established that it is quite theoretically respectable, in practice it is not yet quite socially acceptable" (p. 233). The popularity of the word in Internet incarnations, and perhaps the semantic reaction to neo-Darwinism/evolution/positivism, mitigate against its being selected in certain domains of social scholarship. Hence, Ellison and Flowers (Ch.12) prefer the term 'dominant narrative' while Breslin (Ch. 20) sees routines as constructed via language.

Language, in such accounts, provides its speakers membership of a particular 'tribe' and the ability to label manifest objects in their environment. In Pratchett, Stewart and Cohen's (2002) example, language not only allowed the label 'Lion' to be placed on a particular, and potentially fatal, predator, but also allowed the emergence of narratives about the lion, the lion god, say, which transformed the animal into a metonym for some agency with no ontological reality outside the narrative itself, but yet one sufficiently believed in to confer power and influence on the narrators of the imaginary cult. In essence, language, and the selective competition between linguistically and symbolically transmitted representations, provides a plausible, ontologically real, explanation of the core claim of social constructionism (Berger and Luckmann, 1966), namely, that social reality is constructed via language and that social interactions are an essential part of the process. Darwin could be said to have anticipated them by nearly a century.

Social constructionism has subsequently melded with postmodernism into a broad field of studies of language and discourse in organizations. The field has generated its own subgroups and positional debates, captured now in numerous books and courses on research methodology. In the process (Morrell, 2008) it has come to privilege original accounts over confirmatory studies; despite this, there is a growing body of empirical evidence for the degree to which discourses or narratives shape thought and behavior even if the degree of shaping is uncertain (e.g., Cameron & Markus, 2002; Heath & Siedel, 2005; Musson, Cohen & Tietze, 2007). Further support, and differences of perspective, can be found in chapters in this volume in the evolution of FM (Price, Ch. 7), in supply chains (Ellison and Flowers, Ch. 12) and in the evolutionary failure of a steel company (Breslin, Ch. 20).

To highlight just one other example related to organizational space, consider Musson and Tietze's (2004) analysis of a university business school dispersed across three buildings on two separate campuses. The buildings' names became labels, strictly metonyms, through which occupiers of one building both represented and perceived those of another. The perceptions, sensed as realities, influenced the interaction between individuals from different buildings in ways that reinforced the perceptions themselves. The language became self-referring and realities were 'declared into existence' (Ford & Ford, 1995; Price & Shaw, 1998; Ford, Ford & McNamara, 2002), that is, constructed via speech acts.

In such instances the narrative or representation functions as if it was a replicator bent on the selfish purpose of preserving and copying itself. I imply no teleology, no purpose, in making that statement any more than Dawkins (1976), despite misinterpretation by his critics, intended to imply purpose with the metaphor of the selfish gene. The replication is not, of course, always perfect. The same signifier (such as the trope 'selfish') can be received very differently by those from a slightly different semantic community, but the semantic drift provides a source of variation without which the selection process could not function.

Put simply then, my proposition, offered as ontologically real, is that organizations are ecologies produced by variation, selection and retention, acting on replicating narratives, representations, signifiers or discourses. The detailed semiotic distinctions between the four terms are, firstly, not a concern, and, secondly, a source of discussion in their own right. Following Weeks and Galunic's lumping into modes of thought, I would lump all four and more into a category we might call 'language acts' and identify as cultural replicators or memes if the latter term has not already, *qua* Distin (2010), become too debased, too semantically diverse, in its many different guises.

The proposition is not without some interesting ironies. First, for followers of the finer turns of evolutionary theory, it honors Darwin as a progenitor of, and in fact but not name the originator of, the meme concept.* Second, it challenges but also acknowledges the utility of the postmodern turn. Rather than say there are no realities only texts, I suggest that advocates of ontological relativism have actually assisted in uncovering an ontological fact, social construction as a selection process.

*An accolade that I hope would find favor with Richard Dawkins.

NOTES

1. *Evolution* is another word that has come to be a metaphor for gradual change. Here I use it to describe a process that results in ecologies. The distinction is carefully explored by Weeks and Galunic (2003).
2. As Ian Ellison pointed out, it serves as a metonym for a style of management.
3. In Saussurian terms the sign stays the same but what is signified changes.
4. Lord and Price (2001) did offer an empirical test involving the potential falsification of a memetic prediction.
5. The possibility that we express with our mouths but sense with our hands has implications for the role of mobile space in facilitating organizational and individual learning (Beard, Ch. 6).

REFERENCES

Aldrich, H. E. (1979). *Organizations and environments*. Englewood Cliffs, NJ: Prentice Hall.

Aldrich, H. E. (2008). *Organizations and environments* (2nd ed.). Stanford, CA: Stanford University Press.

Aldrich, H. E., Hodgson G. M., Hull, D. L., Knudsen T., Mokyr, J., & Vanberg, V. J. (2008). In defence of generalized Darwinism. *Journal of Evolutionary Economics, 18*(5), 577–596.

Becker, F. D. (2007). Organizational ecology and knowledge networks. *California Management Review, 49*(2), 42–61.

Bennett, T. (1989). *Formalism and Marxism*. London: Routledge.

Berger, P., & Luckmann, T. (1966). *The social construction of reality*. New York: Anchor Books.

Blackmore, S. J. (1999). *The meme machine.* Oxford: Oxford University Press.

Breslin, D. (2011). Reviewing a generalized Darwinist approach to studying socio-economic change. *International Journal of Management Reviews, 13*(2), 218–235.93 1. .18218–221

Cameron, D., & Markus, T. A. (2002). *The words between the spaces: Buildings and language.* London: Routledge.

Campbell, D. T. (1965). Variation, selection and retention in sociocultural evolution. In H. R. Barringer, G. I. Blanksten & R. W. Mack (Eds.), *Social change in developing areas: A reinterpretation of evolutionary theory* (pp. 19–49). Cambridge, MA: Schenkman.

Csikszentmihalyi, M. (1988). Society, culture, and person: A systems view of creativity. In R. J. Sternberg (Ed.), *The nature of creativity: Contemporary psychological perspectives* (pp. 325–339). New York: Cambridge University Press.

Darwin, C. R. (1871). *The descent of man, and selection in relation to sex.* London: John Murray.

Dawkins, R. (1976). *The selfish gene.* Oxford: Oxford University Press.

Dawkins, R. (1986). *The blind watchmaker.* London: Longman.

Dennett, D. C. (1991). *Consciousness explained.* London: Little Brown.

Dennett, D. C. (1995). *Darwin's dangerous idea.* New York: Simon and Schuster.

Distin, K. (2005). *The selfish meme: A critical reassessment.* Cambridge: Cambridge University Press.

Distin, K. (2010). *Cultural evolution.* Cambridge: Cambridge University Press.

Feldman, C. F. (1987). Thought from language: The linguistic construction of cognitive representations. In J. Bruner & H. Haste (Eds.), *Making sense: The child's construction of the world* (pp. 131–146). London: Methuen.

Ford, J. D. (1999). Organizational change as shifting conversations. *Journal of Organisational Change Management, 12*(6), 480–500.

Ford, J. D., & Ford, L. W. (1995). The role of conversations in producing intentional change in organizations. *Academy of Management Review, 20*(3), 541–570.

Ford, J. D, Ford, L. W., & McNamara, R. (2002). Resistance and the background conversations of change. *Journal of Organizational Change Management, 15*(2), 105–121.

Griffiths, P. E. (2000). David Hull's natural philosophy of science. Biology and Philosophy, *15*(3), 301–310.

Haas, P. M. (1989). Do regimes matter? Epistemic communities and evolving policies to control Mediterranean pollution. *International Organization, 43*(3), 377–403.

Haeckel, E. (1866). *Generelle Morphologie der Organismen: allgemeine Grundzüge der organischen Formen-Wissenschaft, mechanisch begründet durch die von C. Darwin reformirte Decendenz-Theorie.* Berlin: Georg Reimer.

Hannan, M. T., & Freeman, J. (1977). The population ecology of organizations. *American Journal of Sociology, 82*(5), 929–964.

Heath, C., Bell, C., & Sternberg E. (2001). Emotional selection in memes: The case of urban legends. *Journal of Personality and Social Psychology, 81*(6), 1028–1041.

Heath, C., & Siedel, V. (2005). Language as a coordinating mechanism: How linguistic memes help direct appropriate action. Working paper v4.2. Retrieved June 20, 2011, from http://icos.groups.si.umich.edu/Linguisticmemes4.2.pdf

Hull, D. L. (1988). *Science as a process: An evolutionary account of the social and conceptual development of science.* Chicago: University of Chicago Press.

Hurford, J. R. (2003). Why synonymy is rare: Fitness is in the speaker. In W. Banzah, T. Christhaller, P. Dittrich, J. T. Kim & J. Ziegler (Eds.), *Advances in artificial life: Proceedings of the 7ᵗʰ European Conference on Artificial Life (ECAL)* (pp. 442–451). Heidelberg: Springer Verlag.

Kirby, S. (2007). The evolution of language. In R. Dunbar & L. Barret (Eds.), *Oxford handbook of evolutionary psychology* (pp. 669–684). Oxford: Oxford University Press.

Langrish, J. Z. (2004). Darwinian design: The memetic evolution of design ideas. *Design Issues, 20*(4), 4–19.

Lord, A., & Price, I. (2001). Reconstruction of organisational phylogeny from memetic similarity analysis: Proof of feasibility. *Journal of Memetics—Evolutionary Models of Information Transmission, 5*(2), 1–9.

Lumsden, C., & Wilson, E. O. (1981). *Genes, mind and culture.* Cambridge, MA: Harvard University Press.

Morgan, G. (1986). *Images of organization.* London: Sage.

Morrell, K. (2008). The narrative of 'evidence based' management: A polemic. *Journal of Management Studies, 45*(3), 613–635.

Murmann, J. P., Aldrich, H., Levinthal, D., & Winter, S. (2003). Evolutionary thought in management and organization theory at the beginning of the new millennium. *Journal of Management Inquiry, 12*(1), 1–19.

Musson, G., Cohen, L., & Tietze, S. (2007). Pedagogy and the 'linguistic turn': Developing understanding through semiotics. *Management Learning, 38*(1), 45–60.

Musson, G., & Tietze, S. (2004). Places and spaces: The role of metonymy in organizational talk. *Journal of Management Studies, 41*(8), 1301–1323.

O'Mahoney, J. (2007). The diffusion of management innovations: The possibilities and limitations of memetics. *Journal of Management Studies, 44*(8), 1324–1348.

Pratchett, T., Stewart, I., & Cohen, J. (2002). *The science of Discworld II: The globe.* London: Ebury Press.

Price, I. (1995). Organizational Memetics? Organizational learning as a selection process *Management Learning, 26*(3), 299–318.

Price, I. (2009). Space to adapt: Workplaces, creative behaviour and organizational memetics. In T. Rickards, M. A. Runco & S. Moger (Eds.), The Routledge companion to creativity (pp. 46–57). London: Routledge.

Price, I., & Kennie, T. (1997). *Punctuated strategic equilibrium and some leadership challenges for University 2000.* Paper presented at *the* 2nd International Conference on the Dynamics of Strategy, SEMS, Guildford.

Price, I., & Shaw, R. (1998). *Shifting the patterns.* Chalford Gloucestershire: Management Books 2000.

Sammut-Bonnici, T., & Wensley, R. (2002). Darwinism, probability and complexity: Market-based organizational transformation and change explained through the theories of evolution. *International Journal of Management Reviews, 4*(3), 291–315.

Shepherd, J., & McKelvey, B. (2009). An empirical investigation of organizational memetic variation. *Journal of Bioeconomics, 11*(2), 135–164.

Stotz, K., Griffiths, P. E., & Knight, R. (2004). How biologists conceptualize genes: An empirical study. *Studies in History and Philosophy of Biological and Biomedical Sciences, 35*(4), 647–673.

Tietze, S. (2007). Language and international management: Emergent themes and new perspectives. University of Bradford Working Paper No 07/35 Retrieved August 8, 2011, from http://www.brad.ac.uk/acad/management/external/pdf/workingpapers/2007/Booklet_07–35.pdf

Waddington, C. H. (1977). *Tools for thought: How to understand and apply the latest scientific techniques of problem solving.* New York: Basic Books.

Weeks, J., & Galunic, C. (2003). A theory of the cultural evolution of the firm: The intra-organizational ecology of memes. *Organization Studies, 24*(8), 1309–1352.

Whittington, R. (1993). *What is strategy and does it matter?* London: Routledge.

2 Workplace Redesign to Support the 'Front End' of Innovation

Jeremy Myerson

Over the past decade or more large organizations have been experimenting heavily with the redesign of their physical workspace to help them respond more swiftly and effectively to the effects of globalization in business (Davenport, Thomas & Cantrell 2002; CABE & British Council of Offices, 2005). This chapter looks at a particular aspect of this process, namely, the introduction of new office design in response to a growing need for organizations to focus on the 'front end' of innovation—to discover, define, select and appraise new ideas in a knowledge-based economy amid unprecedented global competition.

My purpose here is to show that in reorganizing people and space to meet one of the key innovation challenges of globalization, many large companies have been forced to adopt new spatial and organizational models. These depart in some shape or form from the command-and-control space plans and systems of established bureaucracies and take on new characteristics related to such values as flexibility, agility, community, autonomy and teamwork. By reviewing office design developments between 1998 and 2008, I want to show how an intense search over a decade for better physical work settings to facilitate the 'front end' of the innovation process has contributed to the emergence of some new organizational ecologies and the transformation of others. As part of this, I also want to show how an accelerated phase of innovation development has led to organizations exploring more sustainable approaches to innovation culture in the workplace to counterbalance the effects of an unchecked economic growth model.

SETTING THE CONTEXT

First it is important to set the context for the decade of experiment in office redesign that I will describe. By the late 1990s, it was clear that the physical structure and appearance of the workplace was critical to company performance. It was clear too that large organizations were facing enormous change and uncertainty in business markets as the twin effects of globalization and new technology began to cut a swath through clerical ranks and eliminate the role of middle managers (Turner & Myerson, 1998).

Many companies began the process of cultural change among staff to introduce new business practices to respond to such new challenges, some linking cultural change programs directly to a redesign of the physical work environment and others choosing to ignore the link between the two. The result was that by the late 1990s the picture was patchy with mixed results for adoption of new office design in relation to changing business processes. Four generic organizational models could be identified, which we termed the 'monolith,' the 'makeshift,' the 'moderniser [*sic*]' and the 'mould-breaker.' Two could be described as progressive models (moderniser and mould-breaker); two were entrenched in a soon-to-be-outdated status quo.

The monolith could be characterized as a deeply conservative and stiffly hierarchical organization, resistant to change and a stickler for procedure with a dominant management culture of formal committees and top-down initiatives. Many long-established private sector companies with captive markets or Whitehall departments at the heart of government adhered to the monolithic model. Monoliths often occupied expensive city-center headquarters buildings boasting grand facades. Senior managers were cocooned in expansive cellular accommodation in top-floor suites. More junior staff worked in bleak and cramped open-plan spaces away from natural light; they were also kept in the dark by being given little information.

The makeshift could be characterized as a 'make-do-and-mend' organization, unable to think coherently about redesigning its workspace to meet changing needs and simply overwhelmed by day-to-day operations. We found dysfunctional makeshift organizations in every sector of business from publishing to logistics—untidy, unfocused and living hand to mouth with Portacabins stacked up in the car park and staff working in corridors and basements amid trailing wires and broken furniture. The motives of the makeshift were often less malign than the domineering monolith, but this was an organizational type that simply couldn't cope.

The moderniser could be characterized as a traditional organization (often a monolith) that was determined to change its traits, usually via relocation from the city center to either a docklands site or a greenfield campus. The office move was the impetus for a new culture to flourish amid bright, new, modern surroundings, but staff often felt uneasy and out of place shuffling down foliage-filled boulevards between atrium, artworks, crèche, gym and water fountains in the lobby. Many large organizations from the Ministry of Defence at Abbey Wood near Bristol to British Airways at Waterside near Heathrow adopted the moderniser model, with mixed success. Modernizing a traditional organization proved much harder than many progressive managers imagined.

The mould-breaker could be characterized as a young company determined to rewrite the rules of office design by taking a radical new approach to use of time and space. Typical mould-breaking companies were advertising, media, IT or management consultants—energetic and technologically literate, with a high proportion of employee shareholders and a concern to project a friendly ambience and build a real sense of community. In 1998, mould-breakers were the outliers of office facilities—few in number but highly significant for their capacity to innovate and for the new thinking embodied in their vanguard schemes, which typically featured 'town squares,' table football and all-day cafés.

THE IMPERATIVE TO INNOVATE

By the turn of the new millennium these four organizational types, which we could describe as ecologies in the context of this book, were facing a wave of business change that threatened to engulf them. As globalization continued apace, monolithic bureaucracies were ruthlessly cut down to size, either by vengeful shareholders or reformist governments; and makeshift organizations either smartened up their act or were swept away as new technology demanded greater efficiencies. Modernisers fared better: although many of-out-town campuses quickly proved to be inflexible white elephants, there was at least a physical template in place for new, more collaborative, team-based working in brighter surroundings. Mould-breakers fared best of all: their inherent agility and attractiveness as organizations made them able to attract and retain premium employees amid talent scarcity in key industry sectors (Myerson & Ross, 1999). The problem was that there were so few genuine mould-breakers.

What influenced the planning of office facilities in the early 2000s most of all was a need to innovate. As old business models were overturned, so there was a mounting imperative on most organizations to 'think differently' (in the parlance of Apple's advertising campaign) and to find better and faster ways to take new ideas to market. In this context, there was a growing focus on the 'front end' of innovation—the phase of discovery, understanding and appraisal of ideas, often called the 'fuzzy front end' on account of its ambiguous and open-ended nature. This is the phase of innovation that companies find most difficult to manage through the provision of physical work settings.

Offices grew out of the bureaucratization of industry (Forty, 1986) and were first modeled on rigid factory lines, within the dominant scientific management ideologies of Fordism and Taylorism (Merkle, 1980). As a result, office interiors were best placed to support the more logical and linear processes at the 'back end' of innovation—production, distribution, administration, logistics and so on. Front-end discovery was poorly served by the enduring legacy of factory-style time-and-motion in the workplace, as was that middle phase of innovation typically concerned with design and development once ideas have been discovered and selected.

Another major factor in planning office facilities was the disruptive effect of accelerating globalization on corporate innovation. Many multinational companies had already shifted the back-end delivery phase of the innovation cycle—the manufacturing, servicing and distribution processes—offshore to lower-cost economies, mainly in Asia-Pacific. Now they began to look at also sending the creative phase of innovation—the design and development processes—offshore. China and India, with their fast-rising expertise in design, engineering and software, were the main beneficiaries as Western firms took advantage of lower salaries and rising educational standards to set up innovation facilities from Shanghai to Bangalore.

Different organizations adopted different innovation outsourcing strategies. British engineering and design consulting firm Atkins, for example, opened new creative studios in China and India, while the Dyson manufacturing company moved production of its vacuum cleaners to Malaysia but kept its engineers and designers close to home in the UK. Generally, as the forces of globalization saw the 'create' and 'deliver' phases of innovation move east, US and European corporate headquarters began to put an unprecedented emphasis on the one part of the process that could not be profitably sent offshore—the front end of innovation.

PRIORITY ON FRONT-END ACTIVITIES

By the mid-2000s there was extensive management commentary on shifts in innovation strategy in the global economy and in particular on the high priority being placed on front-end activities. Kim and Mauborgne (2005), for example, advocated intense strategic focus on business organizations finding a 'blue ocean' well away from well-established markets—the 'red oceans' in which companies are directly up against their competitors. Organizations as diverse as Cirque du Soleil and Casella Wines, the Australian winery behind the successful Yellow Tail brand, were cited as finding their own 'blue oceans.'

Christensen (1997) told a similar story of the centrality of the discovery phase of innovation to business, arguing that companies needed to get much closer to customers at the front end so that they could develop products and services that meet real needs and 'get the job done' in people's lives. Christensen cited FedEx and eBay as companies successfully built on getting a job done—and the Sony Walkman and Kodak EasyShare as *brands* that get a job done. Von Hippel, in *Democratizing Innovation* (2005), meanwhile put special emphasis on engagement with powerful user communities at the front end of innovation, citing Lego's development of its Lego Mindstorms product, while Kelley and Littman (2005) described in detail the characters that all companies need to employ in order to handle the discovery phase of innovation: the 'anthropologist,' who watches and listens to users, trying to understand irrational human behavior; the 'experimenter,' who succeeds through enlightened trial and error by making multiple prototypes; and the 'cross-pollinator,' who adapts ideas from other industries and cultures.

All of this analysis both reflected and encouraged organizations to work across discipline boundaries, build new dialogues with users and adopt more imaginative and less predictable innovation methods. Such management commentary also built significantly on calls for a more open innovation model (Chesbrough, 2003) in which the traditional, linear, internally focused world of the closed-off corporate lab is replaced by a vibrant open network of alliances with industrial rivals, universities and research institutes. The result was to present a huge challenge to the designers and managers of corporate workspace—organizations could no longer afford to be monolithic or makeshift, and modernisers were forced to quicken the pace of modernization.

Companies quickly recognized that their most important players at the front end of innovation belonged to the growing international community of knowledge workers (Drucker, 1999), for whom factory-derived office templates were inadequate and inappropriate. The particular demands and contributions of knowledge workers (and in particular *creative* knowledge workers) are dealt with elsewhere in this book (Haynes, Ch.17); here I simply want to point out that, in the early 2000s, there was a wave of experiment in workspace redesign to see what would make knowledge workers more productive—critically so within a creative context of managing innovation.

EXPERIMENTS IN OFFICE REDESIGN

Davenport et al. (2002) and others were critical of this restless experimentation, complaining that companies were not learning much from their experiments. Davenport suggested that 'fad, fashion and faith' was driving most new work environments for knowledge workers. However, I would argue that it is clear from international surveys of new workspace design that the pressure on global companies to enhance their front-end development capabilities led to the emergence of what is described elsewhere in this book as 'socially constructed communities,' with their own constructed design language. These in turn influenced the formation of some new organizational ecologies and the transformation of others.

Over a 10-year period, I worked with technologist Philip Ross to co-author a trilogy of books (1999, 2003 and 2006) on new developments in workplace design. We wrote up 130 case studies from around the world, observing and charting how organizations large and small were responding to changes in business, technology and society through the design and management of their office facilities. By reviewing that body of work now against the specific demands of multinational innovation activity at the front end, a clear picture emerges of workspace redesign dedicated first to supporting a range of creative and collaborative processes deemed essential to catalyzing early stage development, and second to instilling a set of social values conspicuously absent from office facilities for most of the twentieth century. Four generic themes can be identified as making up this picture and are discussed here.

Team Space

The first theme to emerge was that much standard individual workspace was reallocated to *team space*. Innovation has been described as a 'contact sport' in which collaboration is critical within a mix of formal arrangements and informal characteristics (Dodgson, Gann & Salter, 2005). Companies from the late 1990s onwards began to pay closer attention to the dynamics of group working as the old discipline silos were breached and new multidisciplinary teams were formed.

Traditional space planning based on the ruthless divisions of hierarchy and status was ditched along with anonymous meeting rooms bookable by the hour. In their place came dedicated project dens and romp rooms for teams to live, work and create together. Some US technology majors displayed a penchant for enclosed team spaces with translucent screens, billiard tables and domestic rocking chairs. Whole facilities were even turned over to new team-based arrangements. Prominent among the new team players was Interpolis, the Dutch insurance giant, which built an entire headquarters at Tilburg in the late 1990s based on group working. Each team space was given its own identity, dramatically visualized with a café at the entrance to each floor themed as a different world city, from Rio to Barcelona.

Narrative Space

The second theme to emerge was that much neutral corporate office space was remodeled as *narrative space*. Making innovation happen is a mission that requires a strong corporate culture to assert a sense of purpose and direction. Companies from the late 1990s onwards began to explore ways in which the office interior could be redesigned so that innovation teams could 'live' and 'breathe' the brand. The building itself was given an overhaul to be narrative in form—to be a storytelling tool right on the front line of marketing and communication. Offices were no longer designated to be blank boxes betraying little of the inner life of the organization. They were conscripted to a creative campaign to make companies more innovative.

The big global brand owners were the early adopters of this trend. Many had been modernisers; now they pushed beyond the uniform but hardly distinctive light-and-bright look of the standard corporate campus and gave their facilities a branded makeover. At the Newport Beach, California, headquarters of surfing and skateboard clothing brand Quiksilver, designers created a 'beach community' with a polished boardwalk and 'beach shacks' made of slatted wood. At the UK headquarters of carmaker

Toyota at Epsom Downs, the theme was an internal street complete with parked cars and explicit visual reference to automotive styling and materials (curved forms, halogen lights, metallic finishes and lots of glass).

The narrative for innovation was clear to see too in the London office of Sony PlayStation, with its playful and surprising interior features simulating a virtual-reality game, and in the Canton, Massachusetts, campus of sporting goods giant Reebok, with its interior basketball court and plan representing the coiled energy of an athlete on the starting blocks. The thinking was that in branded work environments such as these, the front end of innovation would be more convincingly accomplished. As Paul Brown, vice president of product design at Reebok, commented on his company's new campus completed in 2000: "Products, innovation, marketing . . . This is our church. Everything that comes out of our church represents what we do. When you come into the building you know what you do and who you are" (Myerson & Ross, 2003 p. 11).

Exchange Space

Concurrent with the shift towards team space and narrative space, the third theme to emerge was that much clerical office space was given over to *exchange space*. Instead of operating like paper factories dedicated to repetitive knowledge processing, companies began taking the business of knowledge exchange much more seriously. They explored new ways to build, share, barter and transfer knowledge in environments dedicated to leadership activities, training, mentoring, co-creation with clients and so on.

Knowledge is power at the front end of innovation. Nokia, for example, opened a major new facility at Espoo, Finland, which grouped its offices around two giant redwood atria to create a vast, animated social community for knowledge exchange. Boeing meanwhile opened a dedicated US Leadership Center at St. Louis ('the hot place to meet,' according to the company's design brief) so its senior executives could plan the company's next moves in a highly flexible space away from everyday routines.

As corporate organizations increasingly viewed their facilities as nodes in a global network rather than stand-alone buildings, there was growing emphasis on creating dedicated settings for external knowledge exchange, such as PricewaterhouseCoopers's Zone Complex in Philadelphia, which allows consultants and clients to jointly 'test-drive' new processes in a high-tech suite, or IBM's e-business office in Santa Monica, which allows multi-disciplinary teams to work directly with clients.

Public Space

The fourth theme to emerge was that more private office space was given over to *public space*. This approach manifested itself in a number of different ways, but the catalyst was a singular commitment by companies to get closer to their customers by reaching out to wider society in order to study and understand people's lives. Office buildings were being rightly criticized as aloof, insular and segregated, as doing business behind closed doors and having little connection with the cities and communities in which they were based. In the early 2000s, as models of open innovation caught hold, many organizations resolved to adopt a more open approach to workplace design, blurring public and private.

Some workplace strategies allowed members of the public into office buildings to enjoy restaurants, cafés, viewing platforms and so on. Others deliberately located corporate innovation activities inside civic and cultural buildings in city centers in order to be closer to the action, for example, McKinsey opened an office in the Nemo Science and Technology Museum in Amsterdam.

Space hitherto allocated to private executives was redesignated as public space for all staff and visitors to enjoy. Entire social landscapes emerged that mimicked the public realm of the city with a colorful repertoire of different spaces to enjoy as you might encounter a particular urban area. Linear corridors, the arterial roads of the traditional corporate office that efficiently transported staff from A to B, were replaced by meandering boulevards, lanes and streets that bring people together and create the serendipitous encounters on which innovation thrives.

Some companies went even further in extending into the public realm, recognizing that their most prized knowledge workers at the front end of the innovation process would prefer to work away from the corporate campus and be clustered with their professional peers instead. This thinking led to a new wave of working in revamped business clubs, chambers of commerce, scientific institutes and other alternative settings where like minds could congregate in what has been described as a modern reenactment of medieval craft guilds (Myerson & Ross, 2006). The high-profile refurbishments of the Institute of Directors (2001) and the Royal Society (2003), both in London, can be viewed as key manifestations of this trend.

CONCLUSIONS

If we amalgamate these themes and look closely at the cumulative effect of a significant shift from individual workspace to team space, from neutral workspace to narrative space, from clerical workspace to exchange space, and from private workspace to public space, then we can see that—contrary to the views of Davenport and others— there has been much learning from a succession of experiments in workplace design over the decade 1998 to 2008.

To return to the core argument of this book, namely, that an organization's physical workspace can best be appreciated as a lever of management through a conception of organizations as ecologies (Becker, 2007;

Price, Ch. 1), I would argue here that workspace redesign to prioritize and support front-end innovation processes has changed some organizational ecologies and introduced new ones.

To summarize this, let me return to the models of the monolith, makeshift, moderniser and mould-breaker introduced at the start of this chapter. Slow, large, bureaucratic monoliths were targeted by workplace change and many have not survived—senior executives were forced out of their corporate enclaves, digital technology transformed communication and complacent command-and-control was largely undermined by the sheer pace of global business and its innovation mantra. A lot of inefficient, makeshift organizations have been similarly swept away (cf. Breslin, Ch. 20)—those who could not reform or innovate were always destined to fail.

But what of the moderniser and mould-breaker, those more progressive organizational types? Modernizing organizations have been forced to embrace more profound change than they originally signed up for when they relocated to a modern new campus. Traditional notions of modernity and progress, as signified by simple modernist design with lots of light and air, have been superseded by more complex experiments in social engineering to create working 'communities of practice.'

To provide modernisers with exemplars of change, workspace architects and designers ironically looked not to the future (as the pioneer modernists once did) but to the past: a succession of historical templates from the Greek *agora* and the medieval square to the traditional university college and the craft guild were studied to learn lessons on how communities of a few hundred people could occupy space in a socially cohesive and an economically viable way. If an organization could not develop its own spatial narrative (or 'brandscape' as the technique became known), then one could be readily borrowed from the history books.

The organizational ecology of the moderniser thus became something richer, deeper and more complex. It adapted and adopted much from the disciplines of urban planning and landscape architecture. The reissue and revived popularity as a workplace design primer of Jane Jacobs's famous treatise on cities (1961) during the past decade is telling in this context. So is the contribution of architect Clive Wilkinson whose work for two US West Coast advertising agencies pushed the idea of the retro-community template further than any other design practitioner. One Wilkinson scheme, for Chiat Day (1998), recreated a slice of 1960s Greenwich Village; the other, for Foote Cone and Belding (2001), simulated an entire waterfront to suggest a harbor community.

Mould-breaking organizations, however, went beyond these 'constructed communities' to question the validity of fixed office buildings altogether and formulate a new organizational ecology based on the potential of the digital network. The autonomy of the individual knowledge worker may have been acknowledged by modernisers in providing a range of different work setting free from surveillance inside giant stage sets. But it was the mould-breakers who took things to the next level, challenging every convention of space, time and place in office facilities, and giving their key innovation players the freedom (and the tools) to work anytime and anywhere.

Most recently, organizational ecologies have been re-examined from a new angle in relation to the clamor for business innovation. As a direct result of an accelerated phase of innovation development in the early 2000s, companies have begun to fret about the economic growth model and explore more sustainable corporate cultures (cf. Stuart, Ch.11). Customers, shareholders and employees all want to see organizations developing a more sustainable approach. Office facilities, which clock up commuter miles and waste energy and resources by leaving lights on, ICT and air-conditioning systems running and desks empty, are targets for behavior change. Organizations once motivated by innovation at all costs are now examining whether the costs of sustainability should be borne by the company or employees or a combination of both.

The team-based, knowledge-exchanging, mission-building and customer-facing demands of innovation continue to have an effect on organizational ecologies today. The restless workspace design experimentation discussed in this chapter looks set to continue, albeit with growing environmental awareness injected into many corporate projects. Creative knowledge work now holds the key to future prosperity in a way that mechanized manual labor did a century ago, so we will never stop trying to find the right environments to improve the productivity and flow of new ideas.

REFERENCES

Becker, F. D. (2007). The ecology of knowledge networks. *California Management Review*, 49(2), 1–20.

CABE & the British Council of Offices. (2005). *The impact of office design on business performance*. London: CABE and BCO.

Chesbrough, H. (2003). *Open innovation: The new imperative for creating and profiting from technology*. Cambridge, MA: Harvard Business School Press.

Christensen, C. (1997). *The innovator's dilemma*. Cambridge, MA: Harvard Business School Press.

Davenport, T. H., Thomas R. J., & Cantrell, S. (2002). The mysterious art and science of knowledge-worker performance. *MIT Sloan Management Review*, 44(1), 23–30.

Dodgson, M., Gann, D., & Salter, A. (2005). *Think play do: Technology, innovation and organization*. Oxford: Oxford University Press.

Forty, A. (1986). *Objects of desire: Design and society 1750–1980*. London: Thames and Hudson.

Jacobs, J. (1961). *The death and life of great American cities*. New York: Random House.

Kelley, D., & Littman, J. (2005). *The ten faces of innovation: Strategies for heightening creativity*. New York: Currency Doubleday.

Kim, C., & Mauborgne, R. (2005). *Blue ocean strategy*. Cambridge, MA: Harvard Business School Press.

Merkle, J. (1980). *Management and ideology.* Berkeley: University of California Press.

Myerson, J., & Ross, P. (1999). *The creative office.* London: Laurence King.

Myerson, J., & Ross, P. (2003). *The 21st century office.* London: Laurence King.

Myerson, J., & Ross, P. (2006). *Space to work; new office design.* London: Laurence King.

Turner, G., & Myerson J. (1998). *New workspace new culture: Office design as a catalyst for change.* Aldershot, UK: Gower.

Von Hippel, E. (2005). *Democratizing innovation.* Cambridge, MA: MIT Press.

3 Managing Facilities for Human Capital Value

Jacqueline Vischer

Human capital comprises the skills, knowledge and capabilities of the workforce of a firm, as well as the organizational arrangements and networks of relationships that enable employees to be innovative and productive. The stock of productive knowledge and skills possessed by people is a form of capital that can be acquired and enhanced by various kinds of investments. An organization's accommodation and decisions about facilities are an investment a company makes in its human capital and consequently in employee performance and competitive advantage (Holtham, 2003). The concept of human capital is an evocative and powerful way of approaching FM operations and decisions; it offers an innovative approach to legitimatizing the primacy of the occupant or user perspective for setting FM priorities in terms of the value of its human capital to the organization (Vischer, 2011).

Defining facilities and building operations in terms of human capital in firms is a way of exploring the value and applications of a social constructivist perspective to FM. The space employees occupy affects, but does not determine, how well they work, how much they work and how they feel about their work. The accommodation that an organization selects is largely determined by FM, and the workspace it provides is an important mediating influence on the relationship of the organization to its human capital. The design, configuration and features of occupied facilities affect how well and how much a company benefits from 'the acquired and useful abilities of all the inhabitants or members of the society': its human capital. Investing in human capital provides a viable alternative to the well-established service model of FM referred to elsewhere (e.g., Price, Ch. 7).

As other chapters of this volume point out, the dominant FM model in contemporary organizations is cost-based, in spite of a growing number of useful alternative approaches. Occupancy costs are a budget line item on most corporate accounting sheets, and efforts directed at buildings and space tend to focus on controlling and reducing expenditures. This view has resulted in common workspace features such as the standardization of workstations and furniture, efforts to reduce 'footprint' and increase density and a 'value engineering' approach to real estate decision-making that does not address the human aspect or occupant behavior and can have the effect of discouraging more creative approaches to managing facilities (Stuart, Ch. 11). Investing in human capital as a constructivist alternative to cost-based FM means investing in the physical environment for work to increase the effectiveness of a company's human capital: employee and knowledge retention, more employee learning and commitment, new knowledge creation and sharing and improved performance outcomes.

I examine three key ways in which facilities affect human capital: space as an *organizational resource*, linking accommodation decisions with corporate business objectives (Fischer, 1997; Guillen, 1997); space as a *tool for work*, providing needed support for employees' daily tasks (Leaman & Bordass, 2001; Vischer, 1995); and space as it frames organizational interactions and social network formation, a mediating influence on the creation and operation of *intraorganizational relationships* (Grant, 1996; Kampschroer & Heerwagen, 2005). FM is intimately connected with operations at all three levels.

SPACE AS AN ORGANIZATIONAL RESOURCE

Real estate and facilities are often considered an investment by the firm and managed in terms of realizing and increasing financial value. However, the workspace a firm's facilities provide to employees is typically undervalued as a corporate resource and managed as a cost of doing business (Seiler, 1984; Joroff & Bergman, 2007). Shifting from this perspective to a management objective that sees facilities as an investment in increasing the human capital value of the organization is a way of capitalizing on this resource.

The idea that an organization has a relationship with its accommodation that, like all relationships, ebbs and flows and changes over time is not new but is relatively unexamined (O'Mara, 1999; Morgan & Anthony, 2008). This in contrast with the employee–organization relationship, which has received considerable attention, and in which modern companies do not hesitate to invest (Tsui, Pearce, Porter & Tripoli, 1997). How a company defines and thinks about its facilities can be summed up in its organization-accommodation (O-A) relationship, that is, that unique configuration of land, buildings, interiors (workspace) and technology that every company defines for itself, according to its views of itself and of its workers (Vischer, 1996). Trends such as the rise of the networked organization and the knowledge economy have affected the O-A relationship, as well as corporate views of human capital (Boxall, 2011). Alternative accommodation options, such as hotelling and other nonterritorial workspace, would seem to present a reasonable balance between cost reduction and better returns on the human capital investment. While hotelling accommodation is comfortable and supportive, access to it is limited; and the limitations define ways in which workers can make the company more profitable but not necessarily ways to communicate and collaborate to learn and increase knowledge. A human capital perspective on accommodation is oriented towards finding a balance similar to that which is sought in other organizational systems, namely, between 'exploration', that is opportunities for new knowledge and therefore facilities that offer opportunities for new behavior, and 'exploitation', that is making good use of existing knowledge and therefore facilities that enable and support existing ways of doing things (March, 1991).

FM professionals tend to find themselves managing an unbalanced O-A relationship: accommodation decisions are often more reactive and retrospective than innovative and embracing of change. They are reactive in that companies typically change their accommodation not to embrace new ideas and processes, but to solve problems of too much or too little space. They are retrospective in that decisions about new space are most commonly based on what already exists in the firm, and result in reproducing physical environments that are already known and familiar. This approach serves the need for exploitation better than the need for exploration. And while some change constitutes a shift in FM and organizational narratives, no change can limit innovative thinking and the creation of new knowledge.

On the other hand, modern FM is aware of the opportunity that an accommodation change or move offers to rethink the relationship between built space and human capital. Lowering costs as the single most important objective a company has from its accommodation is slowly being replaced by more diverse and organization-related goals (Ouye & Serino, 2004). These include (a) better customer relations, (b) improving worker productivity, (c) generating opportunities for tacit learning and mentoring and (d) growing and consolidating community and culture. To facilitate a shift towards defining accommodation in terms of how well it attains these human capital-related objectives, it is useful to think of four basic constructs that characterize the O-A relationship. Each has a key influence on the social contract and on the employer–employee relationship. These are 'poor,' 'neutral,' 'positive' and 'active' (Vischer, 2005). Where accommodation hinders work—perhaps people are too crowded or they have to move too often or they are located in widely dispersed accommodation—the relationship is *poor*, adding no value and even detracting from business activities and worker efficiency. This can impair customer relations and over time increase employee turnover, resulting in loss of organization-specific skills and knowledge. A move or other space change provides an opportunity to improve business processes. The relationship can become *neutral*—less adverse to worker activities—and it can become *positive*, supporting people's tasks and improving their ability to perform them. A positive O-A relationship means accommodation that supports information exchange, helps build trust and enables collaboration: all goals of strategic human resources and essential to increase competitive advantage (Lepak & Snell, 1999). Optimally, an organization has an *active* relationship to its accommodation, in which accommodation is viewed as a resource to support human capital and FM has strategies in place to derive maximum value from the firm's accommodation.

Making accommodation decisions explicit and purposeful is one way FM can make the O-A relationship more active. Strategies for involving and engaging workers in planning their own workspace are available to help ensure that both their explicit knowledge (what they do) and their tacit knowledge (how they do it) are applied to workspace decision-making (Dewulf & Van Meel, 2003; Gann & White, 2003; Lennertz & Lutzenhiser, 2006). Increasing employee empowerment in relation to the buildings and space they occupy by providing information and offering opportunities to participate in decisions helps knowledge dissemination, increases commitment and improves their performance (Lawler, Mohrman & Ledford, 1995).

SPACE AS A TOOL FOR WORK

FM is focused on the spatial manifestation of organization (Hudson, Ch. 4). Space structures the relationship between value and time that is basic to human capital (Ng, Tan & Ang, 2011). In this sense, designing facilities for employee use and increasing the value of its human capital connects FM concerns to the core business of every organization.

The physical environment has a powerful effect on human performance at work and can positively or negatively affect creativity and ideas generation, communication and knowledge sharing and individual and group problem solving. The concept of *ba*—that is, space for knowledge creation and sharing—combines physical, virtual, and mental space to signify "a shared space for emerging relationships" (Nonaka & Konno, 1998, p. 40). A recent analysis of physical environments inside organizations concluded that accommodation must provide not only space (*topos*), but also the time, attention from leaders and opportunities for relationship building needed to facilitate the creation of new knowledge (Nenonen, 2004). She proposes a list of 10 environmental attributes needed for high-quality *ba*, which include *ba* in the midst of 'real work,' contact between those who have core knowledge and experience and those 'on the periphery of the system,' no fixed center point but rather a center point that changes 'as the context evolves,' opportunities for co-creation and dialogue and 'self-transcendence' in which teams 'connect to their highest creative possibilities' (p. 236). The *topos* or physical space that is a critical component of *ba* is formed through balancing physical, social and virtual work environments; quality of place is one of the most important factors shaping the quality of knowledge (Nonaka, Scharmer & Toyama, 2001).

Workspace design research has been slow to embrace this paradigm shift away from user preferences and towards human capital priorities. For example, studies of whether workers are satisfied with an open-plan configuration in various office environments demonstrate that they are mostly dissatisfied. This is usually attributed to lack of privacy, too much noise or insufficient storage (Hedge, 1986; McCoy & Evans, 2005; Mital, McGlothlin & Faard, 1992). Limiting the outcome measured to individual satisfaction reinforces the traditional service model of FM and generates little new insight about exactly how people's work is affected by open office conditions, whether new knowledge is slower or faster to be generated, how formal and informal networks of communication are affected or if open-plan workspace increases employee turnover: all factors influencing human capital and investment in it.

FM oriented to human capital understands that it is necessary to go beyond what occupants like and dislike and apply knowledge of how work is affected to managing accommodation. The notion that workspace is one of the tools available to occupants to help them get work done is embodied in the concept of *functional comfort*, that is, how well the physical environment supports users' tasks and activities (Vischer, 2005, 2008). The notion of functional comfort provides a direct link between the environmental psychology of workspace and the value and uniqueness of human capital. An environment designed to provide functional comfort ranges from meeting the practical requirements of daily tasks—such as working on the computer, right lighting, ergonomic furniture—to facilitating the tasks and activities needed for better customer relations, generating opportunities for tacit learning and mentoring and growing and consolidating community and culture. A functionally comfortable workspace improves employee performance and thereby organizational productivity; a functionally uncomfortable workspace slows down work and can legitimately be considered a cause of stress at work leading to errors and fatigue (Vischer, 2007b)

Facilities designed for functional comfort use direct feedback from occupants, creating opportunities for informing and empowering workers. Instead of being asked whether or not they like or are satisfied with a feature of their workspace, they assess its impact on their ability to perform tasks, including decision-making and having new ideas (Vischer, 2007a). Study results indicate that environmental conditions for work can range from comfortable (supportive of employees' tasks) to uncomfortable (stress-generating), and that this bears little relation to users' satisfaction levels. Workers who struggle to hear on the telephone in noisy settings, who squint at their computer screens to deal with glare and who spend time searching for a place to sit down and work together are wasting the company's human capital trying to overcome environmental barriers by expending energy, attention and knowledge that should be invested in their work.

In addition to ambient environmental conditions, users providing feedback on their functional comfort assess key ergonomic features such as furniture configuration and floor layout. Distances to meeting rooms, printers and copiers; time to climb stairs or take the elevator; proximity and accessibility of coworkers and collaborators; access to file storage for both individuals and teams; number and dimensions of work surfaces; and wall or partition height are all influential factors affecting worker productivity in offices (Brill & Weideman, 2001; Hatch, 1987; Sullivan, 1990; Vischer, 1989). Similar lists could be identified for schools, hospitals and other workplaces. However, these factors are all part of *topos*: one of the key components of environment for *ba* and the one over which FM has most control. FM needs feedback from occupants to be able to make changes that result in a better fit between environmental design and employees' use of their tacit and explicit knowledge.

In human capital terms, not only are people's tasks and activities important, but also their knowledge, skills, creativity and connections with coworkers. It is a simple matter to expand the concept of functional comfort to include Nenonen's conditions for creating *ba*. The importance of well-designed shared or collaborative workspace is growing as companies rely more on project teams than on individual work and on collaboration through both formal and informal networks for generating new ideas and sharing new knowledge (Haynes, Ch. 17). While ambient environmental conditions and aspects of furniture and layout influence quality of place, knowledge creation and sharing are most directly affected by the configuration of interactive and collaborative space. Shared or interactive workspace provides opportunities for the four stages of the SECI cycle of knowledge generation in organizations—socialization, externalization, combination and internalization (Von Krogh, Ichijo & Nonaka, 2000)—of which more will follow. The *topos* needed for *ba* is located by and large in shared group space and in the type of accommodation decisions and way they are made, rather than in the features of individual workspace that have traditionally been in the FM purview.

SPACE AS A FACTOR IN INTRAORGANIZATIONAL RELATIONSHIPS

Managing the built environment offers a strategic tool for implementing human resources (HR) policies and philosophies. A dynamic and supportive workspace plays an active part in making a business successful; it is a powerful mechanism in the relationship between employees and the organization. It symbolizes mutual commitment, assuring both sides that each worker has 'a place' and that some degree of territorial control can be negotiated. It is this implicit deal between employee and employer, known as the socio-spatial contract, that gives workspace its symbolic power (Vischer, 2005). This contract, rarely made explicit and unlikely to be acknowledged unless violated, includes space as a key component of the agreement made when an employee joins a company. Although space is not typically part of the HR function of fitting people to tasks and jobs, there is an implicit promise that physical space along with pay, training, supervision and benefits are offered to employees in exchange for their time, energy, skills, knowledge and commitment. In view of the importance of select-ing the right combination of 'core,' 'traditional,' 'alliance' and 'contract' workers for optimal organizational performance, the way their time-space is structured, equipped and provided is likely to be a key influence on the effectiveness of the combination selected (Lepak, Takeuchi & Snell, 2003). FM plays a key role in implementing the socio-spatial contract and apply-ing what is known about how space aids and improves task performance, learning and the management of knowledge.

An FM-initiated participatory space-planning process not only gives employees the chance to voice their opinions and preferences, but also enables the organization to draw on and use their knowledge—especially the tacit knowledge of how they perform their tasks—so as to provide the best-fitting workspace. Both fit and flexibility are essential for organiza-tional effectiveness, so the challenge is to balance fit and flexibility of facili-ties, much as these must be balanced in strategic human resources (Wright & Snell, 1998). A responsive HR system *fits* the strategic needs of the firm but also enables a *flexible* response to a variety of strategic requirements over time. Similarly, the optimal environment meets users' needs at one point in time in order to fit—that is, to support, enable and enhance—how people work. It is also readily adaptable (flexible) to changes such as team reconfigurations and moves, mergers with other companies and sudden facilities expansion or shrinkage that might not have been anticipated.

Similarly, HR strategy distinguishes between organizations operating in a stable predictable environment, which might focus on "a human capital pool with narrow range of skills and . . . behavior," and those occupying a dynamic and unpredictable environment, which will need "a broad range of skills" and "a wide variety of behavior" (Wright & Snell, 1998, p. 758). FM may apply a similar distinction to accommodation decisions, in that firms operating in a stable and predictable environment, such as govern-ment agencies, may thrive in space that is more fixed and less easy to recon-figure—for example, walled offices rather than demountable cubicles—and designed specifically to support the behaviors desired. For companies oper-ating in a dynamic and unpredictable competitive environment, such as software firms, telecommunications companies and consulting firms, the need for a broad range of employee skills and behaviors and an empha-sis on communication will benefit from open-plan layouts that are easily reconfigurable, with mobile furniture elements (worktables, white boards), many informal places to meet and work and comprehensive and respon-sive technology to enable remote work and real-time communications. For many companies, the challenge has been shifting from the fit of a stable and predictable competitive environment to the flexibility needed in a dynamic and unpredictable competitive environment (Vischer, 1999).

As accommodation is defined more flexibly, thought can be given to a better fit between human capital characteristics; strategic HR practices (job design, staffing, training and remuneration), contractual terms, and FM.

Contractual terms may include making the socio-spatial contract explicit: letting future employees know not only what kind of space they will occupy, but also organizational rules and expectations regarding the space they have been allocated. Examples of implicit cultural rules include whether advancement to more senior positions is accompanied by larger and more enclosed (private) space, or not; which communal spaces are accessible and used by which members of the organization; and how supplementary and support spaces for tasks not performed inside individual offices or workstations are made available and used. Most space-related rules and expectations in companies are unstated, and learning them is one of the ways new employees gain knowledge of the organizational culture. However, making them explicit as part of the hiring process is one way to speed up employee acceptance into the culture and help them make optimum use of workspace resources sooner, thus reducing the time between investing in new space and the return on investment.

HOW FM CONTRIBUTES TO KNOWLEDGE CREATION

The SECI sequence referred to earlier promotes the conversion of tacit to explicit knowledge and therefore the creation of knowledge in an organization. Whereas studies of users in buildings have tended to focus on individual space and individual perceptions of environmental conditions, the four behavioral activity categories of the SECI sequence take place primarily in physically or virtually shared space. *Socialization* is focused on the individual, but involves sharing experience with another and is therefore not only an isolated activity, but also requires interaction. *Externalization* requires the articulation of tacit knowledge largely through the use of dialogue that others can understand and use, and therefore requires a place in which to occur. *Combination* results in the appearance of new knowledge that transcends the group in which it has arisen—who perhaps occupy shared workspace—and is diffused throughout the organization because physical and virtual opportunities are there for it to do so. Finally, *internalization* requires learning by doing, training and exercises; activities that mostly take place with others in places designed for that purpose. Although some of these activities are also solitary, for example where reflection is required, or testing, most depend on contact and connecting, for which spatial opportunities are key. Shared and group workspace in offices and other work environments designed according to these principles will enhance the SECI sequence.

As organizations attach more importance to sharing information and creating shared knowledge, space for collaborative work is increasingly important in facilities design and management. FM can facilitate socialization and externalization by providing well-designed group workspace and spatial layouts that encourage contact and communication. They can ensure that robust and accessible communications technology (virtual workspace) is available to advance combination activities. Internalization depends on all of these, as well as on a corporate culture that encourages training, mentoring and continuous learning.

Human capital value (the accumulated knowledge and skills that employees apply to improving processes, increasing efficiencies and providing more and better benefits to customers) and uniqueness (the degree of specialization and specificity of knowledge and skills to the organization) are affected both by HR practices and by facilities design and operations (Morris, Snell, & Lepak, 2005). The distinction between entrepreneurial activities that generate new knowledge—exploration—and cooperative activities that "involve the refining and recombining of existing knowledge in new ways" (p. 20)—exploitation—implies that the same, standardized approach to accommodation may not work for all companies or for all departments in one firm. FM is well positioned to identify whether exploratory, entrepreneurial activities that culminate in new ideas and new processes, rapid development decisions and a short time to market should be guiding facilities design. FM has a perspective on how employees' activities that require cooperation and integration to support the exploitation of existing knowledge can use space that supports them and the value and uniqueness of their knowledge. In practical terms, facilities most often need to supply a combination of the two to ensure the balance of exploration and exploitation characteristic of most modern companies.

TO SUM UP

FM has access to numerous examples of design criteria and building performance guidelines to ensure that the accommodation that facilities provide supports individual tasks, facilitates group processes and contributes to organizational effectiveness (Preiser & Vischer, 2004). Many such guidelines address design outcomes, such as the right lighting for individual tasks, control over accessibility (privacy) in group settings and flexible furniture configurations that can be adapted as work changes. If the desired outcome is increasing human capital value rather than simply raising satisfaction levels or improving task performance, then guidelines and practices oriented to creating *topos* (a physical place) for *ba* (organizational knowledge) offer FM an opportunity to enhance knowledge creation rather than remain limited to more conventional rationales for accommodation decisions, namely, either reducing occupancy costs or increasing worker productivity or both.

Nenonen's 10 qualities of *ba* are not limited to physical space; they also consider virtual space and social and relationship space—the emotional or spiritual dimensions of organizational culture—enabling the complexity and interactivity of the user–space relationship to be incorporated into buildings. These 'design guidelines' promote space for knowledge creation and sharing by going beyond the dualistic concept of environment that artificially distinguishes between built space and people occupying it; they assume that the people occupying space and the way they perceive and interact with space is part of the definition of space. While it is tempting to focus on how people are affected by features of the environment in which they work, a one-way relationship, in reality the relationship is equally affected by what people do in and with their space and their experience of interacting with it.

If FM's goal is to enable knowledge creation and application, then facilities will be designed and managed to support HR objectives such as the exploration of new knowledge and the exploitation of existing knowledge and balancing fit with flexibility. Thus HR and facilities architecture need to be designed in tandem to ensure that the right type of employee is hired, that opportunities exist for training and other activities that increase knowledge and that knowledge is applied and integrated among the firm's work groups and departments. This approach to FM places facilities decisions along with HR as essential considerations in enhancing the value and uniqueness of human capital.

Such an approach implies, first, that feedback and engagement of workers in devising their own space must be activated to ensure that both implicit (what they do) and tacit (how they do it) knowledge is applied to building design and operations. This is a departure from the usual space-planning process in which managers make selections from a limited set of choices offered by facilities and design teams, and workers have to adapt to the environment provided. In instances where FM uses an approach based on human capital considerations, workers will have a chance—indeed they will need—to be involved. Second, it means that workspace will function less as a reward for promotion through the company and more as a functional and supportive tool for work. Employees will seek out spaces, both physical and virtual, that support the work they do and have an enhancing effect on their performance. This likely means changes not only to space for work, but also to spaces for learning, health services delivery and communities (Beard, Ch. 6; Michel, Ch. 14; Macdonald, Ch. 19). Third, it means that FM will focus increasingly on group and shared space and opportunities for communication, collaboration and networking. Valuing knowledge means making sure it is produced and actively used, as well as making sure it is shared inside the organization and accumulates. This requires a balance between comfortable private individualized space for people to perform thinking tasks and reflection and a range of attractive and functional collaborative opportunities. Fourth, it means that communications technology and other tools must be integrated with workspace planning to facilitate "distributed working" and dispersed teams as people collaborate increasingly with partners in other parts of the world (Harrison, Wheeler & Whitehead, 2004). Finally, it means that companies will identify the type of human capital they want to invest in and make facilities decisions to recruit and retain the employee mix that suits the management of knowledge in the organization. An emphasis on exploration (producing new knowledge) may not yield the same facility solution as an emphasis on exploitation (using existing knowledge). Moreover, an optimal fit between employee characteristics, HR architecture and accommodation is likely to be time-limited, meaning that some degree of flexibility must be built into facilities to accommodate changing social and business practices in today's world.

FM will benefit from a better understanding of the socio-spatial contract. Research on the environmental psychology of workspace aimed at identifying the various ways in which people are affected by and interact with their physical environment at work is helpful in this regard. The concept of functional comfort forges a link between the environment's effects on worker performance and the overall productivity of the organization. Linking functional comfort to the concerns of human capital researchers expands the functional comfort model. Rather than focusing on people's experiences *per se*, the expanded framework generates studies that examine how effectively their knowledge is acquired, used, transferred and integrated to attain improved company performance and competitive advantage. The desirability of *ba* and the space-dependent aspects of the SECI sequence offer an important new paradigm for FM to assess dimensions of the organization-accommodation relationship and the effectiveness of facilities in the future.

The space that FM manages structures the relationship between value and time that is basic to fulfilling the human capital potential. Through informed FM, some organizations appear to be recognizing that investing in innovative and high-quality accommodation equates to investing in their human capital, balancing the quality of fit with flexibility as the organization's needs change over time and progressing towards an active O-A relationship. As mediator of key organizational activities such as information flow, social contact and reinforcement of corporate values, facilities need to be recognized for the underutilized asset that they are. As a knowledge area with unique abilities to manage the occupied environment, FM will increase its range and effectiveness—if not the definition of the FM community—by paying more attention to the 'big picture' of the organization-accommodation relationship, by working with HR to make the socio-spatial contract explicit, and by implementing innovative and effective ways to support workers' collaboration and communication as well as their individual tasks. FM has a key role to play in leading organizations towards deriving maximum value from their human capital.

REFERENCES

Boxall, P. (2011). Human capital, HR strategy and organizational effectiveness. In J.-L. Spender and A. Burton-Jones (Eds.), *The Oxford handbook of human capital* (pp. 289–291). Oxford: Oxford University Press.

Brill, M., & Weideman, S. (2001). *Disproving widespread myths about workplace design.* Jasper, IN: Kimball International.

Dewulf, G., & Van Meel, J. (2003). Democracy in design? In R. Best, C. Langston & G. de Valence (Eds.), *Workplace strategies and Facilities Management: Building in value* (pp. 281–291). London: Butterworth-Heineman.

Fischer, G. N. (1997*). Individuals and environment: A psychosocial approach to workspace.* New York: Walter de Gruyter.

Gann, D., & White, J. (2003). Design quality: Its measurement and management in the built environment. *Building Research and Information, 31*(5), 314–317.

Grant, R. M. (1996). Toward a knowledge-based theory of the firm. *Strategic Management Journal, 17*(Winter Special Issue), 109–122.

Guillén, M.F. (1997) Scientific Management's Lost Aesthetic: Architecture, Organization, and the Taylorist Beauty of the Mechanical *Administrative Science Quarterly 42*, 682–715.

Harrison, A., Wheeler, P., & Whitehead, C. (2004). *The distributed workplace.* London: Spon Press.

Hatch, M. (1987). Physical barriers, task characteristics, and interaction activity in research and development firms. *Administrative Science Quarterly, 32*(3), 387–399.

Hedge, A. (1986). Open versus enclosed workspace: The impact of design on employee reactions to their offices. In J. D. Wineman (Ed.), *Behavioral issues in office design* (pp. 139–176). New York: Van Nostrand Reinhold.

Holtham, C. (2003). *Knowledge and space: Why the most important technology in knowledge management is physical space.* Paper presented at Knowledge and Innovation Workshop: Creating physical and virtual knowledge spaces—new opportunities for knowledge management, September, Coventry, UK.

Joroff, M., & Bergman, M. (2007). *Strategies for capturing business in integrated workplace and real estate project markets.* Helsinki, Finland: Tekes.

Kampschroer, K., & Heerwagen, J. (2005). The strategic workplace: development and evaluation. *Building Research and Information, 33*(4), 326–337.

Lawler, E. E., Mohrman, S. A., & Ledford, G. E. (1995). *Creating high performance organizations: Practices and results of employee involvement and total quality management in Fortune 1000 companies.* Cambridge MA: Harvard Business School Press.

Leaman, A., & Bordass, W. (2001). Assessing building performance in use: The Probe occupant surveys and their implications. *Building Research and Information, 29*(2), 129–143.

Lennertz, B., & Lutzenhiser, A. (2006). *The Charrette Handbook: The essential guide for accelerated collaborative community planning.* Washington, D.C. American Planning Association.

Lepak, D. P., & Snell, S. A. (1999). The human resource architecture: Towards a theory of human capital allocation and development. *Academy of Management Review, 24*(1), 31–48.

Lepak, D. P., Takeuchi, R., & Snell, S. A. (2003). Employment flexibility and firm performance: Examining the interaction effects of employment mode, environment dynamism, and technological intensity. *Journal of Management, 29*(5), 681–703.

March, J. G. (1991). Exploration and exploitation in organizational learning. *Organization Science, 2*(1), 71–87.

McCoy, J. M., & Evans, G. W. (2005). Physical work environment. In J. Barling, E. K. Kelloway & M. R. Frone (Eds.), *Handbook of work stress* (pp. 219–246). Thousand Oaks, CA: Sage.

Mital, A., McGlothlin, J. D., & Faard, H. F. (1992). Noise in multiple workstation open-plan computer rooms: Measurements and annoyance. *Journal of Human Ergology, 21*(1), 69–82.

Morgan, A., & Anthony, S. (2008). Creating a high performance workspace: A review of issues and opportunities. *Journal of Corporate Real Estate, 10*(1), 27–39.

Morris, S., Snell, S. A., & Lepak, D. (2005). *An architectural approach to managing knowledge stocks and flows: Implications for reinventing the HR function.* CAHRS series Cornell University. Retrieved August 25, 2011, from http://www.ilr.cornell.edu/depts/cahrs/downloads/PDFs/WorkingPapers/WP05–15.pdf Nenonen, S. (2004). Analysing the intangible benefits of workspace. *Facilities, 9*(3), 233–239.

Ng, K-Y., Tan, M. L., & Ang, S. (2011). Global culture capital and cosmopolitan human capital: The effects of global mindset and organizational routines on cultural intelligence and international experience. In J.-L. Spender & A. Burton-Jones (Eds.), *The Oxford handbook of human capital* (pp. 96–119). Oxford: Oxford University Press.

Nonaka, I., & Konno, N. (1998). The concept of 'ba': Building a foundation for knowledge creation. *California Management Review, 40*(3), 40–54.

Nonaka, I., Scharmer, O., & Toyama, R. (2001). *Building Ba to enhance knowledge creation and innovation at large firms.* Retrieved August 25, 2011, from www.dialogonleadership.org O'Mara, M. A. (1999). *Strategy and place: Marketing corporate real estate and facilities for competitive advantage.* New York: The Free Press.

Ouye, J., & Serino, M. (2004). *Human capital and why place matters.* Paper presented at the Northern California Human Resources Assn Conference, San Francisco, CA.,September.

Preiser, W. F. E., & Vischer, J. C. (2004). (Eds.) *Assessing building performance.* Oxford: Elsevier Science Publishing.

Seiler, J. A. (1984). Architecture at work. *Harvard Business Review, 62*(5), 111–120.

Sullivan, C. (1990). Employee comfort, satisfaction and productivity: Recent efforts at Aetna. Chapter 3 in P. Souter, G. H. Durnoff & J. B. Smith (Eds.), *Promoting health and productivity in the computerized office.* London: Taylor and Francis. 28–48

Tsui, A. S., Pearce, J. L., Porter, L. W., & Tripoli, A. M. (1997). Alternative approaches to the employee-organization relationship: Does investment in employees pay off? *Academy of Management Journal, 40*(5), 1089–1121.

Vischer, J. C. (1989). *Environmental quality in offices.* New York: Van Nostrand Reinhold.

Vischer, J. C. (1995). Strategic workplace planning. *Sloan Management Review, 37*(1), 33–42.

Vischer, J. C. (1996). *Workspace strategies: Environment as a tool for work.* New York: Chapman and Hall.

Vischer, J. C. (1999). Case study: Can this open space work? *Harvard Business Review, 77*(May–June), 28–36.

Vischer, J. C. (2005). *Space meets status: Designing workplace performance.* London: Routledge.

Vischer, J. C. (2007a). The concept of workplace performance and its value to managers. *California Management Journal, 49*(2), 62–79.

Vischer, J. C. (2007b). The effects of the physical environment on job performance: Towards a model of workspace stress. *Stress and Health, 23*(3), 175–184.

Vischer, J. C. (2008). Towards a user-centred theory of the built environment. *Building Research and Information, 36*(3), 231–240.

Vischer, J. C. (2011). Human capital and the organization-accommodation relationship. In J.-L. Spender & A. Burton-Jones (Eds.), *The Oxford handbook of
human capital* (pp. 477–498). Oxford: Oxford University Press.
Von Krogh, G., Ichijo, K., & Nonaka, I. (2000). *Enabling knowledge creation:
How to unlock the mystery of tacit knowledge and release the power of innovation.* Oxford: Oxford University Press.
Wright, P. M., & Snell, S. A. (1998). Toward a unifying framework for exploring fit
and flexibility in strategic human resource management. *Academy of Management Review, 23*(4), 756–772.

4   Facilities in Popular Culture

John Hudson

The study of popular culture might seem an unlikely and obscure way of gaining insights into FM. On the face of it there would appear to be little to be gained from the analysis of media productions intended primarily to provide mass entertainment. Popular culture has often been regarded as debased and unworthy of serious study; however, this view has slowly changed over the years (Mukerji & Schudson, 1986; Traube, 1996) and it is increasingly seen as an important locus for social and management studies. There is a small but well-established research tradition in social and management studies of studying organizations and their management through the lens of popular culture (Rhodes & Westwood, 2008; Hassard & Holiday, 1998). This approach is a valuable addition to existing research into organizations as it raises issues that are often ignored in more conventional approaches. As Hassard and Holiday (1998, p. 1) note: "where organization studies texts present rationality, organization and monolithic power relations, popular culture plays out sex, violence, emotion, power struggle, the personal consequences of success and failure, and *dis*organization on its stage." A variety of popular media and genres have been subjected to studies of this type. A pioneering work was Whyte's (1957) work *The Organization Man*, which included discussion of the representation of organizations in popular novels. There have been studies of the portrayal of particular organizational roles (Lee, 2002; Smith, 1999; Stead, 1998) and genres (Hassard & Holliday, 1998; Rhodes, 2001; Corbett, 1998).

In addition to this material in organizational studies there is also a design-related literature that draws upon popular culture amongst other sources. For example, a number of works explore the relationship between architecture, urban form and the cinema (Shiel & Fitzmaurice, 2001; Shonfield, 2000; Clarke, 1997). Pélegrin-Genel (1996) and Budd (n.d.) have also used cinema to illustrate the development of office design in the twentieth century.

The physical environment is a very strong element in visual popular culture such as TV and cinema. Of necessity the action takes place in a representation of physical space whether realistic or fanciful. This is unlike non-visual media, such as the novel or radio broadcast, where physical space may be suggested but where there is wide scope for interpretation by the reader or listener. In certain productions the portrayal of a place can be a dominant element; the film *Blade Runner*, directed by Ridley Scott in 1982, with its graphic representation of an urban environment degenerating through pollution, is a good example of this. The cinema has a long history of portraying powerful images of utopian, or more often dystopian, urban futures. Fritz Lang's *Metropolis* of 1927 was a seminal film in this respect (Hudson, 2009; Elsaesser, 2000; Neumann, 1996).

FM is focused on the spatial manifestation of organization. The study of visual popular culture such as film may therefore provide insights into aspects of FM that may not be easy to access through more conventional academic study. However, this will not be through treating film as a reality. Although film can be realistic it is not a mirror of reality. Films are the creation of filmmakers and are interpreted by their audiences. Even documentaries are molded by the beliefs and worldviews of their makers; they often have a strong social and even political purpose. This can be seen in the work of John Grierson and the British documentary movement of the 1920s and 1930s (Aitkin, 1998) or more recently in Michael Moore's documentaries on American society. Film, then, constructs worlds in which the man-made environment plays an important role. It can provide us with broad, often idealistic, visions of places. Sometimes these constructed worlds are utopian; often they are the stuff of nightmares. These worlds may be abstracted and over simplistic but may provide archetypes against which general principles can be explored. This can be likened both to the building of scenarios in long-term planning (Bradfield, Wright, Burt, Cairns & van der Heijden, 2005) or the use of thought experiments in philosophical analysis (Baggini, 2005). Scenarios and thought experiments allow "what-if" questions to be asked in the context of a range of potential circumstances and events. Thought experiments often test or explore ideas against extreme, simplified or highly improbable circumstances. Scenario planning is being increasingly employed within the field of FM (International Facility Management Association, 2009), land-use planning (Xian & Clarke, 2003), corporate real estate (Dewulf & van Der Schaaf, 1998) and long-range business planning in general (Bradfield et al.). Xian and Clarke point out the origin of the word scenario in the dramatic arts and Schwartz (1998, p. 137) explicitly likens the development of a scenario to the process of writing a movie script.

The remainder of this chapter is devoted to an analysis of three major films in which the representation of the built environment and the process of managing that environment are central themes. They are: *Jurassic Park*, directed by Stephen Spielberg and released in 1993; *Brazil*, directed by Terry Gilliam and released in 1985; *Play Time*, directed by Jacques Tati and released in 1967. *Jurassic Park* and *Play Time* are strongly focused on particular facilities, the former a prehistoric theme park and the latter an imaginary modern district of Paris. *Brazil* takes a more general view of the environment of a dystopian totalitarian state dominated by bureaucratic procedures. Although of different decades and very different in style, approach and content, all three films have something in common in their explorations of aspects of modern, man-made environments and the ways in which people interact with them.

My adopted method is a critical analysis of the representation of the man-made environment and its management within each of the films. I attempt to draw out the particular relationship between the physical environment and the social, organizational and political order portrayed in the films. A brief characterization of the scenario being explored by the filmmaker is posited. The plot is only dealt with in as far as it provides insights into this representation, and the focus is on particular scenes that highlight the issues under consideration. No aesthetic judgments of the films are made.

JURASSIC PARK

Jurassic Park (1993) was one of the great box-office hits of the 1990s, grossing more money worldwide than any other film up to that time. Directed by Stephen Spielberg, it pioneered computer-generated imagery techniques to take the monster movie genre to new levels of apparent realism. It combined an exploration of the overarching theme of the potential dangers of uncontrolled technologies (particularly genetic engineering) with a series of exciting action sequences involving highly realistic simulations of dinosaurs threatening the human characters in various ways.

Facilities, their management and its potential failings are central to the film. The action is set in a huge, island-based tourist facility in which genetically engineered dinosaurs are contained by elaborate, computer-controlled security measures. The whole establishment is owned by the InGen Corporation, under the control of CEO John Hammond. The action is initiated by an inspection of the facility called for by the project's investors after one of the staff is attacked by a dinosaur. The inspection is carried out by a group of experts accompanied by Hammond's two grandchildren. During the inspection Dennis Nedry, the designer of the park's computer systems, who is secretly in the pay of a rival corporation, shuts down the security systems in order to steal dinosaur embryos. During the shutdown, various dinosaurs escape the bonds of their security enclosures. A dramatic sequence of events takes place as a consequence of which various protagonists, including Nedry, are killed and eaten by dinosaurs. Eventually the survivors return to the central control facility and are able to escape from the island by helicopter.

The overarching theme is of the dangers of uncontrolled technological development, in this case genetic engineering, and its potential to destroy its creators. This is, of course, not a new theme and the monster that terrorizes its creator is, for example, central to Mary Shelley's novel *Frankenstein* and its theatrical and cinematic adaptations. More generally the theme of an unbridled thirst of knowledge and its consequences are found in the legends of Faust or Pandora's box. The film can be seen as a scenario for exploring the ability of humankind to control the technological forces they unleash through technological means. In *Jurassic Park* the facility fails, not through the limitations of technical systems (these largely function as designed) but through the interface between technology and its human users; it is human frailty and greed (Nedry's attempt to steal the dinosaur embryos), and the reliance of the control system on Nedry's individual knowledge, that cause the disaster.

There is a central debate running through the film between the character Ian Malcolm, a chaos theorist, and Hammond. Hammond's background is in circus and theme park development, and he starts out with a belief that it is possible to construct a totally controllable environment, providing sufficient resources are available. He repeats the phrase "no expense has been spared" several times during the film. Malcolm's position, in contrast, is that no such total control is possible and the natural forces will break out of their constraints in unpredictable ways. Hammond's faith in his vision is slowly undermined by force of circumstance. As the survivors escape from the islands the paleontologist Alan Grant tells Hammond, "I cannot endorse this facility." Hammond replies, "Neither can I."

Jurassic Park can be interpreted as a scenario that explores the possibilities and limitations of a completely controlled artificial environment in which even the living creatures are man-made. The conclusion seems to be that although such an environment may be technically possible, the dangers imposed by human fallibility would render it too dangerous.

BRAZIL

Brazil is science fiction fantasy/black comedy released in 1985 and directed by Terry Gilliam. It is set in an Orwellian authoritarian state where the lives of individuals are controlled by the sinister, bureaucratic, yet somewhat incompetent, Ministry of Information. This is a state where security is paramount and there is a vague and unspecified terrorist threat. There is an all-pervasive but inefficient bureaucracy manned by an army of officials and enforced by a well-armed and ruthless police force.

The physical presence of the built environment is a prominent feature of this film. It is set in a bleak and dysfunctional urban environment. This forms the backdrop to a society obsessed by a shallow consumerism, particularly in an ill-fated search for physical perfection through plastic surgery. Building services, especially in the form of ducts, are found everywhere and connected to almost every device. The opening section of the film is a fatuous advert for the latest fashions in ducts. Set sometime in the twentieth century, buildings and fashions are of the 1930s and 1940s but the advanced, though unreliable, technology belies this. The technology mixes elements such as microcomputers and robots with older technologies such as the use of vacuum tubes for document transfer. Although this is in some respects a digital world, it is still dominated by the paper systems that seem particularly suited to its bureaucratic ethos.

The plot centers on the character of Sam Lowry, a downtrodden and unambitious minor bureaucrat in the Ministry of Information. He escapes from the tedium of the daily routine through dreams of himself as a flying knight seeking and rescuing a beautiful woman. The plot is instigated by a mistake in the bureaucracy when a swatted fly causes a printing malfunction that results in the arrest for terrorism, and subsequent death under interrogation, of Archibald Buttle, an innocent shoe repair operative, rather than Archibald Tuttle, a heating repair engineer and suspected terrorist. A chain of events is sparked off that leads Lowry to both meet his dream woman and be implicated in terrorist activities. Eventually this leads to his detention and loss of sanity under interrogation.

The terrorist Tuttle is an elusive and chimerical character. When we meet him we find his apparent offense is to subvert the state systems for maintenance of building services as a guerrilla air-conditioning engineer. He carries out repairs quickly and efficiently before the incompetent state-run Central Services can arrive.

A set of scenes in Lowry's apartment illustrate the film's exploration of the relationship between people and the built environment in the context of an authoritarian state. Lowry first meets Tuttle when a fault develops in the air-conditioning of his apartment. Lowry dutifully reports the fault to the Central Services department, but before they arrive Tuttle makes a dramatic entrance and easily fixes the problem. Before he can leave two aggressive operatives from Central Services arrive, demanding to be let in. Lowry manages to put them off before they discover Tuttle by invoking various bureaucratic procedures. They retreat angrily, threatening to return. In a second scene at the apartment, Lowry returns to find that the Central Services operatives have entered without permission and have caused havoc; ducts and other heating equipment are hanging everywhere. The operatives discover Tuttle's repair and accuse Lowry of employing an unauthorized engineer. In a third scene when Lowry once again returns to the apartment he finds it in a terrible state, icy cold and full of uselessly hanging ducts. The Central Services operatives are dressed in protective suits and announce to Lowry that he has been dispossessed of his apartment pending inquiries. Lowry goes outside and again meets Tuttle. This time Tuttle swaps the sewage duct with the supply of fresh air to the protective suits of the Central Services operatives, thus ensuring that they meet a horrible fate.

The oppressive urban environment is the dominant visual feature of the film. However, the scenario seems to be less about the physical presence of the built environment and more about how the management of that environment can become an oppressive tool in the hands of the authoritarian state. There is a struggle for control of the built environment between state authorities and individual users of that environment. Unauthorized building maintenance becomes a state crime. *Brazil* is a highly stylized fantasy, but interestingly it anticipates some of the same issues of corporate control and individual freedom in the urban environment identified by Minton (2009) as affecting life in the early twenty-first-century British city.

PLAY TIME

Play Time (1967) was Jacques Tati's most ambitious film. Like most of his work, it relies primarily on visual effects and the dialogue is secondary, functioning as a sound track rather than as a dialogue. The plot itself is minimal, and the film is a visual observation of the anonymity and disorienting effects of a modern Parisian urban environment. Tati's bumbling character M. Hulot and a group of female American tourists negotiate their way through this environment over the course of a day, during which their paths cross from time to time.

It is this environment that is the central theme of the film. During its making Tati personally funded the hugely expensive set, an action that led to his eventual bankruptcy. The film is set in a series of modern places: an airport, an office, an exhibition space, residential apartments and a nightclub. These places seem realistic but at the same time exaggerated. The sets are not realistic reproductions of real places; rather, they emphasize the domination of the rational urban order over ordinary human values. For example, Tati famously anticipated the development of the office pod that was to become such a feature of workplace design in later years (Pélegrin-Genel, 1996). The set is clearly intended to represent a business district in Paris. However, it is a part of Paris where modernism has prevailed and we only see glimpses of the historic city in hazy distant views or the reflections in opening windows and doors.

The environment is both transparent and confusing. M. Hulot can often see where he wants to go but is unable to find a way to his destination. One scene takes place in residential apartments with huge glass windows facing onto the street. Within the apartments, family life is played out as if on the television screen.

The bland modern environment provides the context for a series of comic incidents and gags. Just below the outwardly cool and rational facade of the buildings there are all manner of problems and chaos that await their users. We can see this in M. Hulot's difficulties in finding his business contact within the modern office, or in the old doorman's struggle with the baffling electronic communications systems. This dichotomy between the superficial rationality and the chaos lurking beneath its surface is particularly apparent in the long scene set in the Royal Garden restaurant. It is the restaurant's opening night and it is clearly unfinished, with workmen still busy with construction work when the first guests arrive. The evening is dogged by design defects and shoddy workmanship with which the management struggle to cope. The hapless architect is bombarded with problems. As the doors of the restaurant open, the elegance and sophistication of the first rich guests is in marked contrast with the unpreparedness of the staff. As the night progresses, a range of other guests arrive, including the American tourists and M. Hulot. Hulot's entrance is another play on the idea of transparency. He manages to shatter the glass door and the doorman has to retrieve the handle and spends the rest of the evening using it to open an imaginary door for arriving and departing guests.

Guests begin to dance, particularly when the modern jazz group begins to play, and the scene becomes wilder. The unanticipated number of guests results in the food running out; only cold chicken remains. A model of a chef displaying the menu is carried away, corpselike, to strange looks from some of the guests. The air-conditioning fails and the architect finds himself unable to cope with the control system, particularly as the instructions are not in French. He summons an engineer to fix the problem but subsequently the airflow becomes much too strong and noisy.

Hulot, who is tall, tries to retrieve an object high on the wall for one of the guests. This action results in the partial collapse of the poorly constructed building interior. The electrical systems begin to short and fail. Some of the guests, under the direction of a visiting American, use the collapsed material to partition off part of the floor and create their own enclave. Further partial collapse onto the jazz band causes them to cease playing. Barbara, one of the American tourists, takes over and plays the piano. The American takes the plans from the architect and gives them to Hulot, announcing that Hulot will be the new architect. Improvisation and partial chaos triumph over rational order. Around dawn the guests begin to disperse.

Play Time, as a scenario, is about the exploration of how ordinary people interact with a rationalist modern environment. Despite outward appearances, this environment is a human product and suffers from all the imperfections that this implies. The users of this environment, despite their frequent bafflement with its complexities, are able to use it, and sometimes to modify it, in ways that suit them, even in the face of the initial design intentions. There is a sense of optimism that basic human values will win through in the end.

CROSS-CASE ANALYSIS

The three films studied are very different in genre, style and subject matter. However, they also have strong similarities. All contain powerful representations of modern, for their time, environments: in *Jurassic Park* we have the ultimate theme park; in *Brazil*, a nightmare authoritarian urbanism; in *Play Time*, an exaggerated rational modernism. All three can be seen as scenarios for exploring aspects of contemporary design and urban issues. The environments portrayed are all, in various ways, oppressive and controlling. *Jurassic Park* is a totally engineered experience; *Brazil* is about extreme centralized authority; *Play Time* is about an unspecific and diffused, but nevertheless omnipresent, power. Despite this level of environmental control, there is no suggestion of environmental determinism. Rather, people interact with the environment for their own purposes and demonstrate considerable resourcefulness in doing so, whether this is in escaping from dinosaurs, fooling the state security services or adapting a disintegrating nightspot for personal enjoyment. Human values are central, and qualities such as resilience, cooperation, adaptability and bravery are usually rewarded.

The environments are the creation of flawed, or even evil, centralized authorities; the InGen Corporation and its investors in the case of *Jurassic Park*, the authoritarian state and its particular manifestations in the form or the Ministry of Information and Central Services in *Brazil* and the implied, but unseen, property developers in *Play Time*. These central authorities are counter posed with the free spirits of the central characters, who subvert the intended uses and management processes of these environments in a variety of ways.

It is not surprising that the man-made environment features prominently within each film. Film is a visual medium and visual impact is important, even in movies that rely heavily on dialogue. What is perhaps more surprising is that the process of managing facilities is central to each of the films. *Jurassic Park* is about what happens when things go wrong, particularly due to human failings, in a complex and potentially dangerous facility. Information management and services engineering are both featured prominently in *Brazil*. Human incompetence leads to mistakes in bureaucratic control; the act of subverting official channels for the repair of air-conditioning systems is sufficient to brand the perpetrator as a terrorist. Building services are the locus for a power struggle between individuals and central authority.* In *Play Time* individuals struggle to make sense of, and negotiate their way around, an environment that is not of their making and whose processes are obscure and dysfunctional.

CONCLUSIONS

A major value of the study of representations of environments in popular culture is that it can give insights into aspects of facilities that are difficult to investigate using conventional academic approaches. It is important,

---

*Editors note. Lest you think this is artistic licence consider the FMs checking after hours for indentations in the carpet revealing furniture that had been moved and other power struggles described by Ian Donald in 1994 (referenced on page 2 and page 86). The phrase life following art springs to mind.

however, not to treat representations as mirrors of reality. The approach taken is rather to use films as scenarios in which concepts and possibilities can be explored. There are parallels between the film scenario and the scientific experiment. The filmmaker constructs a simplified and often extreme world in which the consequences of particular actions by the characters in a particular context can be observed. In an experiment the scientist constructs a highly controlled environment in which the actions of particular variables can be observed in isolation from the wider world. The analogy should not be taken too far. However, film is a powerful medium within which to explore the ways in which people might behave in, and interact with, the environment in particular circumstances.

The films studied in this chapter date from the period between the late 1960s and the mid-1990s. Since that time the potential for manipulating images and creating complete alternative realities using computer technologies has increased dramatically. This is reflected not only in the techniques of filmmaking, but also in the subject matter. Films such as *The Matrix*, *The Truman Show* and *Inception* explore the possibilities of alternative and differently perceived realities. Although such explorations are not new—there are similar themes in *The Cabinet of Dr. Caligari* of 1920—they have proliferated in recent years. Moreover, the development of computer gaming and avatar worlds in cyberspace is expanding the possibilities of this approach dramatically. The study of these alternative worlds may provide further insights into the ways in which FM is developing.

REFERENCES

Aitkin, I. (1998). The documentary film movement, the post office touches all branches of life. In J. Hassard & R. Holliday (Eds.), *Organization representation* (pp. 17–40). London: Sage.

Baggini, J. (2005). *The pig that wants to be eaten*. London: Granta.

Bradfield, R., Wright, G., Burt, G., Cairns, G., & van der Heijden, K. (2005). The origins and evolution of scenario techniques in long range business planning. *Futures, 37*(8), 795–812.

Budd, C. (n.d.). *The office: 1950 to the present*. Retrieved December 6, 2008, from www.moma.org/exhibitions/2001/workspheres/swfs/theOffice.pdf

Clarke, D. (1997). *The cinematic city*. London: Routledge.

Corbett, J. (1998). Sublime technologies and future organization in science fiction film, 1970–95. In J. Hassard and R. Holliday (Eds.), *Organization representation* (pp. 247–258). London: Sage.

Dewulf, G., & van der Schaaf, P. (1998). Portfolio management in the midst of uncertainties: How scenario planning can be useful. *Journal of Corporate Real Estate, 1*(1), 19–28.

Elsaesser, T. (2000). *Metropolis*. London: BFI Publishing.

Hassard, J., & Holliday, R. (Eds.). (1998). *Organization representation*. London: Sage.

Hudson, J. (2009). Workplaces in the cinema. *Facilities, 27*(1/2), 34–43.

International Facility Management Association. (2009). *Strategic facility planning, a white paper*. Houston: International Facility Management Association.

Lee, M. (2002). Management history as told by popular culture: The screen image of the efficiency expert. *Management Decision, 40*(9), 881–894.

Minton, A. (2009). *Ground control.* London: Penguin.

Mukerji, C., & Schudson, M. (1986). Popular culture. *Annual Review of Sociology, 12,* 47–66.

Neumann, D. (Ed.). (1996). *Film architecture: From* Metropolis *to* Blade Runner. Munich; Prestel.

Pélegrin-Genel, E. (1996). *The office.* Paris: Flammarion.

Rhodes, C. (2001). *The Simpsons,* popular culture and the organizational carnival. *Journal of Management Enquiry, 10*(4), 374–383.

Rhodes, C., & Westwood, R. (2008). *Critical representations of work and organization in popular culture.* Abingdon, UK: Routledge.

Schwartz, P. (1998). *The art of the long view.* Chichester, UK: Wiley.

Shiel, M., & Fitzmaurice, T. (2001). *Cinema and the city.* Oxford: Blackwell.

Shonfield, K. (2000). *Walls have feelings.* London: Routledge.

Smith, P. (1999). Sex, lies and Hollywood's administrators. *Journal of Educational Administration, 37*(10), 50–65.

Stead, P. (1998). The cultural representation of trade unions. In J. Hassard and R, Holliday (Eds.), *Organization representation* (pp. 67–81). London: Sage.

Traube, E. (1996). "The Popular" in American culture. *Annual Review of Anthropology, 25,* 127–151.

Whyte, W. (1957). *The organization man.* London: Cape.

Xian, W., & Clarke, K. (2003). The use of scenarios in land-use planning. *Environment and Planning B: Planning and Design, 30*(6), 885–909.

5 Facilitating Creative Environment*

Birgitte Hoffmann, Peter Munthe-Kaas and Morten Elle

Over the past decade, social debate about creativity in relation to cities, businesses and society as a whole has intensified. Its strength can be seen in the fact that the United Nations (2008) identified the vital importance of creativity in a better future for the global society. Furthermore, the European Union decided that 2009 should be the year of "creativity and innovation." Clearly the winds of creativity have gained momentum, and we explore their origins and direction to provide a basis for the study of the development of the workplace and the potential for FM.

THE WINDS OF CREATIVITY

The global fascination with creativity can be seen in the context of the general reorganization of Western societies as a consequence of economical crises, energy crises, technological development, institutional changes and globalization in general (Harvey, 1989; Ericsson, 2001). In particular, creativity has been promoted as a means of keeping ahead in the competition with the growing economies in Asia, and thus the perception of businesses being able to reinvent themselves and produce innovative ideas is central to the economic thoughts in the Western world (Myerson, Ch. 2). The concept of creativity has become a main driver, not only in the creative industries, but also as an essential guideline of the managerial level in public administration and business in general (Ericsson), producing a noticeable demand for facilitating creative environments within these organizations.

The urban perspective constitutes one of the dominant narratives in the development of the creativity discourse. In *Cities in Civilization* (1998), the British professor in urban planning Sir Peter Hall describes how different cities at different times have constituted creative environments facilitating cultural and technological breakthroughs. However, during the last decade

---

*This chapter was first presented at the Ninth EuroFM Research Symposium in Madrid, May 2010, and is published in an edited form with the permission of the European Facilities Management Network.

the Darwinian struggle between cities for foreign direct investment has been explicitly influenced by the idea of creativity, and urban planning has taken a rather different turn. The question today is not so much about producing effective "business climates"—often in designated enterprise zones—that score highly in information and communications technology (ICT), HQ facilities, geographical accessibility and a well-educated labor market in order to attract corporations. According to the American professor of regional development Richard Florida, it is rather a question of creating the right "people climate" in order to attract the creative people who either develop or attract the contemporary growth engines of the economy, "the creative industries" (Florida 2002, 2003). While he focuses on "technology, talent and tolerance" as the prerequisites for creative cities attracting the "creative class," others target citizens' creativity in general. Charles Landry (2000), a key inspiration in the development of urban planning, focuses on concrete aspects of the city facilitating an innovative culture; Klaus Overmeyer (2007) focuses on the temporary use of urban space to further creative development in cities. The novelty is the direct linking of the physical and cultural aspects with economical development and the deliberate integration of this idea into urban planning and development.

A parallel narrative on creativity can be derived from a managerial perspective with a series of theoretical and practical approaches. *Organizational learning* has been a headline in the development of organizations in the knowledge society (e.g., Agryris & Schön, 1978; Senge, 1990), which draws learning and personal development from formal settings to become an integrated part of the lives of organizations and individuals. Several approaches explicitly dealing with "creativity" can be identified in the fields of design and innovation. A prominent example is "design thinking" (or lateral thinking as opposed to critical thinking), which constitutes a prevailing tool for actively promoting individual or collective creativity (de Bono, 1999). Similarly, Csikszentmihalyi (1996) coined the term "flow" for a harmonious state of intrinsic motivation where people are fully immersed in the task at hand. Currently Otto Scharmer, a German professor from MIT, is a dominant figure in implementing the creativity discourse in businesses with his method of "presencing" for collectively creating "the future that wants to emerge" (Scharmer, 2007).

From the different contexts the idea of creativity as a main driver of social processes of change has fused, Florida's notion of "the creative class" (2002) has become a signpost in the strategic planning of not only many Western cities, but also of international organizations, as well as public and private businesses. The creativity discourse has become manifest in concrete strategies and approaches in both public and private organizations to develop "creative environments." This development is subject to ongoing and local interpretations (cf. Price, Ch. 1); however, for this chapter the important point is that across the different approaches creativity is emphasized as a special potential that should be urged to develop, i.e., a potential that needs facilitation.

Creative environments in workplaces need facilitation in many ways, some of which exceed the field of FM, e.g., process facilitation and general management (cf. Alexander, Ch. 13; Bull & Kortens, Ch. 15; Macdonald, Ch. 19). FM has the potential to contribute to this development in dialogue with other fields, and we therefore proceed to explore the area between facilities and facilitation that FM may contribute to.

THE FIELD OF FM

FM has developed a strong practice around providing a supportive framework for businesses and organizations based on physical facilities. Newer definitions communicate a broader ambition of FM to become "a strategically integrated approach to maintaining, improving, and adapting the buildings and supporting services of an organization in order to create an environment that strongly supports the primary objectives of that organization" (Barrett cited in Alexander et al., 2004, p. 3). As pointed out in the first section, these primary objectives of organizations to a growing extent relate to creativity. Here we explore the potential and challenges for FM when the workplace is to become a more creative environment. Based on a review of FM literature on creative environments and on human factors in relation to workplaces, we outline strategies and methods presented in existing FM as a platform for this development.

Firstly, we need to point out that the review did not succeed in identifying a systematic discussion within FM of roles and strategies in relation to the development of creative environments; however, we did find a series of different input that may be used as stepping-stones in future moves. The fact that workplaces are undergoing radical changes, and the consequent demand for new ways to support these, seems to be recognized by newer FM. Along the lines of Florida (2002), Grimshaw (2004, p. 23) emphasizes that the creativity discourse sets forth new demands for workplaces as "[knowledge] workers need an empowered workplace where their individual skills in creativity and innovation can be exploited and which encourages them to stay." In a review of innovation in FM service delivery, Noor and Pitt (2009, p. 225) further argue for supporting general innovative work in FM not just to produce innovative solutions, but also to establish and develop a creative environment in which solutions can be conceived, developed and implemented.

Approaching the question of how FM may enlarge the engagement in this development, we focus on the notion of "people climate" as the basis of creative environments. In the urban context, people climate is very much related to facilitating a diversity of formal and informal public spaces and cultures (Florida, 2002; Landry, 2000). A similar focus increasingly inspires the development of public and private organizations, and icons of the creative age such as Google and the design company IDEO are examples of how corporations have internalized social and physical aspects of the bustling urban milieu on their own premises in order to reap the innovative fruits of creative people in informal social interaction (Turner, 2009; Radich, 2005; Gladwell, 2000). From inside the field of FM, Noor and Pitt (2009) show how FM strategies have integrated the provision of recreational spaces as well as designated team spaces (resembling what Scharmer [2007] labels "lairs"), supplementing traditional office workspaces in order to make environments conducive to innovation. They state that innovation requires many different creative processes over a sustained period of time and should involve many people. They argue for the need to consider human and process oriented aspects such as "lateral communications" (p. 218) and state (p. 219) that "the FM interface is a strategic approach to create a workplace atmosphere that is able to set an innovative culture and ambiance towards an organization's prosperity."

Other researchers have worked with human aspects and creativity, focusing on office design. Steen and Markhede (2008) investigate openplan offices and discuss disturbances due to noise and distraction against the benefits of enabling more horizontal conversations in the organization. Roper (2008) also describes this dilemma and develops a mathematical valuation model to analyze the value of "adaptable workspaces" that is defined (p. 640) as "supporting the quick transformation of the micro-environment into open, partially open, and closed environments as required by a knowledge worker." Martens (2008) concludes that the office space can be of value to the creativity of organizations and lists several physical factors such as layout, color, light and space for presenting one's work that might express, stimulate and facilitate creativity.

In his work on productivity, Haynes (2007; Ch. 17, this volume) focuses on the human aspects and argues that the behavioral components of the office environment have the greatest impact on office productivity improvements. He therefore argues for a larger focus on the human asset when evaluating workspace performance and calls for a shift in the FM paradigm from "cost reduction" to "value added" (2007, p. 453). He also points to the need for establishing a greater understanding of the relations between work processes and work environment and increased office productivity (p. 460).

Price and Fortune (2008)—addressing space effectiveness—discuss the implementation of new open space in "creative workplaces" (academia) and conclude that space reflects cultural patterns and that change management, therefore, is crucial when trying to change working environments. They state (p. 616), "Facilities Management professionals, trained to deal in the concrete realities of buildings, furniture and projects can find such considerations and the reactions of users as, at best, an irritant, and at worse a major obstacle which they perceive need overcoming." A concrete barrier for FM to engage in the processes relates to the project-oriented world of FM versus the ongoing need for management of space (p. 619).

The work that has been reviewed points to an interest in FM to work within the complex field of social and cultural processes. The review outlines some efforts and challenges that need to be further addressed to exploit this interest into a general development of FM, including the business strategies. In the FM literature studied, it seems that a strong focus on the physical environments and open-plan offices (and the potential and problems with these) is the dominant approach when looking at the physical representation of creativity. The focus of handling human aspects as part of system optimization based on perspectives of space effectiveness and productivity needs to be reflected and developed into more complex and dialogue-oriented approaches.

From a strategic perspective, this might be a challenge that includes reflections on predominant FM practices and research. Grimshaw (2004) claims that FM historically lost the opportunity to work with the more humanistic aspects of the working environment as other fields took over. Thus FM practice was forced into being mainly a cost-cutting function in businesses. In this perspective, FMs have been cut off from working with workplace integration and using their competences and know-how to improve working environments (ibid., p. 16). A case used by Leonard and Swap (2005) illustrates that if traditional FM wants to escape the role as the cost reducing administrator of the physical environment, and develop a future FM that contributes to creative environments, FMs need to engage in dialogues at a more strategic level with other fields.

To sum up, the creativity discourse presents new opportunities to FM, but also challenges. We agree with Grimshaw (2004) that the FM field might play a central role in the effort to improve creative working conditions in businesses. But if the field is to use the potential to move from the boiler to the boardroom (Becker, 1990) in the creative age, it needs to relate to the creativity discourse and focus on the people-centered aspects of creativity. And, as Noor and Pitt (2009, p. 219) point out, "innovation in FM must take place at a more initial stage and tied with the overall organization [of] innovation strategies to enable holistic innovation values, beliefs and attitudes to be adapted at all levels within an organization." In the following sections, we first present concepts and experiences from other fields to provide input to explore the relation between the facilities and facilitation, and subsequently some inputs on how FMs need to reflect on their contributions to the social side of workplaces.

A NEW PERSPECTIVE OPENS

There is much to be learned about supporting "people climates" from the field of urban planning (Larsen, Elle, Hoffmann & Munthe-Kaas, 2011). A central contribution derives from the Danish architect Jan Gehl (2008), who is internationally known for emphasizing "the space between the houses" and the importance of informal meetings taking place therein. The preceding should, however, not be interpreted into an argument for—or against—open-office environments. Landry (2000), with the concepts of "hard and soft" infrastructure, further points to the need for not just physical, but also organizational and process-oriented aspects of the creative environment, which he further labels as open-minded and cosmopolitan. This urban perspective can also be used in regards to workspaces. Malcolm Gladwell, inspired by the American urbanist Jane Jacobs (1961), unfolds this perspective of the city as a metaphor for the creation of creative workplaces. He states, "[We need] to overcome our initial inclination to be office suburbanites" (2000, p. 70), and uses Jacobs's narrative of Hudson Street in Greenwich Village to further his argument: "When sidewalks are used for socializing and play and commerce, the users of that street are transformed by the resulting stimulation: they form relationships and casual contacts they would never have otherwise" (p. 60). Creative work environments, just as cities, need busy public spaces and striving life. The principles used for creating the physical arena for life in the city seem to be well applicable to the design of physical environments in creative businesses. Looking at a firm like IDEO (Radich, 2005), it is striking how this business seems to be using the same principles in the design of their facilities as Gehl (2008) is prescribing as principles for planning of the built environment in an urban context.

Staying in the city metaphor, Gladwell states that "gated communities" in businesses should be avoided when designing creative environments. Likewise, Gehl finds that a number of urban activities are closed in by non-transparent walls with no real reason and claims that it would be better to open the city up, as the activities behind the wall might inspire others. In a business facility, the notion of transparency might also contribute to a more creative environment and it could be the first step towards a deeper contact. It is important to assemble activities, as the density of activities is decisive for the possibility of spontaneous, informal meetings occurring.

To support a more complex and process-oriented approach it might also be beneficial to turn to the field of innovation and design to further argue for opening up the traditional creative organizational setups to support a creative environment within the whole business. The social constructivist analyses of technological development all emphasize that successful innovative processes integrate heterogeneous networks, including different human and nonhuman actors (e.g., Latour, 1987; Law, 1987; Callon, 1987). With this, they break with the perception of innovation as a technology-driven process with separated creative activities driven by especially talented people. Also Binder, Brandt, Horgen and Zack (1998), who look at the workplace from a more concrete design perspective, criticize the often used notion about designing working environments that enable tasks to move easily and undisturbed through the organization. Instead, they argue that creative businesses are better served with working with collaborative inquiry, rather than formal presentations. They describe a case in which temporary space was created for people to meet and participate collaboratively in the process by organizing centrally located and visible common workspaces, where the ideas proposed and discussed could be seen and heard by passersby and other staff members, with the gain of more people being able to contribute. From the perspective of codesign and co-creation, Binder et al. argue for integrating users in design and work processes. This user-driven perspective on innovation currently prevailing (e.g., von Hippel, 2005) pushes organizations even further in opening up to what used to be conceived as external. FMs might gain insights of how to support the dynamic and complex creative and innovative processes from these perspectives. From a strategic perspective, a central feature in the codesign approach is the participation of users in the design of their workspace, which should not be misinterpreted as the personalization of the individual workspace, but as a participatory process where users of the facilities are involved in rethinking and reshaping these.

To sum up, we have argued for a strategy of a dynamic integration of facilities and facilitation in order to enable creative environments. We draw attention to perspectives that seems fruitful to inspire FM to open up towards facilitating creative environments: to perceive the whole organization as a creative environment and open up the facilities and work processes, and to open up the processes of design of the workplace to include more groups (cf. Beard, Ch.6; Bull and Kortens, Ch. 15)

AS WELL AS THE NEED FOR NEW REFLECTIONS

The workplace is an increasingly important point of reference for modern workers and plays a more important part than ever in their lives (e.g., Castells, 1996; Sennett, 1998; Grimshaw, 2004). The ongoing change of organizational structures and workplaces should be systematically reflected and evaluated in regards to the potential negative effects on people and society. Here we focus on the need to reflect what the strong focus on creativity means for employees.

FM has to consider where the winds of creativity are blowing. Even though restructuring workplaces to maximize their creative potential seems like a viable business strategy today, it is important to consider what unwanted externalities might show during the process. The contours of one risk can be detected from research in knowledge work. Flexible workplaces might induce alienation and greater work-related anxiety, and flexible work practices can make people feel isolated, uninspired and uncertain of their responsibilities (Cairns & Beech, 1999; Sennett, 1998). Thus there is a moral point to consider regarding the companies' right to challenge and adjust the internalized values and norms of their employees. Organizations employing what the Danish philosopher Ole Fogh Kirkeby (2009) labels "intimate technologies," such as value management and coaching to support the disciplinary processes of the employee into corporate values, might impose inexpedient pressure on the employees. New research on stress also points out that aspects such as influence, flexibility and meaning—earlier regarded as important to prevent stress—for the knowledge worker impose a duality between enthusiasm and strain that enforce stress (Buch & Andersen, 2009). The American professor Edgar Schein even emphasizes that the organizational developments towards more flexible and creative workplaces mean significant personal readjustments for the workers. He claims (1997) that organizations often (if not always) have to use coercive persuasion to adapt and internalize new modes of work:

> It is quite [unrealistic] to expect that just advocating such new assumptions will bring them into being. Organizations will either have to go through painful periods of coercive persuasion, or they will have to start with new populations of employees and managers who hold such assumptions in the first place. In either case, it is likely to be a long and difficult road so one should not kid oneself that cultures can be ordered up and cooked like restaurant meals. (Online reference unpaginated)

To unfold the creative environment to the whole workplace might set loose unwanted forces. FM has the potential to strengthen the reflective outlook not only about how to navigate in the creative winds, but also about how FM is contributing to the shaping of the winds, asking questions such as: what forms of creative environments should be stimulated? How can the creative environments be developed in accordance with the local context? And, not least, what does it mean for the people involved?

CONCLUSIONS

As the discourse and practice of "creativity" has entered the scene in post-industrializing societies, new agendas are constructed for the planning of future social development and economic growth. The concept of "creativity" has had an especially big and early impact in urban planning, meaning a more people-centered vision of urban development. In the planning for the development of a "people climate" conducive to creativity and innovation, soft issues of tolerance, diversity, participation and informal cultures and public spaces have become increasingly important. The same tendencies have been internalized in quintessentially creative organizations such as Google and IDEO, and in workplace development in general.

As such, the FM research on creative environments is mainly focused on the physical layout, mainly in the form of open-plan offices, but also recreational and dedicated team spaces. A more integrated approach to physical facilities and process facilitation may have a positive impact on the innovative culture of an organization. A central challenge is to develop the workplace for creativity instead of trying to add special creative rooms or zones to an existing workplace. A wide-scale reinvention/redesign of both physical facilities and organizational culture seems to be necessary for developing creative environments. A coordinating FM approach has the possibility to contribute to this development if integrated on a strategic organizational level. The function of FM in a creativity context cannot solely be seen as secondary or supportive in a traditional sense. In a creative organization, the facilities need to be part of a more general strategy regarding the creative environment.

Other fields of work have demonstrated the value-added element of the physical environment in combination with facilitation and organizational restructuring and might thus show ways for FM to contribute more to general organizational strategies. From urban planning, a strong tradition in designing for urban life has yielded a string of tools for the orchestration of exactly those serendipitous meetings and activities so important for a creative organizational culture. Likewise, research in codesign has suggested the advantages of collaborative and relatively exposed creative group processes as well as the user-involved design of workplaces for an innovative culture.

In making strategies for the development of a creative organizational culture, FM research needs to reflect the engagement and especially consider the possible human costs of this. There are limits to everything, and changing the physical and organisational layout of the workplace as well as the everyday work practices, may have detrimental effects such as stress and alienation for employees.

REFERENCES

Alexander, K., Atkin, B., Bröchner, J. & Haugen, T. (2004). Introduction. In K. Alexander, B. Atkin, J. Bröchner & T. Haugen (Eds.), *Facilities Management— innovation and performance* (pp. 1–11). London: Spon Press.

Agryris, C., & Schön, D. (1978). *Organizational learning.* London: Addison-Wesley.

Becker, F. D. (1990). *The total workplace—Facilities Management and the elastic organization.* New York: Van Nostrand Reinhold.

Binder, T., Brandt, E., Horgen, T., & Zack, G. (1998). *Staging events of collaborative design and learning.* Paper presented at the Concurrent Engineering Conference, July, Tokyo.

Buch, A., & Andersen, V. (2009). *Knowledge work and stress—between strain and enthusiasm.* Paper presented at CMS6 Conference, July, Warwick, Warwick Business School.

Callon, M. (1987). Society in the making: The study of technology as a tool for sociological analysis. In W.E. Bijker, T.P. Hughes, & T.J. Pinch (Eds.), *The social construction of technological systems: New directions in the sociology and history of technology* (pp. 83–103). Cambridge, MA: MIT Press.

Cairns, G., & Beech, N. (1999). Flexible working: Organizational liberation or individual strait-jacket? *Facilities, 17*(1/2), 18–23.

Castells, M. (1996). *The rise of the network society.* Oxford: Blackwell.

Csikszentmihalyi, M. (1996). *Creativity: Flow and the psychology of discovery and invention.* New York: Harper Perennial.

de Bono, E. (1999). *Six thinking hats.* London: Little, Brown and Co.

Ericsson, D. (2001). *The creative mystery*. PhD, Economiska Forskningsinstitutet vid handelshöskolan i Stockholm, Stockholm University.

Florida, R. (2002). *The rise of the creative class—and how it's transforming work, leisure, community and everyday life*. New York: Basic Books.

Florida, R. (2003). Cities and the creative class. *Cities & Community*, 2(1), 3–19.

Gehl, J. (2008). *Life between buildings: Using public space*. Copenhagen: Arkitektens Forlag.

Gladwell, M. (2000). Designs for working—why your bosses want to turn your new office into Greenwich Village. *New Yorker*, December 11, 60–70.

Grimshaw, B. (2004). Space place and people: Facilities Management and critical theory. In K. Alexander et al., B. Atkin, J. Bröchner, & T. Haugen (Eds.), *Facilities Management—innovation and performance*. London: Spon Press. (Eds.), *Facilities Management—innovation and performance* (pp. 15–32). London: Spon Press.

Hall, P. (1998). *Cities and civilization: Culture, technology and urban order*. London: Weidenfeld and Nicolson.

Harvey, D. (1989). From managerialism to entrepreneurialism. *Geografiska Annaler*, 71(1), 3–17.

Haynes, B. P. (2007). Office productivity: A shift from cost reduction to human contribution. *Facilities*, 25(11/12), 452–462.

Jacobs, J. (1961). *The death and life of great American cities*. New York: Random House.

Kirkeby, O. F. (2009). *The free organization—balancing between passion and magnanimity*. Copenhagen: Gyldendal Business.

Landry, C. (2000). *The creative city: A toolkit for urban innovators*. London: Earthscan.

Larsen, J. L., Elle, M., Hoffmann, B., & Munthe-Kaas, P. (2011). Urbanising Facilities Management: The challenges in a creative age. *Facilities*, 29(1/2), 80–92.

Latour, B. (1987). *Science in action: How to follow scientists and engineers through society*. Milton Keynes, UK: Open University Press.

Law, J. (1987). Technology and heterogeneous engineering: The case of Portuguese expansion. In W. E. Bijker, T. P. Hughes & T. J. Pinch (Eds.), *The social construction of technological systems: New directions in the sociology and history of technology* (pp. 111–133). Cambridge, MA: MIT Press.

Leonard, D., & Swap, W. (2005). *When sparks fly: Igniting creativity in groups*. Cambridge, MA: Harvard Business School Press.

Martens, Y. (2008). *Unlocking creativity with physical workplace*. Proceedings of the *CIB W070 Conference in Facilities Management*. Edinburgh: Heriot Watt University.

Noor, M. N. M., & Pitt, M. (2009). A critical review on innovation in Facilities Management service delivery. *Facilities*, 27(5/6), 211–228.

Overmeyer, K. (Ed.). (2007). *Urban pioneers—temporary use and urban development in Berlin*. Berlin: Senatsverwaltung für Stadtentwicklung, Jovis Verlag.

Price, I., & Fortune, J. (2008). *Open plan and academe: Pre-and post-hoc conversations*. Proceedings of the *CIB W070 Conference in Facilities Management*. Edinburgh: Heriot Watt University.

Radich, F. (2005). *Physical frames for innovation: Case studies of creativity supporting innovative rooms*. Horsens/Århus, Denmark: Vitus Bering/Strategy Laboratory.

Roper, K. O. (2008). *Providing knowledge worker requirements: A framework for decision-making and evaluation*. Proceedings of the *CIB W070 Conference in Facilities Management*. Edinburgh, Heriot Watt University.

Scharmer, O. C. (2007). *Theory U: Leading from the future that emerges—the social technology of precensing.* Cambridge: The Society for Organizational Learning.

Schein, E. H. (1997). *Organizational learning as cognitive re-definition: Coercive persuasion revisited.* The Society for Organizational Learning. Retrieved December 22, 2009, from http://www.solonline.org/res/wp/10010.html

Senge, P. (1990). *The fifth discipline. The art and practice of the Learning Organization.* New York: Doubleday.

Sennett, R. (1998). *The corrosion of character: personal consequences of work in the new capitalism.* New York: Norton.

Steen, J. & Markhede, H. (2008). Creativity demands new office designs. Proceedings of the *CIB W070 Conference in Facilities Management.* Edinburgh, Heriot Watt University.

Turner, F. (2009). Burning Man at Google—a cultural infrastructure for new media production. *New Media Society, 11*(1/2), 73–94.

United Nations (2008). *Creative Economy—Report 2008. The Challenge of Assessing the Creative Economy: Towards Informed Policy-making.* New York: United Nations.

von Hippel, E. (2005). *Democratizing innovation.* Cambridge, MA: MIT Press.

6   Spatial Ecology
Learning and Working Environments that Change People and Organizations

Colin Beard

Many spaces counterintuitively interfere with learning and working, yet this state of affairs remains largely misunderstood by senior executives. I argue that rapid change to working and learning spaces forms a new ecology, a spatial dynamic that can liberate, or limit, human and organizational capacity. Driven largely by what we know about learning and human development, *working* and *learning* are increasingly regarded as converging phenomena in the knowledge economy: both require a similar range of human functioning, particularly, 'higher'-level thinking through complex information manipulation. These human functions, previously seen as largely cognitive, can be developed through greater comprehension of the role of movement in an ecological context. Synergies exist with human processing tools as movement emerges as key to new gesture-based technologies that align GPS-like human capacities to processes important to learning, creativity and memory retention. I suggest that the human would better comprehend problematic knowledge, so typical in today's complex world, by organizations identifying and creating, although not necessarily owning, more spaces for corporeal applications, as an extra gear to individual and organizational learning (cf. Myerson, Ch. 2; Bull & Kortens, Ch. 15). I propose a new evolution, an ecological alignment of the structural, functional, personal and social milieu of workplaces. Through sensitive design work that acknowledges human fears and the need to *belong*, new spatial ecologies can liberate individuals and organizations.

WHAT DO WE KNOW ABOUT LEARNING?

In the past our schools used to seat our children in rows of separate desks, suitable, it was thought, for the dissemination and reception of information. Offices did much the same, and universities pursued a similar focus of linear form within classrooms. However, academic institutions, and a handful of corporate organizations, are now leading the way with new changes in the design of working and learning environments (Beard & Price, forthcoming), partly because the *business of learning and knowledge creation* is taking center stage in faculty and corporate building design. Without proposing a neat sequential timescale, theorizing about adult learning has been exposed to continual critique. Notions of 'deficit' and limitations about what we know about human capacity have confronted the prevailing hegemony. This evolutionary process searches for more 'complete' ideas about adult learning, and has almost subconsciously influenced office and building design.

By the early twentieth century behaviorism had emerged. As a dominant view of its time it was linked to ethology, focusing on, for example, animal conditioning and stimulus-response patterns behaviors (Pavlov, 1927; Skinner, 1974). The Hawthorne studies symbolized such stimulus-response approaches to human productivity experimentation. Cognitivist theories surfaced in the late 1950s, seeing the 'human' as unique, intelligent and rational (e.g., Lewin, 1951; Bloom, 1956; Gagne, 1974). The dominant metaphors were computational: processes of thinking, remembering, analyzing and seeking ways to explain and make sense of the world were of great concern. By the late 1960s humanist theories were emphasizing personal agency and the fulfillment of human potential. Perhaps the most well-known proponent was Carl Rogers, whose seminal text, *Freedom to Learn* (1969), articulates a liberatory metaphor, a theme I develop later. Such ideas gave rise to *learner-centered* methods, currently dominant in educational institutions where the student experience is a business priority.

Cultural and social context became increasingly recognized as important (e.g., Vygotsky, 1978), giving rise to a range of social constructivist theories, with learning seen as active and contextualized. It was accepted that people 'constructed' knowledge, both individually and through social interaction, and the now rather ubiquitous café design approach to corporate and educational institutions has been driven partly by constructivist views about knowledge creation and social interaction. Today constructivist thinking is positioned amidst a vast milieu of alternative, although mostly complementary, views about human learning. The result is enormous changes in what we know about how adults learn: psychoanalytic theories (Britzman, 1998); the questioning of a single intelligence (Gardner, 1983); major advances in neuroscience (Damasio, 1995); and a widening recognition of the role of the body in learning (Lakoff & Johnson, 1999; Sheets-Johnstone, 2009), specifically bodily gestures (Gallagher, 2005), the human senses (Abram, 1997) and human emotions (Illeris, 2002; Mortiboys, 2005). Such diversity highlights the ongoing search for more integrative theories of learning within and across disciplines (Dillon, 2007). Although far from presenting a comprehensive picture, this brief chronological sketch highlights a continuing trajectory towards a complex, web-like ecology of learning involving *mind, body and environment*.

Few contemporary models of learning go beyond the primacy of cognition and social construction. Heron (2001, p. 208) voiced concern that "the old model of education, going back to classical times, dealt only with the education of the intellect, theoretical and applied." He noted that "nowadays we have people who are learning by thinking, feeling and doing—bringing all these to bear on the acquisition of new knowledge and skills." Illeris (2002) likewise broadened his theorizing to include emotions, suggesting three dimensions as central to learning: the social, cognition and emotion. He noted (p. 157) that "in order for learning to be characterized as formation of experience, the learner must be actively present and be self-aware in his or her interaction with the social and/or material environment." This marked a further recognition that our biological inheritance is to sense and understand the world through many connected processes.

Beard and Wilson (2002, 2006) argue for a greater understanding of the relational and dynamic nature of a number of core aspects of learning. Using integrative thinking they present a new model (Figure 6.1), which specifically recognizes the importance of the learning environment, including the relationship between space, place and cultural and sociopolitical contexts, to five other core dimensions. The location and context of learning is anchored within the philosophical notion of *belonging*: a human sense in which the built environment plays a major part. The second dimension concerns what learners *do* (an active component); the third dimension concerns *sensing* (how information and the experience is received internally for processing); the fourth dimension concerns *feeling* (emotions); the fifth concerns aspects of *thinking* (cognition); and, finally, the sense of *being* (self, identity, learning and change).

Beard and Wilson's work is not, however, common in the language of the workplace. Using an 'ecological' approach to space design in the workplace, Becker (1990) suggested we observe *tribes* and their *territoriality* in spaces. Conflict between tribes can center on language incompatibility between space providers (facilities and estates managers), space

SIX PRACTICAL QUESTIONS FOR LEARNING AND DEVELOPMENT					
WHERE?	**WHAT?**	**HOW?**	**HEARTS?**	**MINDS?**	**CHANGE?**
WHERE DOES LEARNING TAKE PLACE?	WHAT WILL THE LEARNERS ACTUALLY DO?	HOW WILL LEARNERS RECEIVE THE EXPERIENCE?	CONSIDER THE EMOTIONAL ENGAGEMENT?	WHAT DO LEARNERS NEED TO KNOW?	HOW CAN LEARNERS BE ENCOURAGED TO CHANGE?
SIX PHILOSOPHICAL CONSIDERATIONS					
BELONGING	DOING	SENSING	FEELING	THINKING	BEING

Figure 6.1   Increased complexity: six core dimensions of learning.

consumers (workers), space designers (such as architects) and institutional senior managers. The FM tribes have traditionally focused on efficiency of use, durability in performance and density of occupation, with operational management expressed through measures and costs, inventories, equipment lists, 'service' offerings, durability, efficiency of utilization and occupation and consumption density of seats and desks. The number of rooms used, investment cycles, health and safety issues, theft and security problems also became the dominant statistical data that formed the basis of important managerial decision-making. The CEOs and educationalists largely failed to comprehend that this language falls short in its alignment with the language of productive working involving individual and organizational learning, innovation and continuous positive change. As a result physical and virtual learning environments, and workplace offices, have until recently remain rooted in the false efficacy of fixed, simplistic and linear arrangements, rather than mirroring the rich ecology of human learning.

Paper and fixed telephones originally created a need for desks/workstations, yet the processing tools of control and efficiency that once tied us to the work*station* now have the potential to liberate people from the view of work as a sedentary process. The workplace is not an inert container but a coalescence of social and artifact dynamics with learning and working experiences is in constant flux. New mobile human tools, including portable, gesture-based computing technology, support human hand and body mobility, allowing rotational capacities of multidimensional form. First the pod, then the larger pad and next the *i-wall*, permitting large wall spaces to be functionally productive, rather than a space for unused coat hooks.

The linear format of the written and spoken word, as with computer screens, may also limit human development: the spoken language and the textbook, symbols of the uniqueness of the *human* being, are presenting new problems. Sheets-Johnstone illustrates this point nicely (2009, p. 362): "Everyday language is clumsy and inadequate when it comes to dynamics" and "bodily feelings are not easily or readily describable, especially when it comes to affectivity and movement."

Mobility within and between spaces can accelerate complex thought and social interaction. After all, as Lakoff and Johnson note (1999, p. 555), "our conceptual system is grounded in, neurally makes use of, and is crucially shaped by our perceptual and motor system." They also point to the lineage inherent in our habitual cognitive processing metaphors. They are clearly sensorial and kinesthetic: 'I *see* what you mean now,' 'I think I have *grasped* the concept,' 'We *support* our argument with.' Lakoff and Johnson also note that "reason is not disembodied, as the tradition has largely held, but arises from the nature of our brains, bodies, and bodily experience." They posit that referring to the period before written and spoken as *prelinguistic* implies a language vacuum. Reframing this notion, utilizing the term *post-kinetic*, acknowledges the bodily sensorial evolutionary precursor to the spoken and written, still evident in pictographic languages such as Chinese (Abram, 1997) and in gestures (Gallagher, 2005).

MIRROR IMAGE: LEARNING ENVIRONMENTS EMULATE LEARNING THEORY COMPLEXITY

Some contemporary working and learning environments are beginning to mirror the ecological complexity found in the theories of adult learning: an asynchronous coevolution becomes apparent. Organizational ecology is no longer restricted to immediate organizational boundaries: the FM supply chain is extending into the community, generating wider relationships, and outsourcing building services. The ecology can be illustrated by reference to a recent definition of a 'learning environment' as:

> A sufficiently diverse and varied, physical or virtual, natural or artificial place and/or space that, wherever and whenever, can facilitate and engage people in the wide range of learning activities, through connectivity and community, cultivating and sustaining psychological, intellectual, emotional, social and political development. (Beard, 2008, p. 184)

The same definition increasingly holds true for *working* environments. Working and learning have, or should have, mutual affinity in the knowledge economy: learning impels work and vice versa. If this definition is applied to working environments the result would be eco-diversity: more varied working settings, inside and outside the 'office.' Ecology becomes an appropriate metaphor with contemporary currency for FM. An empty niche, a new space, becomes a place when we endow it with our culture and functional artifacts. A work*place*, historically part of our identity, also contributes to the sense of belonging: it is a place to work, to learn, to socially interact, to think, write and to just 'be' and 'belong.' Yi-Fu Tuan (1977) notes that we transform space and dwell in it: space, says Tuan, is freedom; place is security. Place enables, but it can also limit. Let me further explore some limiting aspects. The human sense of *belonging* can be problematic in open-plan, hot-desk designs, largely because the personal becomes depersonalized and the *territory* has little perceived ownership.

Battery hens are reluctant to leave their cages. After a long period of occupation, liberation is frightening. Similarly, human habits influence the choice of human habitat. New interactions, providing memetic diversity, are necessary for organizational survival: although new habitats require adaptation as people evolve to work and learn out of the original and very artificial single habitat of the secure corporate office environment. The shift towards a more natural ecological web of opportunity and spatial complexity demands FM change. I will explore this evolutionary phenomenon by reference to two corporate buildings. Changing the nature of social encounters through spatial design can, however, prove problematic: the adaptive changes don't always occur in the short term. Spatial changes can create conditions that initially disturb, interfering with established working practices; it takes time to agree on fresh rules of the human encounter.

Let me illustrate this by referring to the pragmatism that guided the redevelopment of the London headquarters of the global property consultancy EC Harris. ECHQ, as it was labeled, was rebuilt as a solution to several strategic challenges, most notably differentiation and rejuvenation of their surveying practice. The project is credited with dramatic increases in profitability as well as a significant reduction in space requirement per head and CO_2 emissions (Stuart, Ch. 11). What I saw in their building, however, was an evolving spatial ecology, involving three key layers of the workplace. These were as follows: layer one created public areas available to anyone, including the practice's clients and collaborators. This area was welcome 'public' space, for staff and visitors involving the café/social dynamic as a conversational form. Layer two was available, although less formally recognized, for 'friends' of ECH to have space to work, online, with a desk. Layer three was a restricted 'staff' hot desk and milieu of varied light office spaces, designed to achieve a richer range of spaces for different conversations, with efficient density without packing, and allowing for 'clusters' of mobile teams. The result was that the traditional desk is no longer the fixed space at which a worker is expected to sit. The ECHQ approach, for me, was significant in that if it were to be replicated in collaboration with other businesses in the City of London (cf. Hoffman, Munthe-Kaas & Elle, Ch. 5; Alexander, Ch.13), then, possibly for the first time, there would be an ecology of spaces and places providing a networked web of home and 'away' spaces for inner and outer conversations that mirror the understanding of the whole person spatial-functional awareness of management learning and knowledge creation in a rapidly changing world (Beard & Price, forthcoming).

THE HUMAN BODY IN THE NEW SPATIAL ECOLOGY

We can make sense of many spatial issues if we understand that *working* is no longer synonymous with *doing* (work); work functionality is diversifying. In the knowledge economy socially constructed knowledge is important; the process requires human exchanges through mobility, having different conversations in different spaces. Aristotle's habit of walking whilst lecturing gave rise to the name *peripatos*, a process important in early university cloisters. This emphasis on bodily movement and social interaction requires further translation. Physical exercise and routine movement can provide opportunities not only for social conversations, but also synthesizing thought through silence. Silence, and the space to think with depth, is important to business functions. How does this work? More importantly, how can physical space support this human function?

Typically heightened sensory alertness and increased cognitive receptiveness occurs in novel locations. Furthermore, these other spaces have the potential to divest us of sensory habituation and elements of (social, political and cultural) belonging that can inhibit change. The 'other space' is less inculcated with our organizational and individual identity: a new collective identity has to be forged in new locations. Such spaces appear exemplary for specific kinds of organizational and individual learning. Reflection can be a significant or perhaps vital element of learning (Wood-Daudelin, 1996). Solitary and group reflective processes are important for workplace learning: Wood-Daudelin lists performance appraisal, project review sessions and mentoring as examples of group reflective processes. Individual, solitary reflective activities, on the other hand, are facilitated by repetitive, rhythmic routine: so-called 'mindless' activities such as jogging, swimming laps, lawn mowing and routine habits such as ironing, shaving or showering. Such bodily acts, she suggests, reduce or suspend incoming sensory information, allowing for a mental rewiring and refocus on sorting existing data about previous experiences. Significantly, she is proposing that reflection is operating in a state of flux between mind and body, and higher cognitive functions are facilitated by bodily movements. The *sand walk* (Beard and Price, 2010) honors Charles Darwin's original example of a route around which he would walk so as to develop his thinking by creating a 'synthesizing mind state,' which resulted, of course, in him having some of the most original insights in the history of thinking (Price, Ch. 1). Similar functionality has already been incorporated into leading-edge building design. GCHQ is a government organization concerned with for example anti-terrorism measures. They too benefited from redesigning the workplace (Green, foreword). Their new circular building encouraged new ways of working, reducing response times. A work anywhere culture developed through more open-plan areas, greater desk and knowledge sharing, and agile team working (Crabb, 2005). Significantly, the design included a huge outer circular ring of walking space, the modern equivalent of the *peripatos*, known by staff as *The Street*.

SPACE FOR CRITICAL THINKING TO WORK AND LEARN

Silence is required for certain mental functioning: to 'concentrate,' to 'think' or 'write' with critical depth. These activities require different spatial properties for efficacy. Behuniak argues for a pedagogy of silence as a research topic, suggesting that public spaces are diversifying whilst private spaces are declining; for example in the academy:

> Given the need for solitude, it is ironic that what most universities do is to create an environment in which students are rarely alone. Intent on forming a campus community, campus architecture creates communal

spaces: classrooms, student living quarters, outdoor quads, dining halls, recreation centres, and now even libraries are places to be designed to be with others. Where, then, do they go to be alone . . . Where is the private space? (2005, p. 11)

Many workplaces and universities have little or no space to concentrate, to think and write with depth. One approach to encourage critical reflective work, referred to as *Coffee and Papers* (Beard, 2010), got its name from training settings in hotel lounges, where the experience was designed to be comparable to reading the Sunday newspapers in a relaxed environment and focused mind state. Essentially it consists of an invitation to individuals to read themed articles and to intentionally relax in an environment that is personally special. Articles are taken from scholarly and professional journals: *Harvard Business Review, People Management, Management Learning* and many others—hardly conventional Sunday morning reading! *Coffee and Papers* typically generate high levels of learner engagement and knowledge generation through the process of individual reading in a retreat simulation, followed by social conversational learning. The experience is designed to develop a specific sensory cognition, or body–mind state of 'relaxed alertness.' Individuals experience comfort, with a degree of solitude, to enhance concentration and thinking. Coffees, teas, fruit juices, croissants and fruit add to the sensory experience. After a period of quiet solo reading the group reassembles and constructs collective conversations, critically exploring the range of readings. The acquired collective knowledge can be substantial. During these sessions, differing views concerning the same articles are discussed and new insights are developed based on individual experience outside the articles. This leads to a spin of ideas that spur more new ideas and reshape initial thoughts of the articles. It appears that many of the participants share this experience regarding the sessions. Senior executives admit to the pleasure at effectively being given permission to experience an extended period of *thinking* and *concentrating*. A CEO sat in her stocking feet on a stool in a hotel lounge and said: "Colin, I am in heaven. I never have the time to read anymore. I have lost the power to think or read with any depth these days . . . I am enjoying this experience so much!"

The *Coffee and Papers* experience had a profound effect on a whole organization. Staff members in the UK's National Health Service (NHS) have responsibilities to sustain professional development through reading of evidence-based clinical practice. Time to read about such clinical practice is, however, diminished by the dominance of everyday activities—the *doing* dimension of learning. Concentrated reading and the subsequent collective sharing may not happen for a number of reasons, including guilt associated with relaxed reading at work. Reading might not be interpreted as *doing* work. However, the staff of one primary care trust, having experienced *Coffee and Papers* in a training program, put forward what turned out eventually to be a successful proposal brought to senior managers under the workplace umbrella. The proposal, as part of an 'Inspiration Award' scheme in 2009, included some of the following required actions suggested in order to implement this idea:

- Encourage staff to write reading time into their objectives.
- Develop a marketing campaign across the organization showing that it's okay to sit and read clinical material.
- Provide education for managers to help them understand how to enable staff to absorb current evidence.
- Understand the cost of allowing staff time to absorb evidence, but also calculating and understanding the cost, service and other benefits.
- Purchase resources to make reading easier.

The *place* signifies that *time* for concentration is important and a legitimate extension of work. Organizations often require a diversity of *spaces*, for staff to *go away*, for example, to innovate, to learn and think more deeply about change. Many spaces belonging to other organizations are used for 'away days': hotels, retreats, outdoor centers, on board yachts, up mountains and around golf courses to name a few. Going on *away* days or retreats for staff development or training is also an interesting term: *away* from what? To get away from the computer station, the incoming e-mails, incoming calls and the company culture, to find other spaces to 'concentrate,' to 'think,' to 'write' or to innovate? These *away* environments need not be the same as space to process paper at a work*station*. If working and learning is more mobile it can occur in a diverse range of spaces and places, thus a tension between *doing* and *thinking* becomes apparent. Spatial diversity aligned to human functionality appears key.

SPATIAL SEPARATION: CONVERSATIONS AND DATA MANIPULATION IN TIME AND SPACE

Osborn (1963) has argued that a major block to creativity is the tendency to prematurely evaluate ideas and suggests that it is useful to separate idea generation from idea evaluation. Amabile (1983) suggests that managers habitually damage creativity by looking for reasons not to use a new idea instead of searching for reasons to explore it further. Her research "shows that people believe that they will appear smarter to their bosses if they are more critical"—and it often works. "In organizations increased professional status can arise from the ability to react critically to new ideas" (p. 83). The Disney Corporation, as masters at providing visual and spatial experiences, worked with this problem. According to Robert Dilts (1994, p. 163), a major element of Walt Disney's original genius was his ability to explore something from a number of different perceptual positions. One of his animators noted: "There were actually three different Walts: the

dreamer, the realist and the spoiler. You never knew which one was coming into your meeting." Based on this insight, Dilts identifies the structure
of creativity as a synthesis of different processes or phases. Specifically,
dreamer conversations enable new ideas and goals to be formed; realist
conversations transform those ideas into concrete expressions; critic conversations act as a filter to counter overly creative or ambitious ideas and
also provide a stimulus for refinement. These conversations, when separated in time and space, allow for constructive alignment. Critic conversations, which can so easily destroy the creative conversation of the dreamer
if occurring simultaneously, take place in a different room and at a different
time than the dreamer and realist conversations. Tensions associated with
left–right brain supremacy are solved by spatial and temporal separation.

In today's complex world, solving problems requires an appreciation of
the nature of complexity. Over 20 years ago Peter Senge (1990) suggested
five disciplines that should be practiced by every employee for an organization to become a learning organization. Two of these were an awareness
and examination of *mental maps* and developing the ability for *systemic
thinking*. Clues as to the nature of complex problems are found in the work
of Meyer and Land (2005). Troublesome threshold concepts, they suggest,
occur within any subject or discipline area, including business. The troublesome knowledge consists of several epistemological concepts that are
hard to grasp; although they suggest that once people have understood such
threshold concepts, deep transformative learning can occur. Significantly,
such concepts are said to be a weblike network of bites of knowledge. They
also suggest a dimensional complexity: the spatial and relational connect-
edness of the bites of knowledge cannot be easily relayed through one-di-
mensional communication such as speech, text or computer screens. Space
and time dimensions may prove to be at the root of this problem.

DISCUSSION

Contemporary, experience-based models of learning (Beard & Wilson, 2006)
highlight how the physical environment affects a complex milieu of learning
dynamics. Through practice examples I have sought to open up a new vista
so as to highlight the underappreciated and sophisticated nature of the con-
nectedness of space to the bodily senses and to internal and external reflective conversations. I have explored the important role of rhythmical physical
bodily movement, the separation of cognitive and social conversations in different spaces, the use of quiet space to develop mind states of relaxed alertness
and the experiencing and understanding of problems that have a relational
complexity in terms of time and space dimensions. At the heart of these brief
explorations of practice is a suggestion that greater flexibility and mobility of
the space-learning-working dynamic is required. Mobility and flexibility are
required for the movement of people, for the movement and reconfiguration

of information, for the movement of technology itself as well as other arti-facts and for the reconfiguration of spaces to facilitate different conversational types that are essential for learning. The learning and working have great poten-tial to migrate out into the corridors beyond the office and classroom, into informal spaces, out across the city, relocating within other spaces beyond immediate ownership and creating an ecology of spaces. I have highlighted a complex ecology of what Neuro-Linguistic Programming calls *mind, body and field*, the latter being the environment. Those responsible for workplace design do need to understand the important and interrelated contributions of space (s), cognition (c), kinesthetic bodily movement (k) and the separation (s) of conversation (co) to overall cognitive understanding and performance. An inability to know the world in a more complex relational way through space unsuited to complex learning might have long-term consequences of limiting the learning function and brain capacity. The recognition of the need for such *satellite* spaces might be a compromise interpretation of Becker's notion of the elastic organization. Such space is devoid of cultural embellishments. Traditionally, the workplace has a population density, creating close proxim-ity of humans. Close proximity represents noise and potentially excessive sensory stimulation, sometimes at inappropriate times: complex problems require a synthesizing of the complexity, which is not solely a cognitive/men-tal function. Synthesis demands connective and relational thinking. Granting physical expression to modern views of the learning process as mobile and corporeal can accelerate learning.

REFERENCES

Abram, D. (1997). *The spell of the sensuous*. New York: Vintage Books.

Amabile, T. M. (1983). *The social psychology of creativity*. New York: Springer-Verlag.

Beard, C (2010) The Experiential Toolkit, Blending Practice with Concepts, London: Kogan Page.

Beard, C. (2008). Space to learn? Learning environments in higher education. In J. Buswell & N. Beckett (Eds.), *Enhancing student-centred learning*. pp. 179–188. Berks, UK: Threshold Press.

Beard, C., & Price, I. (2010). Space, conversations and place: lessons and questions from practice, *International Journal of Facilities Management*, 1(2), 1–14

Beard, C., & Price, I. (Forthcoming). Mobility, physical space and learning.

Beard, C., & Wilson, J. (2002). *The power of experiential learning*. London: Kogan Page.

Beard, C., & Wilson, J. (2006). *Experiential learning: A best practice handbook for trainers and educators*. London: Kogan Page.

Becker, F. D. (1990). *The total workplace: Facilities Management and the elastic organization*. New York: Van Nostrand Reinhold.

Behuniak, S. (2005). *Finding solitude: The importance of silence and space for thinking*. Paper presented at Design for Learning, the 12th International Conference on Learning, July 11–14, Granada, Spain.

Bloom, B. S. (1956). *Taxonomy of educational objectives, handbook 1: The cognitive domain*. New York: David McKay.

Britzman, D. P. (1998). *Lost subjects, contested objects: Towards a psychoanalytic inquiry of learning*. New York: State University of New York Press.

Crabb, S. (2005). Out in the open. *People Management*, October 13, 4.

Damasio, A. R. (1995). *Emotion, reason and the human brain*. New York: G. P. Putnam's and Sons.

Dillon, P. (2007). *A pedagogy of connection and boundary crossings: Methodological and epistemological transactions in working across and between disciplines*. Paper presented at Creativity or Conformity? Building Cultures of Creativity in Higher Education, University of Wales and the Higher Education Academy, January 8–10, Cardiff.

Dilts, R. (1994). *Strategies of genius*. Capitola, CA: Meta Publications.

Gagne, R. M. (1974). *Essentials of learning instruction*. Hinsdale, IL: Dryden Press.

Gallagher, S. (2005). *How the body shapes the mind*. Oxford: Oxford University Press.

Gardner, H. (1983) Frames of mind: the theory of multiple intelligences, New York: Basic Books Inc.

Heron, J. (2001). *Helping the client: A creative practical guide*. London: Sage.

Illeris, K. (2002). *The three dimensions of learning*. Malabar, FL: Krieger Publishing.

Lakoff, G., & Johnson, M. (1999). *Philosophy in the flesh*. New York: Basic Books.

Lewin, K. (1951). *Field theory in social science*. New York: Harper and Row.

Meyer, J. H. F., & Land, R. (2005). Threshold concepts and troublesome knowledge (2): Epistemological considerations and a conceptual framework for teaching and learning. *Higher Education, 49*(3), 373–388

Mortiboys, A. (2002) *The emotionally intelligent lecturer* (Birmingham, SEDA Publications).

Osborn, A. F. (1963). *Applied imagination*. New York: Scribner's.

Pavlov, I. (1927). *Conditioned reflexes: An investigation of the physiological activity of the cerebral cortex* (G. V. Anrep, Trans.). London: Oxford University Press.

Rogers, C. R. (1969) *Freedom to learn: a view of what education might become*, Columbus OH: Charles E. Merrill http://www.panarchy.org/rogers/learning.html (accessed 13 April 2011)

Senge, P. M. (1990). *The fifth discipline: The art and practice of the learning organization*. New York: Doubleday.

Sheets-Johnstone, M. (2009). *The corporeal turn, an interdisciplinary reader*. Exeter: Imprint Academic.

Skinner, B. (1974). *Adult behaviour*. London: Jonathan Cape.

Tuan, Y. F. (1977). *Space and place: The perspective of experience*. Minneapolis: University of Minnesota Press.

Vygotsky, L. (1978). *Mind in society: The development of higher psychological processes*. Cambridge, MA: Harvard University Press.

Wood-Daudelin, M. (1996). Learning from experience through reflection. *Organizational Dynamics, 24*(3), 36–46.

Part II

Social Constructs and Contradictions

7 The Social Construction of FM Communities*

Ilfryn Price

This book's core argument is that an organization's physical workspace is an underappreciated managerial lever best understood through a conception of organizations as ecologies (Alexander and Price, Introduction). I have argued (Ch. 1) that those ecologies can be understood via the emergence of cognitive communities (cf. Breslin, 2010) that are enabled by shared interpretations of key signifiers or narratives. FM is a label that can, indeed the editors would say should, express the process of using workspace to assist in the achievement of an organization's goals. It is, however, a label redolent with its own contradictions (cf. Vischer, Ch. 3; Cairns, Ch. 8) that arguably provides an example of the very emergence of separate, socially constructed communities and helps corroborate the theory of organizational ecologies. Other chapters discuss the strategic contribution of space. My purpose here is only to examine the emergence of FM and the various discourses that have developed therein, as an example of emergent cultural evolution. It displays, I suggest, an example of mutation of meaning.

FM AND MANAGEMENT FASHIONS

The term 'management fashion' has found scholastic favor to describe and understand the diffusion of what others would call fads or, according to taste, business recipes. Citations in business-oriented literature have become accepted as a tool for tracking a fashion's popularity through cycles in which they wax then wane (Abrahamson, 1996), often to the point of either near extinction (Abrahamson & Fairchild, 1999) or displacement by a partly synonymous alternative (Scarbrough & Swan, 2001). More recently, as memetics has come to slightly greater prominence in organizational research, management fashions have been considered as possible examples of linguistic memes (Price & Shaw, 1996, 1998; Williams, 2004; Heath & Seidel, 2005) spreading in business discourse (O'Mahoney, 2007).

---

*This chapter draws on a commissioned study of the history and development of FM (Price, 2003).

Fashions come into existence via 'ontic dumps' (Price, Ch. 1) when one, or several, individuals coin a term to describe a new action or process that they have found useful or want to persuade others of. For example the term 'benchmarking' began to claim a place in business discourse when operational researchers with Rank Xerox used an older word, from surveying, to represent the concept of openly comparing business processes with another firm (Price, 2000). The concept thus labeled found a ready niche and spread through the actions of various companies, consultancies and academic groups. It became, as Williams (2000, 2004) puts it, a meme in "the ecology of consultobabble" peaking, at least in book titles, in the late 1990s and acquiring a range of subtle differences in meaning. The signifier 'benchmarking' came to signify various different levels of comparison and even, in policy circles, the setting of targets. Benchmarking has arguably survived longer than many fashions. Some would argue it has achieved a permanent, socially constructed, niche in business discourse, albeit with various shades of meaning from the original comparison to something more akin to standard setting (Walgenbach & Hegele, 2001). Viewed as a word competing with others for replication space, the meme's-eye perspective, such generalization is an example of what Dennett (1995) calls a good trick for a replicator.

FM, in its early inception, showed all the hallmarks of a management fashion. Early descriptions in business-oriented journals suggest the term was coined in the late 1960s or early 1970s to describe the outsourcing by banks of their data-processing operations (Scott, 1971; Anon., 1972). Other surviving references from the early 1970s take a similar perspective but the term itself did not become widespread.[1]

Meanwhile technological developments and cost pressures were forcing companies to invest in newer office designs, a trend encouraged by large providers of office furniture. In 1978 the research branch of one such, Herman Miller Corp., hosted a conference, Facility [*sic*] Influence on Productivity, in Ann Arbor, Michigan. It is not clear why they chose the term *Facility* but my coeditor recalls claims that the label came via Herman Miller's IT department.[2] Three attendees at that meeting agreed on a need for an organization comprised of "facility professionals from industry." One went on to host, in May 1980, a meeting that agreed on a constitution, bylaws and temporary officers for a new organization the National Facility Managers Association (NFMA).[3] The event appears to represent a significant mutation in the meaning of FM and the emergence of an organization dedicated to its replication. As Roper (Ch. 16) notes, the practice of managing buildings was much older. Giving it a label raised its profile.

From the constructionist perspective the mutation of meaning opened up a new niche for the construct so labeled, the word or meme. Both practicing managers and the furniture suppliers had an interest in replicating the term 'Facility Management.' In a sense, and viewed metaphorically from the meme's perspective, it was lucky in this second coining. It had a critical mass of would-be champions. By 1985 the use of FM to convey systems outsourcing had faded from the literature and Kaufman (1985) could ask, "Who Should be Running the Office? You or the Experts?" Kaufman (p. 171) claimed, "Facilities management [*sic*] involves an outside company managing one or more of a firm's in-house needs." The two early senses of FM were merging.

In 1982 NFMA became international, changing its name to IFMA when a Canadian chapter opened. FM had also begun to spread in other ways. In the process several separate communities were to emerge, each emphasizing subtly different interpretations as to what was represented by either Facility or Facilities Management. FM, as a term, began to become institutionalized (*sensu* Powell & DiMaggio, 1991). It was core to the narrative of various organizations that existed because they transmitted it. In the process it acquired greater permanence than most fashions as its global spread and diversification were to testify.

FM AS INSTITUTION

In North American academic circles, the term (representation/signifier) 'Facility Management' was adopted by researchers concerned with workplace design, especially Becker (1990), who called, largely in vain, for FM to understand the patterns (Schein, 1990) of an organization. Becker was, as we have seen, ahead of his time in construing the organization as an ecology of which the workplace and its artifacts were part. Unfortunately, FM did not get the message (Alexander, 2003; Price, 2004; Price, Ellison & Macdonald, 2009). The term did, however, propagate globally, spread by more than the simple growth of IFMA.

Dispersal in the UK

Becker and his coworkers inspired, among others, the UK-based architects Frank Duffy and John Worthington, who founded a workspace consultancy, DEGW, in London in the early 1980s. In 1983 DEGW launched an in-house journal with the title *Facilities*. Despite aiming to bring Facility Management to the UK, they inadvertently triggered a minor semantic mutation. One of *Facilities*' earliest issues[4] (April 1983) quoted an eminent British industrialist, Sir Monty Finniston, addressing the Manchester Society of Architects:

> I should like the architect to become involved in what I believe the Americans call facilities management, giving constant attention to improving the efficiency of the building . . . enhancing the environment inside . . . and keeping it in good repair, (providing the after sales service which is often lacking).

Workplace design was expanded to include building maintenance how-ever the term 'facilities,' as then used in the UK, was synonymous with the North American 'facility.' Another prominent UK pioneer, Tony Thomson[5] (1988), wrote an MSc thesis on the early development of the discipline in the UK. He cited Duffy's address to a 1987 conference:

> Facilities management has been around a long time. Now it has become a profession. It is strongest and most active in Britain in two main sec-tors, electronics and financial services. This already gives us the clue as to why it is becoming so prominent today and why it is certain to grow in importance in the future: because the organisations [*sic*] which need facilities management most are those which are changing most rapidly, particularly through the adaptation of that great catalyst of yet more change information technology.

What had started as a fashion was again becoming defined, or some would say promoted, as a profession! Others challenged that designation, querying whether the 'profession' had the necessary code of ethics (Grimshaw, 2003), while those offering FM services showed little interest in the designation (Green & Price, 2000). In the process of spreading, the term was acquiring a different shade of meaning as an umbrella term for the management of vari-ous operational aspects of a building. By 1988 in the UK there were two sep-arate bodies. The Association of Facilities Managers saw themselves as the doers, responsible for running buildings, while a more cerebral architectural movement, the Institution of Facilities Management, saw FM having a more strategic design role. Neither, as Roper (Ch. 16) notes, had the technical/ professional experience and education that might make them sensitive to the cultural constructs of organizations. Fashionable new offices, conceived and executed as projects, were perceived very differently by the occupants who saw themselves as on the receiving end. As Donald (1994) expressed it, FM professionals, trained to deal in the concrete realities of building furniture and projects, found considerations of the reactions of users as, at best, an irritant, and at worse a major obstacle they perceived as needing overcoming! In similar vein, Thomson (1988), who was one of the few individuals who had a foot in both camps and understood the cultural dimension, quoted the then president and founder of the association:

> For too long the area of facilities management has suffered from the "anyone can do it" syndrome. Well they can't. But because of the situ-ation too many designers have been getting away with too much. They haven't had enough discipline imposed on them. There's too much attention to aesthetics, not enough to function. Our aim is to improve the relationship with designers, which is not too good at the moment. We want them to talk to facilities managers first. If we can talk about their designs we can get the aesthetics and function right.

Yet by August 1990, after he had by moved from Hewlett-Packard to DEGW, Thomson argued, in *Facilities*[6], that *Real Facilities Management* was to be found in Facilities Planning, and that the failure of FM in the UK was in missing this "most central of issues" and immersing itself in long and complicated explanations, together with producing lists of activities that seemingly encourage more and more diverse skills into the fold and add to the overall confusion. It was, but the confusion nonetheless persisted. Rather like a virus, the word *FM* had acquired a momentum of its own: an observation consistent with a recent view of management fashions (Røvik, 2011).[7]

In the UK in particular it perhaps helped that FM also developed as a business sector from around 1990. An economic downturn prompted cost-cutting and increasing corporate interest in the outsourcing of various building services. Firms began to advertise themselves as providers of FM. Under financial pressure IBM (UK) divested its former in-house property and facilities operations as an independent company, Procord, in 1991. The new firm was acquired by Johnson Controls four years later. Politics favored the new industry that developed with a vengeance. Various engineering, maintenance, construction, surveying, cleaning and catering firms competed to enter a new, fluid and emergent market (Lord, Lunn, Price & Stephenson, 2002). Many simply rebadged their existing services. One marketing director interviewed for that research graphically testified to the trend: "Xxx FM Ltd was formed in 1993/4 in response to the *wonderful new buzzword of FM* that had appeared. People wanted to see the word *management* in an outsourcing contract" (ibid. p. 361–362. emphasis added).

Most companies entering the new market did not, in fact, stray far from their original competencies. Lord et al. (2002) examined the business sectors served and services offered by the 25 largest firms competing in the UK's FM market. They used pairwise matching of characteristics (Lord & Price, 2001) such as shares of different markets and services offered to construct a taxonomy (reproduced here as Figure 7.1) based on similarity. Most firms clustered in terms of their origin selling, as FM, the same services they had previously. In effect, much as Walgenbach and Hegele (2001) described for benchmarking, the new term *FM* was absorbed into the old 'modes of thought' (*sensu* Weeks and Galunic, 2003; Price, Ch. 1) of the companies doing the absorbing. FM took to describing itself, enthusiastically but overly simplistically (Price, 2004), as 'non-core' and, in the process, ceased to have any concern with organizational outputs; however, the term itself continued to be replicated.

The spread was not confined to the private sector. The UK's Conservative government, which had spent the 1980s divesting publicly owned but privatizable entities (e.g., steel, gas or telecoms) turned its attention to outsourcing. As part of a move to bring 'market forces' into the National Health Service (NHS) hospital trusts were required to submit all their support services to compulsory competitive tendering, a discipline also

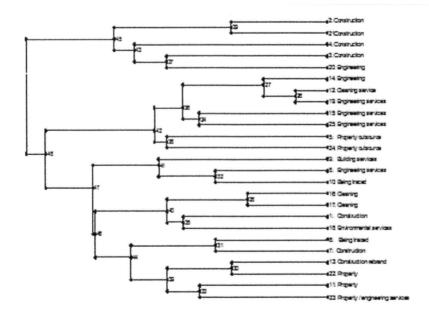

Figure 7.1   A phenogram of the 25 largest FM firms in the UK created by pairwise mapping of similarities (after Lord et al., 2002).

mandated for local authorities under what was promoted as 'best value'; a phrase that became a euphemism for cutting costs. In the NHS in particular there was a growth in the creation of FM departments as in-house managers sought to defend their departments against imposed competition (Payne & Rees, 1999).

In 1994 the, smaller, Institution of Facilities Managers and the larger Association of Facilities Managers merged (as the union was euphemistically described). To the chagrin of some of the dominant figures in the Aassociation the merged group elected to describe itself as an institution, hence the creation of the British Institute (BI) of FM. Despite, therefore, having become less virulent, in the sense of exerting strategic influence, FM acquired a further, self-asserted, degree of institutional image. In the words of an ex-IFM member (personal communication to author 2001), "We were more strategic—it was a blow to the AFM founders when the membership voted for institution in the title of the new organization."

Other International Developments

IFMA actively encouraged the development of affiliate associations. In Japan the term "was imported from the US" around 1985 (Makoto, 1990). The new Japanese FM association was keen to stress FM's link to the Deming Cycle, as illustrated by a copy of its then website I made in 2000 (Figure

7.2), which I offer as an example of a new fashion being expressed in terms that will blend with the discourse into which it is being introduced.

IFMA continued to internationalize successfully. As of August 2011 it has 126 chapters worldwide. Holland, Australia and South Africa also saw, as in the UK, separate national bodies formed. In the process different definitions took hold. IFMA *remained true* to what they term the *classic* definition of Facility Management as "the practice of coordinating the physical workplace with the people and work of the organization," integrating "the principles of business administration, architecture and the behavioral and engineering sciences." For BIFM, Facilities Management was "the integration of multidisciplinary activities within the built environment and the management of their impact upon people and the workplace." The South African FM association laid great stress on outsourcing government services. The Australians were bolder. By 2003 they were defining FM as "the practice of integrating the management of people and the business process of an organization with the physical infrastructure *to enhance corporate performance*" (emphasis added). Unfortunately, by 2011 they had reverted to defining FM's function as maintaining the efficient operation of buildings. Ensuring that services contribute to the productivity and profitability of those people who utilize a facility is merely one of several subordinate goals[8].

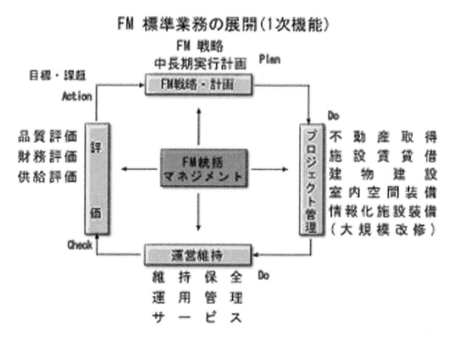

Figure 7.2   FM was clearly promoted for the Japanese FM association, as related to the Deming Cycle.

In Europe, by 2002, the then existing national FM associations had developed very separate approaches. While the Dutch saw it as *the integrated planning realization and maintenance of building, equipment and services*, the Danes stated it to be more comprehensive than building operations. The German association promoted the size of the FM market (in-house or outsourced), whereas the Austrians emphasized not cost-cutting but adding value. Unsurprisingly perhaps, there was a move to standardize, but also generalize, as the IFMA-assisted European network, EuroFM, grew in influence. Having been a significant force in its development, in 2006 EuroFM adopted the European standard definition: "Integration of processes within an organisation [*sic*] to maintain and develop the agreed services which support and improve the effectiveness of its primary activities." In practice their website emphasized FM as "the largest business services market in Europe" and the firms competing in that market still emphasize competence in managing provision of particular services.[9]

However, the emphasis given by the new executive board has been strongly contested by the membership, composed of mainly educationalists and researchers, who endorse the original mission and objectives of EuroFM as an open network to advance knowledge in FM for application in research, education and practice. A new strategy was debated and nominally decided in autumn 2011. In practice, however, there remain at least three communities. Some see FM as an engineering discipline; others see it as a service one (Coenen & von Felten, Ch. 10). Both perspectives have lost sight of the role of space in business. Instances of real contributions to 'core businesses' remain the exception, often steered from other directorates, yet the institutions devoted to the spread of FM thrive as do journals, books, models, definitions, standards, conferences and educational offerings. What is going on?

A SOCIAL CONSTRUCTIONIST EXPLANATION

The Constructionist Summary

The historical sketch just outlined offers numerous examples of the emergence of communities attached to different constructs of FM, grounded partly in the prior training and partly in the interests of their members. First was a group dedicated to promoting, or writing about, IT outsourcing. That construct flared briefly from about 1970, but disappeared in the early 1980s. It was replaced by FM as, in broad terms, a discipline concerned with the design, procurement and management of buildings, especially initially offices. From early days that new sense of the word was promoted both by 'designers' and 'engineers.' I have provided examples of struggles between the two communities and their constructs and the tension persists to this day (Roper, Ch. 16). In North America, IFMA managed, successfully, to embrace both camps.

As the term spread, different constructs became prominent in different states. In Japan FM was firmly embraced and championed as scientific building management. In the UK, in contrast, FM arrived as a concern for workplace design but came to be used also by a community of building managers championing, in their terms, function over form and, in the process, their own professionalism. The wider context (a recession and a government with a radical market-driven agenda) favored the development of a third construct, the market for outsourced building services. FM's umbrella extended to embrace the so-called 'soft services,' such as cleaning, catering and, in hospitals, people movement. There were communities with an interest in professionalizing FM (academic departments and the Institute) and others with an interest in expanding the market. Elsewhere around the globe various different constructs dominate national associations. The result was not planned; it emerged or evolved as variations in how a single term was understood became the accepted wisdom, the dominant 'mode of thought,'(cf. Price Ch 1) in those communities.

An Evolutionary Perspective

A theory of social construction as a selection process cannot be proved by a single example. Evolution by selection is ultimately a theory that explains a wide range of observations concerning the observed properties, distribution and history of life on earth; phenomena bound up with selection on genes encoded in DNA. In the 'selfish gene' view of evolution a gene's 'success' is determined by the number of copies that are replicated, with the same gene expressing itself differently in different lineages.

If indeed "the survival or preservation of certain favored words in the struggle for existence is natural selection" (Price, Ch. 1) then FM as a word has done very well surviving and spreading for over 40 years, representing itself differently in different communities dedicated to its replication. It has mutated to fit the different business contexts into which it spreads.[10] In the terms suggested by Weeks and Galunic (2003), it is part of the fabric of a diverse ecology of modes of thought. If FM is indeed a meme it has proved a successful one. Unfortunately, from the perspective of users of buildings, it has arguably dumbed down.

NOTES

1. In a global 'snowball' survey of FM practitioners the oldest date offered for first hearing the term was 1968. Scott's (1971) paper was the oldest electronic record I could locate.
2. Intriguingly, according to a chronological history of the Division of State Facilities I downloaded in 2006, the state of Wisconsin created a Bureau of Facilities [sic] Management in 1971 that was clearly intended to operate functions that would be seen today as building-related FM.
3. From a history of the International Facility Management Association (IFMA) communicated to me in 2000.

4. Ironically the paper archive I relied on for the 2003 history was the victim of FM practice when nominally retievable files were fed to an incinerator. This is admittedly the first time their absence has been missed.
5. As note 4
6. As note 4
7. It is interesting to speculate that FM became less virulent in the process.
8. All quotes in the paragraph were taken from the web sites of the relevant associations in 2002
9. As note 8
10. When Episcopalian religions reached North America they underwent a blooming or evolutionary radiation of different denominations (Lord & Price, 2001). Did a similar bloom happen in reverse when FM reached Europe, where it was less obviously subject to the influence of IFMA?

REFERENCES

Abrahamson, E. (1996). Management fashion. *Academy of Management Review, 21*(1), 254–285.

Abrahamson, E., & Fairchild, G. (1999). Management fashions: Lifecycles, triggers and collective learning processes. *Administrative Science Quarterly, 44*(December), 708–740.

Alexander, K. (2003). A strategy for Facilities Management. *Facilities, 21*(11/12), 269–274.

Anon. (1972). Facilities Management is here to stay. *Administrative Management, 33*(7), 16.

Becker, F. D. (1990). *The total workplace: Facilities Management and elastic organization.* New York: Praeger Press.

Breslin, D. (2010). Generalising Darwinism to study socio-cultural change. *International Journal of Sociology and Social Policy, 30*(7/8), 427–439.

Dennett, D. C. (1995). *Darwin's dangerous idea.* New York: Simon and Schuster.

Donald I. (1994). Management and change in office environments. *Journal of environmental psychology, 14*(1), 21–30.

Green, A., & Price, I. (2000). Whither FM? A Delphi study of the profession and the industry. *Facilities, 18*(7/8), 281–292.

Grimshaw, R. W. (2003). FM: The professional interface. *Facilities, 21*(3), 50–57.

Heath, C., & Seidel, V. (2005). *Language as a coordinating mechanism: How linguistic memes help direct appropriate action.* Paper to Academy of Management, Honolulu. Retrieved June 20, 2011, from http://icos.groups.si.umich.edu/Linguisticmemes4.2.pdf

Kaufman, M. (1985).Who should be running the office? You or the experts? *The Office, 102*(1), 172–173.

Lord, A., Lunn, S., Price, I., & Stephenson, P. (2002). Emergent behaviour in a new market: Facilities Management in the UK. In G. Frizelle & H. Richards (Eds.), *Tackling industrial complexity: The ideas that make a difference* (pp. 357–371). Cambridge, UK: Institute of Manufacturing.

Lord, A., & Price, I. (2001). Reconstruction of organisational phylogeny from memetic similarity analysis: Proof of feasibility. *Journal of Memetics—Evolutionary Models of Information Transmission, 5*(2), 1–9.

Makoto, T. (1990). Facility Management enhances usefulness of buildings. *Business Japan, 35*(10), 97–102.

O'Mahoney, J. (2007). The diffusion of management innovations: The possibilities and limitations of memetics. *Journal of Management Studies, 44*(8), 1324–1348.

Payne, T., & Rees, D. (1999). NHS Facilities Management: A prescription for change. *Facilities*, 17(7/8), 217–221.

Powell, W. W., & DiMaggio P. J. (1991). *The new institutionalism in organizational analysis*. Chicago: University of Chicago Press.

Price, I. (2000). Benchmarking higher education and UK public sector Facilities Management. In N. Jackson & H. Lund (Eds.), *Benchmarking for higher education* (pp. 139–150). Milton Keynes, UK: Open University Press.

Price, I. (2003). The development of Facility Management. In R. Best, C. Langston & G. De Valence (Eds.), *Workplace strategies and Facilities Management: Building in value* (pp. 49–66). Oxford: Butterworth-Heinemann.

Price, I. (2004). Business critical FM. *Facilities*, 22(13/14), 353–358.

Price, I., Ellison, I. & Macdonald, R. (2009). Practical post-modernism: FM and socially constructed realities. In *European Facility Management conference: 8th Euro FM research symposium*. Unpaginated, electronic only original source Retrieved July 5, 2011, from http://shura.shu.ac.uk/912/

Price, I., & Shaw, R. (1996). The learning organisation meme: Emergence of a management replicator or parrots, patterns and performance. In T. Campbell (Ed.), *Proceedings of the third ECLO Conference*. Copenhagen: European Consortium for the Learning Organization *unpaginated* Retrieved February 21, 2012, from http://shura.shu.ac.uk/4837/

Price, I, & Shaw, R. (1998). *Shifting the patterns*. Chalford, Gloucestershire: Management Books 2000.

Røvik, K. A. (2011). From fashion to virus: An alternative theory of organizations' handling of management ideas. *Organization Studies*, 32(5), 631–653.

Scarbrough, H., & Swan, J.A. (2001). Explaining the diffusion of knowledge management: The role of fashion. *British Journal of Management*, 12(1), 3–12.

Schein, R. H. (1990). Organizational culture. *American Psychologist*, 45(2), 109–119.

Scott, C. R. (1971). Why Facilities Management. *Bankers Monthly*, 88(10), 38.

Thomson, T. (1988). *Facilities Management consultancy: The development of a plan for its proposed implementation in an architectural company*. MSc dissertation, University of Reading.

Walgenbach, P., & Hegele, C. (2001). What can an apple learn from an orange? Or: What do companies use benchmarking for? *Organization*, 8(1), 121–144.

Weeks, J., & Galunic, C. (2003). A theory of the cultural evolution of the firm: The intra-organizational ecology of memes. *Organization Studies*, 24(8), 1309–1352.

Williams, R. (2000). The business of memes: Memetic possibilities for marketing and management. *Management Decision*, 38(4), 272–279.

Williams, R. (2004). Management fashions and fads: Understanding the role of consultants and managers in the evolution of ideas. *Management Decision*, 42(6), 769–780.

8 Philosophical Contradictions in FM

George Cairns

This chapter builds upon my earlier writing (Cairns, 2003) in search of a Facilities Management philosophy for the changing workplace. In that work, I highlighted theoretical contradictions inherent in different social science and built environment approaches to understanding workplaces. I discussed the conflict between positivistic approaches, based upon rationalist philosophies, and social constructionist approaches grounded in interpretivist and postmodern philosophies. I set out a conceptual framework for addressing the 'multiple realities' of the workplace, to explore contextual solutions to complex and ambiguous workplace problems for which there is no one 'right answer.' In this chapter, I develop a more nuanced approach that addresses the philosophical and methodological contradictions inherent in dealing with these multiple realities and outline a framework for contextual investigation and problem analysis, engaging with multiple stakeholders with different beliefs and value sets. In this, I build on later writing (Cairns, 2008) on theorizing the built environment, referring to Aristotelian philosophy and the concept of *phronēsis*, or practical wisdom, and its contemporary social science interpretation in the works of Flyvbjerg (2001, 2003).

PHILOSOPHICAL INFLUENCES AND CONTRADICTION IN FM

In my 2002 keynote address to the Facility Management Association of Australia (FMA) and subsequent papers in *Facilities* (Cairns, 2002, 2003), I asserted that the developing field of Facility/Facilities Management (FM) was theoretically weak and fragmented. I identified a lack of methodological rigor for much of what was expounded as FM 'theory,' pointing to the adoption of concepts such as homeworking and outsourcing within the rhetoric of FM, without development of a substantial body of empirical studies that might validate them. Also, I pointed to quantitative empirical studies in which the statistical analysis did not support the conclusions presented, due to weak research design and the use of unrepresentative samples. I challenged studies from which generalized conclusions were proposed as universalisms rather than merely as case-specific conclusions that might inform other situations by implication. In addition, I highlighted the lack of transfer of knowledge between the emerging field of FM and other domains of study with which it would appear to have areas of commonality, pointing to the lack of substantive engagement of FM thinkers with extant theories in fields such as organization theory, organization behavior, architecture and built environment studies; theories that might inform the development of better theory within FM. Finally, I highlighted the absence of reference to the physical environment in the fields of organization theory and organization behavior, based upon decades of research in these fields in which human relational factors were seen as dominant determinants of both performance and satisfaction. From these discussions, I argued that the discipline of FM must seek to build linkages to related fields that should both inform it and be informed by it and, in so doing, must establish a philosophical foundation for its theoretical bases, where "philosophy refers not to esoteric, academic abstraction, but to the basic theory and general principles of knowledge that underpin everyday activities" (2003, p. 95).

Since publication of these works, there has been considerable progress in establishing stronger theoretical foundations for the areas with which FM engages—the nexus of the organizational, physical and social environments of workplaces. These have come both from within the community of FM scholars, and from those in other fields in which there has been a growing interest in the physical environment of work. Such developments include moves towards higher levels of theory development in the field of built environment studies (e.g., Koskela, 2008) and growth of interest in engagement with the physical environment of work in the field of organization theory (e.g., Clegg & Kornberger, 2006). In addition, the FM literature demonstrates more considered theoretical approaches, with papers that acknowledge the contextual limitations of studies (e.g., Bigliardi & Dormio, 2010) and that link extant theory from other fields to the FM practice arena (e.g., Straub, Koopman & van Mossel, 2010). Development of new, theoretically informed literature sets within and relevant to FM points to a maturing of the field and justification for its recognition as both an academic and a practitioner endeavor. However, review of the breadth of theories that might be considered relevant to the scope of FM research and practice points to several potential sources of conflict or, at minimum, obstacles to bridging theory to practice. The first of these relates to the continuing possibility of conflict between philosophical stances underpinning theoretical approaches, where some are grounded in positivism and others in social construction. For some, the positivist/constructionist divide is unresolvable due to incommensurability of philosophies, and in some instances this unresolvability is referred to in terms of 'paradigm wars.'

The second potential area of blockage or conflict lies between the domains of theory and practice, even where the former has been developed and defined through empirical study in the domain of the latter. Duffy, Craig and Gillen (2010, p. 111) consider how "some models of social science research tend to be too fine-grained, too sharply focused and too inflexible, too remote from the context of action . . . to cope with the considerable operational challenges of applied research." They imply that even theories that deal with social context, rather than noncontextual generalization, may not be sufficiently adaptable to changes in time, place and action to inform thinking in a context other than that where they originated. In response to a perceived need for context specificity in undertaking research, they refer to the Harvard Business School case study, and suggest the possibility of a similar case archive to inform thinking on the interrelationship between work process and place. I would propose that whilst such case studies might provide valuable exemplars of completed projects to inform teaching and learning on principles and issues in FM, they represent 'historical archives,' and, as such, are unlikely to inspire creativity and innovation directed towards understanding future needs and identifying future opportunity.

In order to foster and develop a creative and challenging FM future that is both theoretically informed and of practical value, I propose that there is a need to recognize the differentiation between positivist and constructionist paradigms, but to accept both as simultaneously valid and applicable. The key requirement is that the user of this complex 'bag' of research resources must distinguish research that is empirically and theoretically rigorous from that which is based upon nonsignificant data analysis or that presents insubstantial generalizations from highly contextual studies. I would posit that both historical studies, of 'best-case' and 'worst-case' examples, and futures-oriented speculations should be drawn upon in order to build robust theories of FM that can inform practice. Based upon the preceding, I propose a framework for FM research that accommodates both positivist and constructionist philosophies and, in particular, is directed at understanding the impacts of decisions on the full range of involved and affected stakeholders and making explicit the mechanisms of power that underpin these decisions and impacts.

RESOLVING CONTRADICTIONS CONCEPTUALLY

In rejecting the idea that inherent contradictions between theoretical stances, based upon different philosophical principles, should be seen as insurmountable, I acknowledge that I face certain risk of critique. For some, such an approach may be seen as inconceivable or, at least, impractical. For others, it may seem to advocate relativism, whereby all approaches are vested with equal validity and all voices are accorded equal prominence in the discourse. However, the inquiry framework that I propose is not based upon moral relativism and equality of status of arguments and voices, only upon equality of access to the discourse. Hopefully, in setting both positivistic and constructionist approaches into a common research methods context in which the value, limitations and boundaries of each is clearly enounced, I will convince at least some skeptics of the value of the proposition.

Living with Ambivalence

In previous writing (Cairns, 2008), I have posited that development of theories of the built environment that have practical significance, an argument that applies equally to the wider domain of FM, requires acceptance that 'multiple realities' (Beech & Cairns, 2001) of the workplace exist through the active involvement of user stakeholders. I argue that, no matter what the origins and nature of the inputs to the workplace environment—physical space and artifacts, hard and soft systems, prescribed controls and negotiated behaviors—the ultimate 'reality' of each individual's environment is that which they socially construct through their personal actions, interactions, interpretations and mediations. Whilst the purpose of management structures and systems is frequently to mold individual behavior and action to achieve 'organizational fit,' the act of 'managing' must acknowledge that this organizational 'mold' and 'fit' will frequently be imperfect. Here, I posit that the key attribute of the successful FM researcher or practitioner who seeks to engage with the 'messy' realities of what practice is, rather than with just a sanitized and idealized conceptual model of what practice should or might be, is the ability to recognize, accept and live with a state of ambivalence. Contrary to common usage, where the term is often read to mean 'not caring,' ambivalence is read here in its dictionary sense, of holding two seemingly contradictory views to be simultaneously valid. This means that the investigator must be willing and able to recognize and accept inherent philosophical contradictions between the objective and positivist, and the subjective and constructionist. She/he must be capable both of understanding and using 'hard' quantitative data that defines parameters of the FM environment to be managed, and of engaging with and making sense of 'soft' data on how these parameters are deconstructed, redefined and reconstructed to form user stakeholders perceptions of the environment—their own 'lived reality'—and to inform their personal behaviors and actions. As stated in the preceding, to understand, accept and live with these multiple realities in a managerial role is not to promote FM as a model of management based upon relativism and thereby to posit that all interpretations are equally valid. Rather, it is to accept that FM is a complex and ambiguous field of endeavor in which the manager is faced with often difficult decisions and choices between conflicting demands and interests. As such, it is a role that requires both an understanding of the power inherent in it and of the mechanisms of power that others will seek to bring to bear upon it. Similarly, for the FM researcher, there is a need to recognize the existence of these complexities and the ambiguous nature of the social, physical and work-related environment that is being studied.

Philosophies of Complexity and Ambiguity

Having set out a stance of ambivalence, I will not engage further here with philosophies of singularity, whether positivist or constructionist. Rather, I will seek to build an argument for FM research that transcends philosophical contradictions and that provides a theoretically sound framework for engagement with the messy field of practice. In order to explain the theoretical foundations of ambivalence in FM in greater detail, I will first outline key conceptual frameworks.

Lefebvre (1991) clarified the difference between what he referred to as 'spatial practices' and 'representations of space.' The first of these refers to space as an entity that is defined in objective terms. These spatial practices are understood in the same way by different actors by applying the same metrics. Representations of space, on the other hand, are defined in subjective terms as mental, cognitive or ideational spaces. They are, therefore, spaces as perceived by the individual, and these perceptions are not necessarily shared with others. The intersection of objective and subjective understandings in the domain of human action generates what Lefebvre refers to as 'space of representations,' lived space in which individuals may have shared perceptions of what the space is, and also very different perceptions of what the space means; how it promotes, constrains or is irrelevant to each individual.

Lefebvre's exploration of space as both objectively and subjectively defined leads him to a resolution of the difference between the two conceptualizations through a synthesis into a 'space of representations.' Thus, it does not set up an ambivalent understanding. The concept of ambivalence has been discussed and analyzed empirically in the work of Albert Rothenberg (1979) and the application of what he terms 'Janusian thinking.' Rothenberg posits that human beings are capable of holding, and commonly do hold two opposite and contradictory propositions as being simultaneously true; that ambivalence is a fairly normal human condition. This process differs from the Hegelian dialectic where, as in Lefebvre's spatial analysis, there is resolution through synthesis, in that there is no synthesis in order to resolve a paradox that "is intrinsically unresolvable" (1979, p. 256). Rothenberg conducted both archival studies on the works of and writings about creative individuals such as Mozart, Picasso and Frank Lloyd Wright, along with empirical studies in conjunction with a poet. He concluded that the creative process is not linear and that complex structures—whether textual, musical or physical—are underpinned by the ability of the creator to hold two, or more, competing ideas in mind simultaneously and to be able to work with them without either collapsing or condensing them into a singularity. As Rothenberg outlines how individuals can hold contradictory meanings to be simultaneously valid, Michel Foucault presents a conceptual framework on how spaces may hold multiple, contradictory meanings for a society.

Foucault (2000) introduces the concept of 'heterotopia,' which he describes in terms of spaces in contemporary society that "are sorts of actually realized utopias in which the real emplacements, all the other real emplacements that can be found within the culture are, at the same time, represented, contested and reversed, sorts of places that are outside all places, although they are actually localizable" (p. 178). I have argued previously (Cairns, 2003) that, whilst it is a spatial category that Foucault does not address, the contemporary workplace is a heterotopian space, in that it is not merely an 'activity container' (Hillier, 1996) for those who work within it or who visit it. Rather, it has achieved a status in contemporary socioeconomic structures, albeit primarily in Western or para-Western business contexts, that elevates it to being a space that contains representations of all other major social places. For example, for many working in the high-pressure business world, the workplace is a place that represents and reverses family place, whereby they spend more and more time in and around the workplace, rather than in home space. For the single city worker, social life in the workplace—and the adjacent cafés and wine bars into which it spills—may be read as a representation of home and family spaces, thereby contesting and reversing these. On the other hand, for many who do maintain the 'norm' of the nuclear family, home space has become workplace, as information and communications technologies (ICTs) expand the boundaries of workplace such that it becomes ubiquitous. Similarly, workplaces may also be read as the new 'sacred' places that, to a large extent, contest and reverse the sacred places of earlier periods. They are secular places devoted to the 'worship' of commerce, generating a sense of econo-spiritual well-being and, thereby, contesting the dominant role of the church as the center for religio-spiritual well-being.

In relation to physicality and location, modern workplaces can be conceived and understood both as physically manifest in concrete, steel and timber, and at the same time as being *not* constrained by their physical situatedness. That is to say, they can be read as being both situated in and existing outside their physical location. Where workplaces are elements of an organizational domain of the multinational company that is not part of the community in which it sits, they may deprive that community of a degree of decision-making power and control over its own physical locality, where the space becomes subject to a higher level of remote authority. Yet, at the same time, they can be localizable in terms of being symbolic representations of the community and a center of economic activity for the population of the community. It can thus be argued that the contemporary workplace fits within Foucault's broad conceptualization of heterotopia.

Foucault defines heterotopias according to six principles (2000, pp. 179–185), which I have considered in full in earlier writing (Cairns, 2003).

Here I reprise those principles that are of key significance in informing the approach that follows to engagement with the ambivalent workplace in the context of practice. Foucault's (2000) third principle states that a heterotopia "has the ability to juxtapose in a single real place several emplacements that are incompatible in themselves" (p. 181). This can be argued to be a defining principle of contemporary workplaces that differentiates them from their immediate predecessors. Whereas, prior to the industrial revolution, work and family space were largely contiguous for the majority of the population, since the Industrial Revolution workplace has largely existed as separate and distinct from home and family space in most if not all industrial societies. In the contemporary socioeconomic context, the introduction of concepts of homeworking, teleworking, etc., in the 1990s led to a situation in which home–work boundaries became blurred and broken down, with many other spaces that were previously functionally defined by name now absorbed within the blur: airports, hotels, restaurants and even public and private transport. These juxtapositions of multiple emplacements are accepted in the service of contemporary work and organization, but can be seen to be incompatible where work and social environments within the home become contested zones, or where, in other contexts, 24–7 ICT-enabled, multidevice workers conflict with fellow diners intent on enjoying their meal, or commuters focused on their Sudoku or their crossword therapy.

The fourth principle of heterotopias is that, in most instances—Foucault does not say all here—they are "connected with temporal discontinuities (*découpages du temps*): that is, they open onto what might be called, for the sake of symmetry, heterochronias" (2000, p. 182). Such temporal discontinuities exist, but may go largely unnoticed in the contemporary workplace, where time is compressed by ICTs that enable instantaneous communication across the globe. Spatial and temporal discontinuities combine in the organizational form in which the individual can dial a local telephone number or can use voice over Internet protocols at any time of day and night and be connected to a service center that may exist in any time zone or in a hyperspace of voice recognition. In the new service economy, terms such as 'day' and 'night,' 'the working day' and 'the weekend' can no longer be assumed to have a common meaning within organizational space, or even between two individuals in synchronous communication with each other.

Foucault's fifth principle of heterotopias states that they "always presuppose a system of opening and closing that isolates them and makes them penetrable at the same time" (2000, p. 183). In contemporary society, the organizations with which we engage on a daily basis, such as banks, insurance companies and government offices, will generally offer a public and welcoming face through the imagery of the workplace, both in physical space and in Internet hyperspace. However, these organizations are now by and large subject to rigid security, with staff and customers subject to constant surveillance and with access capable of being switched on and off at any moment. In the aftermath of violent attacks, even those public buildings and spaces that society previously considered to be most accessible (such as hospitals, schools and shopping malls) have become surrounded and pervaded by security systems such that they are both open to yet isolated from society.

The sixth and final principle of heterotopias states that "they have a function in relation to the remaining space" (2000, p. 184), a principle that Foucault then discusses in relation to two polar extremes of function. First, he states that heterotopias may "have the role of creating a space of illusion that denounces all real space." Second, he posits that they may serve the function of "creating a different space, a different space as perfect, as meticulous, as well-arranged as ours is disorganized, badly arranged, and muddled" (p. 184). The space of illusion—the 'perfect' space—that we are supposed to observe in the contemporary workplace may be one that is defined by the rhetoric of empowerment, distributed leadership, paperless working and autonomous workers. However, for many working within these perfect spaces, the reality may be one of emotional labor, panoptical observation, systems complexity and implicit control. In summarizing Foucault's concept of heterotopias as a framework for analyzing the contemporary work environment, I suggest that it enables us to grasp an ambivalent reality in which there is no clear delineation of workplaces and non-workplaces, no capacity to define workplaces as being in the 'here and now' as opposed to the 'everywhere and every time,' and the likelihood that what is apparently open, inclusive and enabling may in reality be enclosed, exclusive and constraining. It enables us to challenge the grand illusion of freedom and empowerment in the new workplace.

The Multiple Realities of Workplace

Having expounded the notion that philosophical contradictions may inhibit but may also inspire FM research and practice, and that a philosophy of contradiction—or ambivalence—is the most appropriate 'umbrella framework' within which to research and practice, I must reiterate that this opens the need to deal with the 'multiple realities' (Beech & Cairns, 2001) of the workplace, and to deny the notion that there is a 'single reality' to be discovered and understood. The FM researcher and manager must find the means to engage with the different socially constructed realities (Berger & Luckman, 1966) of different groups of actors. Beech and Cairns (2001) set out an ontological framework of such multiple organizational realities, drawing upon Wittgenstein's (1958) philosophical investigations and his attention to language. They draw upon their own empirical engagement with various organizational contexts in order to discuss how 'realities' may be constructed across different metaphorical strata; 'single reality,' 'multilayered reality,' 'multiple realities' and 'no-such-thing-as-reality.' They posit that the first of these is nonexistent—or, at best, transitory—in organizations and that analysis of language usage and interpretation in communication will lead to a more complex understanding. In some contexts, different individuals may have the same understandings, but based upon different reasoning. In others, they may have very different understandings, whilst expressing these using the same words but with different value meanings attached to them.* Finally, an individual may use the same words but with different value meaning attached when discussing different subjects or addressing different audiences. Beech and Cairns posit that the role of the manager in 'coping' with these language issues and games is not to seek to 'get it right' at all times, but to 'be all right' in the management process. Here, the term 'coping' is used in its correct sense of 'grappling with success,' rather than its normal usage, which may be taken to imply *not* coping—i.e., struggling to survive. In order to seek to offer one framework for 'getting it right' in researching or practicing FM, I draw upon the philosophy of Aristotle (2004) and his concept of *phronēsis* or 'practical wisdom.'

MANAGING AND LIVING WITH CONTRADICTIONS IN PRACTICE

Building upon the preceding, I would argue that FM research and practice is not primarily concerned with how to manage 'facilities'—nonhuman organizational resources—per se, rather it is about managing the process of human actors' engagement with these facilities, with "what meaning and what value (they have) for the subjects who have been and who will be involved?" (Strati, 1998, p. 1383). Placing primary emphasis on meaning and value for the involved and affected stakeholders, the FM researcher or practitioner must find a means of engaging with the multiple realities and understandings of both the physical and social environments that are generated by the different stakeholders, as addressed earlier. I posit that the way towards meaningful engagement is through critically reflective thinking on the purpose to be served by the interaction of actors and facilities. The challenge set here is to move thinking beyond instrumental purpose, as in attaining financial return to shareholders through extracting emotional labor from workers in a workplace of illusion. Rather, I seek to promote critical thinking on moral purpose, in Aristotle's (2004, p. 150) words, the ability of "man [*sic*] to be able to deliberate about what is good and advantageous for himself" and to be "capable of action with regard to things that are good or bad for man." Aristotle promotes *phronēsis* as the intellectual value that informs action towards a greater good, rather than merely thinking on that good. In pursuing phronetic inquiry towards action and purpose, the contradictions between different understandings

---

*Editors note. Chapter 7 provided examples from within the field of FM. In Chapter 1 Price provided his interpretation of the phenomenon.

and interpretations will be surfaced, addressed and, hopefully, resolved. The resolution will not derive from moral relativism and acceptance of all standpoints—what is good for each individual—but will involve 'coping' with often difficult questions and conflicts in order to seek the good of 'man'—in contemporary language 'society.'

Flyvbjerg's Contemporary Interpretation of Phronetic Inquiry

Whilst the ancient Greek word *phronēsis* has not found its way into modern Western language, the concept has been subject to much consideration and development in recent times across various academic fields. Here, I draw upon its incorporation into the field of social science through contemporary interpretation in the works of Danish academic Bent Flyvbjerg (2001, 2003). Flyvbjerg (2003, p. 364) proposes that we can interrogate a proposed social intervention by application of the following, seemingly simple set of value-rational questions:

- Where are we going?
- Is this development desirable?
- What, if anything, should we do about it?
- Who gains and who loses, and by which mechanisms of power?

In the field of FM, application of these questions to interrogate existing or proposed strategic and operational plans from the perspectives of and with consideration of the interests of the broadest range of stakeholders will surface conflicts and contradictions. What is desirable for one group of stakeholders, such as financial stockholders, may be highly undesirable for another, such as workers who will be retrenched or made redundant. Also, what 'we' should do about a particular course of action is likely to vary widely according to who the 'we' is. The final question is the most important in informing a critically reflective management process, where issues of power and agency are overtly addressed, and it is recognized that management decision-making will most frequently involve there being 'winners' and 'losers,' albeit these may be in relative rather than absolute terms.

A Phronetic Model of FM Research and Practice

In conclusion, I acknowledge that there are clear philosophical contradictions in the field of FM, both in the literature and in the field of practice. I posit that these contradictions are not resolvable through some form of synthesis into a new singularity, but neither is their incommensurability an impenetrable barrier and a source only of conflict and 'paradigm wars.' Rather, I see the diversity and complexity inherent in the contradictions as being a source of richness and depth in understanding, where the ambivalent state is embraced. In seeking to maintain the contradiction and ambivalence in the field of practice, without resort to moral relativism, I propose engagement with Aristotle's virtue of *phronēsis*, or practical wisdom, through Flyvbjerg's framework for social science inquiry.

REFERENCES

Aristotle. (2004). *The Nicomachean ethics* (J. A. K. Thomson, Trans., 1953; H. Tredennick, Rev., 1976). London: Penguin Books.

Beech, N., & Cairns, G. (2001). Coping with change: The contribution of postdichotomous ontologies. *Human Relations, 54*(10) 1303–1324.

Berger, P., & Luckman, T. (1966). *The social construction of reality.* Garden City, NY: Doubleday.

Bigliardi, B., & Dormio, A. I. (2010). A balanced scorecard approach for R&D: Evidence from a case study. *Facilities, 28*(5/6), 278–289.

Cairns, G. (2002). Aesthetics, morality and power: Design as espoused freedom and implicit control. *Human Relations, 55*(7), 799–820.

Cairns, G. (2003). Seeking a Facilities Management philosophy for the changing workplace. *Facilities, 21*(5/6), 95–105.

Cairns, G. (2008). Advocating an ambivalent approach to theorizing the built environment. *Building Research & Information, 36*(3), 280–289.

Clegg, S. R., & Kornberger, M. (Eds.). (2006). *Space, organizations and management theory.* Copenhagen: Liber Abstrakt and Copenhagen Business School Press.

Duffy, F., Craig, D., & Gillen, N. (2010). Purpose, process, place: Design as a research tool. *Facilities, 29*(3/4), 97–113.

Flyvbjerg, B. (2001). *Making social science matter: Why social inquiry fails and how it can succeed again.* Cambridge: Cambridge University Press.

Flyvbjerg, B. (2003). Making organization research matter: Power values and phronesis. In B. Czarniawska and G. Sevón (Eds.), *The northern lights: Organization theory in Scandinavia* (pp. 357–382). Copenhagen: Liber Abstrakt and Copenhagen Business School Press.

Foucault, M. (2000). *Aesthetics: Essential works of Foucault 1954–1984* (J. D. Faubion, Ed.). Harmondsworth: Penguin Books.

Hillier B. (1996) *Space is the machine.* Cambridge, MA: Cambridge University Press,

Koskela, L. (2008). Is a theory of the built environment needed? (Editorial). *Building Research & Information, 36*(3), 211–215.

Lefebvre, H. (1991). *The production of space* (D. Nicholson Smith, Trans.). London: Blackwell.

Rothenberg, A. (1979) *The emerging goddess: The creative process in art, science and other fields.* Chicago: The University of Chicago Press.

Strati, A. (1998). Organizational symbolism as a social construction: A perspective from the sociology of knowledge. *Human Relations, 51*(11), 1379–1402.

Straub, A., Koopman, M., & van Mossel, H-J. (2010). Systems approach and performance measurement by social enterprises. *Facilities, 28*(5/6), 321–331.

Wittgenstein, L. (1958). *Philosophical investigations* (2nd ed.). Oxford: Blackwell.

9 The Usability of Facilities
Experiences and Effects

Göran Lindahl, Geir Hansen and Keith Alexander

Usability is an intriguing challenge for architects, designers and FM as it concerns how a space, an artifact, is actually used and the effects of that use. It is an equally challenging concept for organizational strategists as it includes the physical setting in which an organization performs its activities. This makes usability of facilities a topic at the center of the relationship between what we do and where we do it.

Since it was formed almost 10 years ago, the International Council for Building Research and Documentation (CIB) working group on usability (W111) has been exploring concepts, methods and tools, developed in the evaluation of all kinds of consumer products, applied to the built environment (Alexander, 2005, 2008, 2010). In the most recent phase of this work, conducted over the past three years, an international network of partners has collaborated to focus on the usability of learning environments achieving their objectives through a series of case studies and associated workshops. They sought to identify and evaluate the ways in which users (and other stakeholders) in projects were involved in decision-making about building use and the methods and tools they used to understand, as well as to design and manage, the relationship between activities and space.

A starting point was the definition of usability in ISO 9241–11 as "the extent to which a product can be used by specified users to achieve specified goals with effectiveness, efficiency and satisfaction in a specified context of use" (ISO, 1998). Usability in the built environment is context dependent, a product of user experience related to the social relations amongst users and to the interaction between users and facilities (Fenker, 2008). Usability has been found to be strongly related not only to relationships between people and physical settings, but also to clear strategies for the organization of work and the use of facilities. The approach of looking at buildings as a means to fulfill strategic objectives and not only as a way to house people and activities is supported by the work of Becker and Steele (1995), Horgen et al. (1999) and Grantham (2000).

The research has enabled broad conclusions to be drawn about the nature of usability as a concept and its application in the built environment and has challenged the basis of conventional approaches to briefing and post-occupancy evaluation. In summary, the group sees usability as "a cultural phenomenon that can only be improved through a better understanding user experience, considered as situated action in a specific context" (Alexander, 2008 p. 1). Here we elaborate the concept of usability, discuss practical implications for FM and for the development of management processes and raise specific issues for usability research in the built environment. We argue usability as a core concept for managing organizational ecology.

CHANGING THE PERSPECTIVE

Studies of the usability in the built environment originate from the field of FM and other disciplines, where the focus and interest have shifted from a technical perspective on building quality to the actual use of buildings. This shift represents a significant change from looking at buildings as end products and measuring their technical qualities and functional performance to looking at buildings as a means for the occupying organizations, or core businesses in the prevailing language of FM, to achieve their overall goals and objectives. Another consequence of this shift has been for buildings to be regarded as artifacts that interact with organizational processes and information technologies rather than defined objects (Gjersvik & Blakstad, 2004a, 2004b; Fenker, 2008; Nenonen & Nissinen, 2005).

Much recent effort in construction research in Europe and the UK has been focused on creating a client-oriented, knowledge- and value-based industry. Interest in considering the client and user perspective has increased. A growing number of international research networks have recently been established, including various working groups of CIB. CIB concerns construction and built environments, and many working groups take a sectorial perspective, i.e., they are concerned with the actors in the building process rather than the users of the output, the building. A sector-based perspective is clearly needed in order to develop and stimulate innovation in a field such as construction. However, the logics of use must also be recognized as a governing factor for the planning of facilities rather than a focus on professional knowledge to determine what is correct, best practice or what have you. The most recent CIB workgroup (W118) was created as a clients and users forum. This is a step towards trying to understand this relationship, albeit in a project context.

However, CIB W111 is the only group that focuses specifically on a user perspective. The application of the concept of usability in the built environment presents a number of key challenges to conventional construction and property perspectives. Nine characteristics of a usability approach have been identified and contrasted with, for example, conventional built environment approaches (Jensen, Alexander & Fronczek-Munter, 2011):

1. User focus—usability places a focus on the user and the organization rather than the building.
2. Demand driven—usability recognizes the dynamic requirements of organizations (and communities), derived from the strategic objectives.
3. User experience—usability is primarily concerned with the perceptions of users rather than the intentions of designers and service providers.
4. Contingency quality—usability is contingent on user values rather than an inherent function of the built environment.
5. Context of use—usability considers facilities in the context of use rather than as a project (context of action).
6. Process oriented—usability is considered as a process rather than as product or service provision.
7. Service production—like all services, facilities are coproduced by service users.
8. Relationship management—usability implies changing relationships with users.
9. Learning process—usability exchange of knowledge amongst users, managers and service providers.

These characteristics are rooted in a pragmatist philosophy, ultimately derived from Peirce (1905), starting from what works well is what is worth achieving. This is also based in the work of Dewey (1977) and his development of activity-based pedagogy where theory, practice, reflection and action are connected. This approach is based on the development of knowledge derived from use, which is what understanding usability also is about. It is the effect of what is done that is at the core of usability, not the specification of what functions shall be performed. Elsewhere, Granath and Alexander (2006) reflected on some of these theoretical aspects of usability research.

USER EXPERIENCE—THE CORE OF USABILITY

If use is what happens, how do we grasp it, understand it and deal with it? There must be ways of describing and thereby understanding the effects of use; otherwise, it cannot be communicated and reflected upon. Fenker (2008 p. 16) describes usability as a process that can only be understood as a social construction where the building acts as a sort of stage. According to him, "the artefacts are bearers of a set of possibilities and constraints as well as, most importantly, activity and social practices." Alexander (2010) argues for greater emphasis on user experience and suggests reconsidering the original triumvirate of efficiency, effectiveness and satisfaction to substitute experience for satisfaction. Recent work on service design and space management draws upon work about experience design (Shedroff, 2011).

This development is also denoted in service management, where customers' experiences rather than specification of service gain more importance. Ultimately the customer is considered a co-creator of the service experience. The use of facilities has the same characteristic; we as humans interact with it. In Chapter 13, Alexander extends the thinking to consider the co-creation of value in FM.

Usability evaluations are based on different user's experiences and assessments on how well the buildings perform regarding different parameters. A building's performance can never be seen or understood in isolation from an organizational and technical perspective, as those aspects interact and influence each other. Discussing use implies a view on who is the user, and one has to be critical of conventional concepts of users. Olsson, Blakstad and Hansen (2010) suggest a tendency to oversimplify the way that users are addressed and challenge the predominant assumption that there is only one group of users. They identify categories of users and their roles at different stages of the building life cycle. They highlight different user roles and perspectives at different project phases. The perspective that is applied determines which user groups are included in a planning process or discontinuities in user involvement. In a usability perspective, different tools for usability analyses may be needed when studying usability from different user perspectives. This opens up a debate on value beyond value management and it brings culture and governance into the discourse. Who is a user and why are they a user? Whose needs and interests should be at the core of usability analysis and guide possible design?

Themes that have been central to usability research were reflected in the chosen theme of the CIB work group W70 on FM conference in São Paulo—FM and the Experience Economy—following Pine and Gilmour's (1999) seminal work in service marketing. Da Graca (2010) argued that this should now be the focus of FM responsibilities and stressed the need to open the way to demand management focusing on the user experience. Professionals working with facilities need to understand user behavior, user needs and user experiences and need to manage and systematize the user experience. There is a need to learn how to understand and design experiences as good FM briefing leads to effective design. There are necessary tools but they need to be put to work. He suggests that research in this area is essential and that FM practice should focus on the user experience, looking at the demand side, managing experiences and putting the resources to work.

Contingent user values are not easy to explore using conventional techniques such as post-occupancy analysis, and there have been calls for multitimethod approaches (Blakstad, Hansen & Knudsen 2008) and a greater range of methods for understanding user experience (Alexander, 2008). This is highly important as there must be methods that manage to bridge from the facilities' professionals, architects and engineers to the everyday user without imposing professional knowledge in such a way that the user's perceptions are depreciated.

THE USABILITY BRIEF—A KEY INSTRUMENT IN FM

Much recent effort in the research has been focused on developing tools to operationalize the usability concepts, particularly for briefing and evaluation. To date, those who work in the building industry have not been sufficiently interested in evaluating the use of buildings they have helped to create. Does the building function as intended? Are there problems related to function or room use? How efficiently is the building utilized? How satisfied are the users? By not evaluating the use of buildings through asking such questions, vital opportunities for improvement and for coming up with new solutions have probably been missed.

A usability perspective has consequences for methods used in design and planning today. Briefing has been highlighted in several studies as a bearer of clients' and users' needs and requirements and a key instrument in getting what one wants. The recent work by CIB W111 on usability has similarly highlighted the importance of briefing as a means to achieve usability. However, this finding itself raises a further series of issues and a possible agenda for future research and has interesting implications for the way we think about briefing, particularly when usability is seen as a contingent quality rather than as the inherent functionality of the physical environment.

Hudson (forthcoming) argues that much of the existing work on briefing is based on premises that it can be reduced to a rational process, that it is part of a finite project, that the final outcomes of this project are buildings or other physical facilities and that user requirements have an external objective existence that can be captured in the briefing process. He goes on to suggest that the usability work suggests the limitations of these premises and argues that a new approach to briefing may be necessary. This approach might be characterized by an emphasis of briefing as creative exploration of possibilities rather than requirements capture, a focus on the social construction of requirements and their evolution over time and a focus on human satisfaction rather than physical facilities. The professionals' capability to integrate and translate becomes important here and implies a responsibility to manage user needs and feed them forward to the subsequent project without losing the understanding of the social processes from which the facilities have emerged.

USABILITY APPRAISAL—HOW TO UNDERSTAND AND INTERPRET THE USE OF FACILITIES

Usability evaluations are based on different user's experiences and assessments on how well the buildings perform regarding different parameters. By considering a building as a tool, we should be interested not only in how the building itself functions, but also how the building impacts value creation in the user organization. The user organization should ask itself: what do we want to achieve? What do we want the building to contribute? How can our premises create added value for the organization? We have seen that many user organizations have little awareness of those aspects. Instead a building is merely seen as floor space or workplace, without much consideration: a return for the rental. For instance, a business that wants to stimulate cooperation and learning should be interested in how the workplace supports these goals; a kindergarten that wants to encourage involvement by the children should consider how the facilities promote their mastery of their environment.

For building owners and users, an increased focus on usability represents both a challenge and an opportunity. The challenge lies in the fact that the user organization may want quick changes and a high degree of customization to achieve maximum effectiveness. If not handled wisely, this may result in unnecessary tailoring for tenants, which can drive costs up and be difficult to change later. In this type of situation it is essential that solutions are flexible so that they can readily be changed as needs change. At the same time, an increased focus on effectiveness represents an opportunity for building owners and FMs, as having expertise and premises that can contribute to increased customer satisfaction may be an advantage.

A building's performance can never be seen or understood in isolation from an organizational and technical perspective, as those aspects interact and influence each other. Hence, usability is complex and has been described as a "wicked problem" (Blakstad et al., 2008). Such problems are characterized by no definitive formulation of solutions, and they are open to multiple interpretations (Rittel & Webber, 1973). The solution is simply the one that in a certain context is most satisfactory. According to Blakstad, addressing "wicked problems" requires multimethod strategies using a triangulation of methods and evaluations with multiple perspectives.

This aligns with findings from studies showing that evaluations work best when they are based on several methods and aspects, depending on objective, purpose, focus, competence and resources (Frechtling, 2002). All this implies that usability evaluations are complex, that there is a need for simplification and that the evaluator possesses both theoretical and practical knowledge and skills (Baird, Gray, Isaacs, Kernoghan & McIndoe, 1996). Blakstad et al. (2008) describe how different methods and tools were explored and tested according to their relevance and validity for evaluation of usability in several Norwegian cases. As pointed out earlier, few of the available methodologies aim directly at evaluation of usability related to organizational objectives. However, they found that many traditional research and evaluation methods had potential to be developed for the purpose of usability evaluation.

Hansen, Blakstad and Olsson (2012) review usability evaluations and the feedback on users' experiences of their environment. The value of such evaluations for feed forward into new projects or improving existing facilities lies mainly in the ability to understand users' experiences and to translate them into adequate products and solutions. Consequently, the results of research related to evaluation should be quickly and easily accessible to clients, designers, decision-makers and others involved in the building process.

USABILITY OF LEARNING ENVIRONMENTS—A THEMATIC FOCUS

From 2009 to 2011 the work of CIB W111 on usability has mainly focused on the usability of learning environments. The lead was taken by the UK, in collaborative work with the Centre for Effective Learning Environments (CELE) at the Organisation for Economic Co-operation and Development (OECD), in a project to develop tools for evaluating the quality of educational environments (EQES). Research by PricewaterhouseCoopers (2010) concluded that school context must be taken into account when assessing the impact of a school building program and that new buildings alone are insufficient to change pupils' attitudes and behavior. They suggest that the real challenge is to link the transformational agenda to changes in pedagogy and leadership in schools.

Reporting on evaluation research conducted in the UK, Alexander (2008) argued that school facilities should be considered in the context of the communities they serve and as a prime means of transforming education. Effective learning environments successfully combine appropriate social and digital environments with the physical environment (cf. Beard Ch. 6). Creating quality learning environments, which are more broadly accessible in the community, can also play a catalytic role in regeneration. To improve usability, the parallel processes of pedagogy and facilities planning must be reconnected, users must be empowered and communities must be offered the opportunity of managing their assets. And professionals must utilize a usability perspective concerning for whom and why. The majority of conventional evaluation methodologies, particularly Post Occupancy Evaluation (POE) and Practitioner-focused Facility Evaluation (PFE) methods and tools, fail to address strategic objectives, consider buildings out of context and tend to focus on the characteristics and performance of the physical environment, rather than on the effects on users and on benefits realization. The evaluation of schools must take account of three key dimensions according to their role in the development of sustainable communities, in educational transformation and in the quality of the learning environment.

Assessing the usability of learning environments against these criteria, using appropriate research-based methods and tools, will require the development of new skills. It also suggests the need to develop different relationships amongst key actors in coproduction processes. This is a challenging agenda for the FM of learning environments.

The objective of FM is to provide the setting and services that support the effectiveness of organizations that contribute to the development and creativity of the occupants and provide community benefit. The key is establishing the strategies and processes that connect effective utilization of the physical, environmental and human resources to create positive outcomes for all stakeholders, through the whole life of the facilities. Stakeholders include owners, occupiers and operators of the facility, all service users and providers, the local community and representative agencies.

Seen in this way, FM is the brokerage of processes amongst all stakeholder interests and between stakeholder constructs. Myerson (Ch. 2) and Vischer (Ch. 3) argue that, in the experience economy, learning and co-creation are key processes. Elsewhere, Beard (Ch. 6) and Thomas (Ch. 18) describe learning itself as a complex process conducted via conversation, in a broad sense, including symbolic change and reflection or silent conversation and kinaesthetics.

MANAGEMENT FOR USABILITY

Jensen (2010) has suggested that a focus on buildings in FM is concerned with how the corporate needs for facilities can be provided and optimized in both a short- and long-term perspective. Therefore, every phase of the life cycle of buildings is important. He proposed that continuous briefing and continuous commissioning are two interrelated concepts that, together with the concept of learning buildings, can be used to integrate the management of buildings and usability. Just as learning organizations need a specific form of management, where traditional hierarchical structures are removed and a shared vision is defined and accepted, so learning buildings need a similar specific form of management.

The management tasks to obtain usability include formulation of visions, strategies and requirements for the long-term development of buildings in the planning phase; involvement of users in defining needs and requirements and deciding on design solutions in continuous briefing; and ongoing monitoring of performance and usability to capture new needs and requirements for changes during the use phase of buildings. In short, FM is about connecting use and space. FMs should be the obvious profession to take on this important management role in close collaboration with the top managers and users in the organization.

FRAMEWORK FOR USE—A STRUCTURE FOR DISCOURSE

Recent reflections on Nordic contributions to the usability research have led to the introduction of a framework—USE*frame*—to conceptualize contextual dimensions of usability. The framework is based on a perceived need to bring usability studies into one structure and to relate what had been done in the different studies. This led to a discussion about a framework that also would enable the positioning of previous research by the research team members as well as the positioning of other research related to usability.

A framework developed by the research team is illustrated in Figure 9.1 and further discussed by Lindahl, Hansen, Nenonen and Blakstad (2012). It illustrates steps in a process of understanding and mapping use to support action in projects or FM processes. It is a framework that can be used to describe processes as well as to map and relate projects or studies. A typical FM loop could be from "as is, use" via development of new knowledge, supported by the USEtool and back to daily use, i.e., to "as is, use" in "context of use." This is an iterative process of change and possibly improvement. New knowledge can also be forwarded in a structured form, in a proprietary information system, to projects and action to create new workplaces via projects in the "context of action" domain. This then results in plans for new or changed facilities, the future use, "to be."

Based on the research carried out in Nordic FM and usability projects we argue that there is a substantial amount of research and development (R&D) concerning facilities in use that already today allow for the possibility of sustaining usability of facilities. However, these are not clearly related and there is a mix between management-oriented research that focuses on the "context of action" and usability-oriented research that focuses on "context of use" and subsequent development of knowledge and briefing. The framework USE*frame* provides a possibility to map and discuss this material (Hansen et al., 2012; Lindahl et al., 2012). With the creation of CIB W118 clients and users and the previous CIB workgroups W65 Organization and Management of Construction, W070 FM and Maintenance, W096 Architectural Management and W111 Usability, understanding and delivering what the users need appears well covered. However, much of

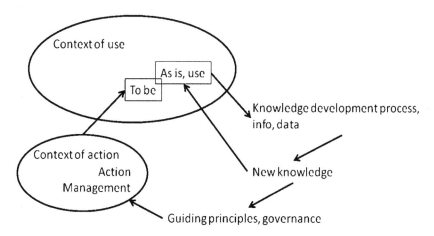

Figure 9.1   The basic framework—USE*frame*.

the research has focused on methods and processes. While this is relevant, we already know that clear information, participation and knowledge dissemination is beneficial. While continued development of methods and processes is needed, there is also a lack of R&D of theory concerning users and their activities in the facilities the construction and FM sectors deliver. As much as researchers like to practice nearness in cases, there is now a need to step back and reflect in order to develop a theory to sustain the field of understanding the effects of facilities in use.

The development of knowledge and tools within USE*frame* will help structure the further implementation of usability knowledge and tools in practice. A crucial question is how research can contribute to, on one hand, strategic/practical development in organizations and, on the other, the design and construction processes. USE*frame* illustrates this and aims to support discussion at the interface of research and practice. This will then also address the validity, reliability and generalizability of usability research.

The delivery world of methods and processes has its own set of social constructs—i.e., it is one ecology; the user world is another. Usability research needs to think through the mind and narrative of the user world. Macdonald (Ch. 19) shows that, in a healthcare setting, strategic FM can be seen as a translation between the two. Higher usability was delivered by FMs who reached out to relate to the users and translated user requirements into appropriate service delivery.

USABILITY—A CORE CONCEPT FOR
ORGANIZATIONAL DEVELOPMENT

A building's usability is never dependent just on the building itself. It should be seen in the light of the relationship between building and user. This is essential for understanding the concept of usability. The users have their own history, experiences and perceptions in relation to the building and the activities that take place there. Further, the way they perceive the building will always be influenced by both individual and psychosocial considerations that have little to do with the building itself.*

Having reviewed and described development within the field of research on usability it is clear that the action and the use of facilities are strongly related to experiences by the users and thus their possibility and will to perform. People create their places in the facilities created by professionals, and there has to be an approach that opens up for questions like what use and why does an organization want a specific solution. If professionals and laymen could meet and understand and define the emerging properties of a workplace they could better manage and design the facilities to

---

*Editors note. Cairns's calls for *ambivalence* and *phronesis* (Ch. 8) might well enrich this line of research.

be. What can be defined by planning should already have been dealt with. So, if a facility can be interpreted and analyzed based on how it is socially constructed we can achieve an integration of organizational use and the facilities provided to arrive at an understanding of usability. The concept of usability brings the organizational space to the fore and by doing so supports the actions needed. Usability will not be fully understood without understanding the social constructs of the users—the organizational ecology of narratives or constructs.

REFERENCES

Alexander, K. (2006). *Usability of Workplaces: report on case studies* CIB Report 906, Rotterdam: CIB.

Alexander, K. (2008a). *Usability of Workplaces—Phase 2*. Report 316. Rotterdam: CIB.

Alexander, K, (2008b), *Usability: philosophy and concepts. in Usability of Workplaces—Phase 2*. Report 316. Rotterdam: CIB.

Alexander, K, (2010a). *Usability of Workplaces—Phase 3*.Report 330. Rotterdam: CIB.

Alexander, K, (2010b). *The usability of learning environments, in Usability of Workplaces—Phase 3*. Report 330. Rotterdam: CIB.

Baird G., Gray, J., Isaacs, N., Kernoghan, D. & McIndoe, G. (1996). *Building Evaluation Techniques*. New York: McGraw-Hill.

Blakstad S. H., Hansen G. K., & Knudsen W. (2008). Methods and tools for evaluation of usability in Buildings, in *Usability of Workplaces, Phase 2*. Report 316. Rotterdam: CIB.

Da Graca, M.E.A., (2010), Preface: FM in the Experience Economy, in *Proceedings, CIB W70 Conference*, University of Sao Paulo.

Dewey, J. (1977). *Essays on pragmatism and truth, 1907–1909*. Carbondale IL: Southern Illinois University Press.

Fenker, M. (2008). Towards a theoretical framework for usability of buildings. in *Usability of Workplaces: Phase 2* CIB Research Report 316. Rotterdam: CIB.

Frechtling, J, (2002), *The 2002 User-Friendly Handbook for Project Evaluation*, Arlington VI: National Science Foundation.

Granath, J.A. and Alexander, K, (2006) A theoretical reflection on the practice of designing for usability, in *Proceedings EuroFM Research Symposium*. Frankfurt.

Hansen, G K, Blakstad, S H and Olsson, N O E, (2011), Usability Reviewed: summing up on Norwegian research on usability', *Nordic FM Conference*, August 2011. Copenhagen: DTU.

Hudson, J, (forthcoming), Briefing for Usability, in Alexander, K, (Ed.) *Usability in the Built Environment* (forthcoming).

Jensen, P A, (2010), Management for usability of the built environment. in *Usability of Workplaces—Phase 3*, Report 330, Rotterdam: CIB.

Jensen, P.A., Alexander, K., & Fronczek-Munter, A. (2011), Towards an agenda for user oriented research in the built environment. in *Proceedings 6th Nordic Conference on Construction Economics and Organisation*, April 2011, Copenhagen.

Lindahl, G, Hansen, G.K.Nenonen, S. & Blakstad, S.H., (2011). Facilities in use —Nordic studies about usability of workplaces, in *Proceedings Nordic FM Conference*, August 2011. Copenhagen: DTU.

Olsson, N., Blakstad, S.H. and Hansen, G. (2010). Who is the User?, CIB Proceedings: Publication number 336. CIB W70 International Conference in Facilities Management. *FM in the experience economy.* Rotterdam: CIB 25–36.

Peirce, C.S. (1905), Issues of pragmaticism, *The Monist* v XV(4). 481–499.

Pine, B.J., & Gilmore, J. H. (1999) *The Experience Economy*, Cambridge MA: Harvard Business School Press.

PricewaterhouseCoopers, (2010), *Evaluation of building schools for the future (BSF): 3rd Annual Report*, London: DCSF.

Rittel, H.W.J. & Webber, M.M. (1973), Dilemmas in a general theory of planning, in *Working papers from the Urban and Regional Development*, Berkeley CA: University of California.

Shedroff, N. (2011). *Experience design 1.1 a manifesto for the design of experiences.* San Fransisco: Experience Design.

10 Service-Centric Logic of FM

Christian Coenen and Daniel von Felten

In research and practice, FM is mostly considered to be a discipline where aspects of the built environment play an important role for increasing efficiency and reducing costs. Research into FM terminology has attempted to define the meaning of the term, and since 2006 a common European Norm has been established to create a terminological foundation for this field of management. In this norm, FM is defined as the "integration of processes within an organization to maintain and develop the agreed services which support and improve the effectiveness of its primary activities" (CEN,[1] 2006, p. 5). Additionally, facility services are defined as provision of support to the primary activities of an organization, delivered by an internal or external provider. They are services related to 'space and infrastructure' and to 'people and organizations' (CEN, 2006, p. 7).

Even though the term 'service' is included several times within these definitions, there is still a need for a well-established management understanding of FM that reflects this service character in addition to its engineering focus and that at the same time accounts for its multidimensional management challenges. The field of services management offers such an understanding and can be applied to FM. According to Johnston and Clark (2005), services management covers the activities, decisions and responsibilities of managers in service organizations. Based on this proposition, it can therefore be stated that FM is responsible for:

- Support service operations—the configuration of resources and support processes that create value and deliver service to customers (e.g., provision of working space, catering, cleaning).
- An organization's resources, including materials, equipment, staff, technology and facilities. These resources often account for a very large proportion of an organization's total assets, so FM is responsible for much of an organization's cost base.
- Some or all internal customer segments (e.g., departments, employees) and various external customers (e.g., visitors) and/or the items belonging to their internal/external customers.

Taking this perspective, FM is interpreted as a services management discipline while service is defined as an "intangible experience performed for a customer acting as co-producer" (CEN, 2011, p. 10). According to CEN (2006, p. 5), the term 'customer' has to be differentiated as: (1) *client*, meaning "organization that specifies needs and procures facility services by means of an FM agreement"; (2) *customer*, meaning "organizational unit that specifies and orders the delivery of facility services within the conditions of an FM agreement"; and (3) *end user*, meaning "person receiving facility services in a permanent or temporary way." In the following section of the chapter the term 'customer' includes all three of these customer types. Our primary objective is to provide a service-centric understanding of the field of FM and describe the role services management plays in successful FM. The objective is achieved by:

- Applying the main characteristics of services management to FM.
- Describing the service-specific perspectives of FM.
- Analyzing the specific quality attributes of FM as a service management discipline.
- Introducing important services management implications for FM.

SERVICE CHARACTERISTICS AND CONSEQUENCES FOR FM

It is generally agreed that goods and services differ and that the distinctive characteristics of services result in certain challenges for services management (Parasuraman, Zeithaml & Berry, 1985). Identifying certain service characteristics and acknowledging them as significant for FM is crucial. This knowledge enables researchers and practitioners to recognize that achieving cost awareness and quality in FM requires specific management tools. The most relevant characteristics and their implications for FM are as follows.

Intangibility

The most obvious and basic characteristic of services is intangibility (Wilson, Zeithaml, Bitner & Gremler, 2008). Because services are performances and actions, rather than objects, they cannot be seen, felt, tasted or touched in the same way one can sense tangible goods. Despite the fact that brick–and-mortar facilities can in fact be seen and touched, the field of activity involved in managing these facilities is intangible because it can't be touched or seen by the customer. For example, maintenance services are actions performed by providers and directed towards the client's properties. These services cannot be touched or actually seen by the client, although the client may be able to see or touch certain tangible components of the service (e.g., tools, documents).

Consequently, intangibility presents several management challenges for FM. FM cannot be patented easily, and new FM concepts can therefore easily be copied by the competition. Another challenge is that FM cannot be readily displayed or easily communicated to (internal) customers, so clients may find quality dimensions difficult to assess. Additional decisions about which elements to include in certain service product bundles or promotional materials are challenging. Finally, the actual costs of a 'unit of service' are hard to determine.

Customer Integration

As a second characteristic of services the integration of the customer or one of his/her properties into the service delivery process can also be considered relevant for FM. FM cannot be performed without the customer participating in the process. In the field of FM, this customer integration can refer to the integration of clients, customers and/or end users in the sense of CEN (2006). Due to the fact that FM is a very diverse field of business, the customer's participation can vary greatly across different FM segments. For example, interior greenery maintenance services require a fairly low degree of customer participation during the service delivery. This standardized service only requires the presence of the customer's plants, and payment may be the only additional customer input. In contrast, a moderate level of customer participation can be observed when considering catering services. In this case, the customer's request for a special meal is necessary for an adequate outcome of the service, and the service is only provided because of the customer's purchase. Finally, services with the highest degree of customer participation can be found when customers co-create the service product and act as coproducers of the service. Taking property consulting for cost reduction as an FM example, it makes perfect sense that the active participation of the customer's employees is mandatory to achieve the project's objectives. One of the implications for FM resulting from customer integration is the fact that FM products are hard to standardize and the customer's perspective should be taken into account when it comes to designing FM processes. Even though the provider's perspective can also be considered relevant for the process, the customer's or client's final authority imperative has to be emphasized.

Heterogeneity

Because services are performances, frequently produced by humans, no two services will be exactly alike (Zeithaml, Bitner & Gremler, 2006). In the customer's eyes, the employees performing the service are the service; there is nothing else. Thus, heterogeneity arises, on the one hand, because service employees may differ in their performance from day to day; on the other hand, customer's demands can differ over time and they will therefore experience the service differently. When considering catering, a typical FM segment, this heterogeneity becomes obvious and is largely a result of human interactions between the service provider and the service customer. As a result of heterogeneity, ensuring consistent service quality may be a challenging management task for FM. The quality of FM actually depends on many factors and cannot be fully controlled by the service supplier. For example, the ability of the customer to articulate his needs, the service provider's ability to satisfy the stated needs or the level of demand for a specific service at a particular time are only a few possibilities that can influence the perceived quality of FM. These factors make it difficult for FMs to know with any certainty whether the service is being delivered in the way planned and promised. Often, facility services are provided by third parties (i.e., outsourcing partners), which might further increase the perceived heterogeneity of the offering.

SERVICE PERSPECTIVES OF FM

After introducing the three most important characteristics of services and describing their consequences for FM, we now explain the three-stage model of service consumption and refer to its relevance for FM. The delivery of an appropriate service package for different groups of customers and the management of core and support services are vitally important to FM companies. Managing the different stages of the customer's experience from a service manager's perspective is vital (Gilmore, 2003). Taking account of the complete experience for the customer in terms of their pre-service, during service and post-service experiences can help managers plan and implement all relevant aspects of service delivery in a balanced way. With this in mind, FM can be seen from three perspectives: resource-based, process-based and outcome-based.

Resource-Based Perspective: FM as a Promise

The resource-based perspective of FM becomes obvious when considering the service as the provider's ability and readiness to perform. From this perspective, FM consists only of a promise to the customer to perform a certain task. The FM service provider is willing and able to integrate certain resources into the proposed service process, such as employees, material, technology, knowledge, etc. In this pre-purchase stage, FM can only present the promised service offerings without the customer being able to actually perceive the service at this stage. Nevertheless, in this pre-purchase stage, the customer is searching for solutions and alternatives that match his expectations and needs. The customer evaluates alternative solutions and suppliers by reviewing their offerings in regard to various features (Lovelock & Wirtz, 2007).

Process-Based Perspective: FM as a Process

In addition to the resource-based perspective, FM can also be seen from a process-based perspective. From this point of view, FM is a process of which the customer is an essential part. FM becomes not only a promise, as the actual deeds of the service provider involve the customer in the creation of the service. Because FM consists of actions or performances done for and with customers it typically involves a sequence of steps, actions and activities (Zeithaml et al., 2006). Customers evaluate the combination of steps, the flow of activities or the experience. The service process is the customer's direct experience of the service and concerns the way the customer is dealt with by the service provider (Johnston & Clark, 2005). It contains aspects of how a customer-facing staff member interacts with the customer. Aspects of the service experience include: the extent of personalization of the process; the responsiveness of the service organization; the flexibility, courtesy and competence of customer-facing staff; the ease of access to service staff or information systems; and the extent to which a customer feels valued by the organization. In this service encounter stage, the customer perceives several episodes of services that are termed 'moments of truth' (Carlzon, 1987). The customer is able to perceive and evaluate the service, thus taking several FM quality dimensions into account. Whether or not the FM provider acknowledges the experiential character of the FM activities, it seems inevitable that the customer will have an experience—good, bad or indifferent (Zeithaml et al., 2006).

Outcome-Based Perspective: FM as a Result

In the post-encounter stage of services, the outcome-based perspective can be applied to FM. Hence, FM is seen as the result of the service delivery process. The term 'service outcome' is used to describe the effect of service delivery for the customer (Johnston & Clark, 2005). The optimal combination of FM and customer resources and the efficient operation of FM processes lead to these results. Basically, the customer is demanding this output and not the resources and processes that lead to it. The most obvious result is the expected output, such as the flawless condition of building services engineering equipment after receiving regular maintenance, or the final report on the energy consumption of the organization. Another example of expected output is the reduced destruction of property, due to the hiring of security services to protect the site.

SERVICES QUALITY ATTRIBUTES OF FM

Following the description of the three different FM perspectives, we turn to the specific considerations implied by the proposition that FM's quality evaluation is determined not only by objectively measurable technical or financial indicators, but also by the subjective perceptions of individual customers. The primary objective of service producers can be stated as the development and provision of service offerings that satisfy customer needs and expectations, thereby ensuring their own economic survival (Johnston & Clark, 2005). To achieve these objectives, FM service providers have to understand how customers choose, experience and evaluate their service offerings. Research shows clearly that customers have a more difficult time evaluating and choosing most services partly because of the aforementioned characteristics, namely, intangibility, heterogeneity and customer integration (Wilson et al., 2008). These characteristics lead to differences in customer evaluation processes in all stages of the buying and experience process. Here we explain the differences in detail.

Generally speaking, there are three relevant attributes that customers refer to when evaluating a product or service (Zeithaml et al., 2006). Firstly, *search qualities*, i.e., attributes that can be evaluated before ordering and purchasing a service or a product. Search qualities include items such as color, size and price. Traditionally, products such as cars, clothing or furniture are high in search qualities, because their attributes can be almost completely determined and evaluated before the purchase. Secondly, there are *experience qualities* that only can be evaluated after purchase or during the service experience. Examples of experience qualities are taste, time and reliability. Service products, such as vacations and restaurant meals, are high in experience qualities because their attributes cannot be fully known or assessed until they have been purchased and are being consumed. A third category, *credence qualities*, includes characteristics that customers may find impossible to evaluate even after purchase or consumption. Examples of service offerings high in credence qualities are surgical operations or brake repairs on cars. Few customers possess medical or mechanical skills sufficient to evaluate whether these services are necessary or are performed properly (Lovelock & Wirtz, 2007).

Products and services high in search qualities are easiest to evaluate; products high in experience qualities are more difficult to judge because they must be purchased and consumed before assessment is possible. Products and services high in credence qualities are the most difficult to evaluate because the customer may be unaware of or may lack sufficient knowledge to appraise whether the offerings satisfy certain wants and needs even after consumption. As can be seen from this threefold differentiation, FM as a service offering provides only few search qualities (e.g., price or references) and offers more experience qualities or credence qualities. Thus, the customer actually has to experience the service (reliability of security access services or friendliness of reception service staff) to evaluate its quality. The customer will have great difficulties in properly evaluating the service quality of hygiene conditions or the healthiness of ingredients in a catering kitchen because of the high degree of credence qualities in this type of setting. The higher the degree of credence qualities for the customer, the harder it is for them to evaluate the quality of FM.

MANAGERIAL IMPLICATIONS FOR FM AS A SERVICES MANAGEMENT DISCIPLINE

Taking the FM characteristics and the corresponding insight regarding the evaluation of quality in FM described in the preceding into account, various managerial challenges can be identified that should find a place in the educational programs of FM (Roper, Ch. 16) as they determine the success of FM. We now describe these implications.

Process Management

Considering the fact that FM services are often perceived by customers as processes, there is a need for a well-designed process management that focuses on the customer's perspective. Every service consists of several customer contact points where the customer perceives FM quality, or indeed the lack of quality. Thus, it is essential for FM service providers to establish a solid process routine for every contact point.

FMs need to be able to manage the total chain of processes that link together to deliver a service to customers. Failure to manage end-to-end processes can lead to inefficiencies across the organization, which in turn leads to lack of consistency, poor reliability in terms of quality and lead times and increased costs (Johnston & Clark, 2005). FMs must not only deal with the individual issues in managing back-office and front-office processes, but also with the challenge of integrating their activities with the core activities across the value chain of the core business. Managers frequently have the tendency to draw a boundary around their processes that coincides with the physical or geographical boundary of their responsibility. However, the problem faced by many customers is often located at the interfaces between the many back-office and front-office processes that together create the total value chain. Nevertheless, by assessing and designing service processes from the point of view of the customer, one can expose the problems that occur at the interfaces (Johnston & Clark, 2005). Thus, it is necessary for managers to take a process rather than a functional perspective and understand its entirety and the way it fits in.

A process management tool that is called 'service blueprinting' offers the possibility to design the internal and external process steps around the customer path (Shostack, 1984; Fliess & Kleinaltenkamp, 2004). It differentiates between activities that are performed by customers and by employees ('line of interaction'), activities that are visible or invisible for the customer ('line of visibility') and activities that are performed by customer contact employees or back-office employees ('line of internal interaction').

Blueprints are particularly helpful in the design stage of service development. A service blueprint visually displays the service by simultaneously depicting the process of service delivery, the points of customer contact, the roles of customers and employees and the visible elements of the service (Zeithaml et al., 2006). It provides a way to break a service down into its logical components and to depict the steps or tasks in the process and the means by which the tasks are executed and to identify the evidence of service as the customer experiences it. A good blueprint should draw attention to points in service delivery where things are particularly at risk of going wrong (Lovelock & Wirtz, 2007). The initial steps of transferring this process management tool to FM have been made in the form of FM blueprinting within the field of healthcare (Coenen, von Felten & Schmid, 2011).

Tangibility Management

Taking the intangibility of services into account, the successful FM has to be aware of the fact that customers perceive and pay for something they cannot see and touch; thus, the perceived value is difficult for the customer to grasp. The successful FM is able to minimize this by making the intangible tangible. Thus, emphasizing the brand name, employee uniforms and logos on physical elements of the service product can become one element of tangibility management. The logos and marketing communication should emphasize the perceived value customers are receiving, such as support services that make their core business more profitable. To reduce the perceived client's uncertainty about what they are buying, the FM provider should offer some search qualities, e.g., service guarantees or flat-rate pricing.

Personnel Management

Most of the services offered by FM providers include interpersonal contact between customers and the FM service provider's employees. The behavior of these employees plays a vital role in the perceived quality of the entire FM service offering (Coenen, 2002; Homburg, Wieseke & Bornemann, 2009; Di Mascio, 2010). Organizations, with their demanding requirements for services to be performed in an appropriate way, can be a source of pressure for service employees (Johnston & Clark, 2005). Customers may also be a source of potential pressure for service employees, e.g., through unrealistic expectations or their own incompetence. These pressures may lead to issues of low motivation, poor customer relationships and stress. Therefore, clear leadership is essential for counteracting the pressure on FM service employees. Teams and teamworking can provide a powerful mechanism for support and also for building ownership of certain service processes. Well-designed FM blueprints or scripts enable consistency and provide useful hints for employees. Supervisors facilitate good services by reducing role conflicts and ambiguity and increasing role clarity for their employees. One of the key aspects in this context is defining the degree and type of discretion required for each role, thus empowering the employee (Bowen & Lawler, 1992; Argyris, 1998; Chebat & Kollias, 2000; Bull & Kortens, Ch. 15).

Thus, it is inevitable not only that employees require education and training in methodological and skill-based issues (e.g., tools, technology, procedures), but also require the necessary training in customer-contact situations (Coenen, 2011). This bundle of activities is often referred to as 'internal marketing,' which consists of certain HR-related tools (e.g., recruiting, incentives, leadership), as well as marketing-related instruments such as communication or behavioral training (Rafiq & Ahmed, 2000; Wieseke, Ahearne, Lam & van Dick, 2009). Internal marketing is generally not a discrete activity, but is implicit in quality initiatives, customer service programs and broader business strategies. It has an important role to play in reducing conflicts between the functional areas of the organization and is more successful when there is commitment at the highest level, all employees cooperate and an open management style prevails (Lovelock & Wirtz, 2007).

Relationship Management

In addition to the fact that FM has to professionally manage processes, tangibility and personnel to create sustainable value for the customer, relationship management also plays a vital role. This is due to the fact that customers evaluate their relationship with the provider, meaning that they not only evaluate the quality of the service of a FM provider, but also the quality of the entire relationship (Bruhn & Georgi, 2006; Ellison & Flowers, Ch. 12). Thus relationship quality becomes an important driver of perceived value and customer satisfaction. Service quality and relationship quality interact with one another. As the FM services used are an important characteristic of a provider from the customer's perspective, consecutive positive experiences with these services cumulate to a positive perception of the relationship in total. Moreover a highly perceived relationship quality facilitates customer interactions. The better the FM provider and customer know and value each other, the more open and constructive are the interactions between them (Georgi, 2000). 'Relationship quality' stands for the customer's perception of the relationship to the FM provider and is defined as the ability of the provider to fulfill the customer's relational needs (Bruhn, 2002). It is not just the sum of the qualities of all the interactions within a customer relationship, but also concerns aspects that are central to the concept of the relationship (Macdonald, Ch. 19). Thus, the following two central dimensions of relationship quality also have to be managed by professional FM (Georgi, 2000): (1) 'trust' as the customer's willingness to forgo any additional investigation and just rely on the corporation's behavior in the future; (2) 'familiarity,' which is closely related to trust, but is based on past experiences. These two dimensions characterize the degree of convergence with the other party in terms of their attitudes and modes of behavior.

CONCLUSION AND OUTLOOK

Our primary objective was to provide the reasoning for a service-centric understanding of the field of FM. Based on insights from services management and the theory of FM, we have clearly shown that FM is to be considered a services management discipline. Thus, FM has to take into account certain management challenges that go beyond the current perspective of FM being a mainly engineering- and cost-driven discipline that deals with the built environment. Therefore, further research in the proposed overlapping fields of FM and services management is needed. This includes topics such as the triple dimension of FM customers (client/customer/end user) and their specific needs and requirements, the dimensions and drivers of perceived value in FM, the concept and measurement of FM services quality and FM relationship quality and the FM service profit chain as well as the FM service value chain. Services management knowledge and expertise certainly have the potential to position FM as an even more professional business discipline for successfully managing organizational ecologies.

NOTES

1. CEN is the acronym for the European Committee of Standardization.

REFERENCES

Argyris, C. (1998). Empowerment: The emperor's new clothes. *Harvard Business Review, 76*(5), 98–105.

Bowen, D., & Lawler, E. (1992).The empowerment of service workers: What, why and how and when. *Sloan Management Review, 3*(3), 31–39.

Bruhn, M. (2002). *Relationship marketing—management of customer relationships.* Harlow, Essex: Pearson Education.

Bruhn, M., & Georgi, D. (2006). *Services marketing—managing the service value chain.* Harlow, Essex: Pearson Education.

Carlzon, J. (1987). *Moments of truth.* New York: Ballinger.

Chebat, J., & Kollias, P. (2000). The impact of empowerment on customer contact employees' roles in service organizations. *Journal of Services Research, 3*(1), 66–81.

Coenen, C. (2002). Prosocial service behaviors and their role in influencing perceived service quality. In Rust, R./Lemmink, J. (Eds.), *Conference Proceedings of 11th Annual AMA Frontiers in Service Conference, Maastricht (NL),* AMA—American Marketing Association, Chicago, 456–465.

Coenen, C. (2011). Auf dem Weg zu Service Centricity [On the way to service centricity]. *Marketing Review St. Gallen, 28*(1), 41–47.

Coenen, C., von Felten, D., & Schmid, M. (2011). Managing effectiveness and efficiency through FM blueprinting. *Facilities, 29*(9/10), 422–436.

Di Mascio, R. (2010). The service models of frontline employees. *Journal of Marketing, 74*(4), 63–80.

European Committee for Standardization. (2006). *EN 15221–1: European standard in Facility Management—part 1: Terms and definitions.* Brussels: CEN.

European Committee for Standardization. (2011). *EN 15221–3: European standard in Facility Management—part 3: Guidance on quality in Facility Management.* Brussels: CEN.

Fliess, S., & Kleinaltenkamp, M. (2004). Blueprinting the service company—managing service processes efficiently. *Journal of Business Research, 57*(3), 392–404.

Georgi, D. (2000). *Entwicklung von Kundenbeziehungen* [Development of customer relationships]. Wiesbaden: Gabler.

Gilmore, A. (2003). *Services marketing and management.* London: Sage.

Homburg, C., Wieseke, J., & Bornemann, T. (2009). Implementing the marketing concept at the employee–customer interface: The role of customer need knowledge. *Journal of Marketing, 73*(4), 64–81.

Johnston, R., & Clark, G. (2005). *Service operations management—improving service delivery* (2nd ed.). Harlow: Pearson Education.

Lovelock, C., & Wirtz, J. (2007). *Services marketing—people, technology, strategy* (6th ed.). Upper Saddle River, NJ: Prentice Hall.

Parasuraman, A., Zeithaml, V., & Berry, L. (1985). A conceptual model of service quality and its implications for future research. *Journal of Marketing, 49*(4), 41–50.

Rafiq, M., & Ahmed, R. K. (2000). Advances in internal marketing: Definition, synthesis and extension. *Journal of Services Marketing, 14*(6), 449–462.

Shostack, L. (1984). Designing services that deliver. *Harvard Business Review, 62*(1), 133–139.

Wieseke, J., Ahearne, M., Lam, S., & van Dick, R. (2009). The role of leaders in internal marketing. *Journal of Marketing, 73*(2), 123–145.

Wilson, A., Zeithaml, V., Bitner, M., & Gremler, D. (2008). *Services marketing—integrating customer focus across the firm* (1st European ed.). London: McGraw-Hill/Irwin.

Zeithaml, V., Bitner, M., & Gremler, D. (2006). *Services marketing—integrating customer focus across the firm* (4th ed.). Boston: McGraw-Hill/Irwin.

11 Value Rhetoric and Cost Reality

Colin Stuart

All successful species have evolved. They adapt to changes in their environment and take advantage of the opportunities presented. Homo sapiens is no exception. From our early beginnings we have changed our behaviors, hunter-gatherers migrated with their prey, the hunter-gatherers then became farmers and the early farmers founded settlements that became mighty ancient civilizations. We traded, invented commerce, developed new economic models, founded corporations and ultimately developed the modern office. Innovation has been at the forefront of adaption to our environment; it is the mechanism for driving change and improving the way we do things, making us more efficient and effective.

The modern workplace can trace its routes back to Fredrick W. Taylor and his principles of efficiency, which were further evolved by the mechanistic thinking of the Bauhaus Institute. Until recently the workplace has remained largely unchanged for a hundred years. We have had minor adaptations to suit emerging technologies, the telephone, the typewriter, the PC and most recently the Internet. The last 10 years has, however, seen the beginning of a radical shift in how the workplace is perceived (Myerson, Ch. 2).

In the past, the office was viewed as somewhere you simply went to work; more space was taken on when required, where required. Organizations steadily started to wake up to the cost of space and started to look harder at how to reduce it. The focus was on consolidation and utilization. With the advent of the "new ways of working" a greater balance was struck. Work was now something you did, not just a place you went, and the FM community was challenged to ensure it was in the right place, the right size and with the right mix of facilities. It was, however, still largely seen as an overhead. Now leading organizations have realized the fundamental impact that FM can have on corporate culture, staff behavior, productivity and ultimately the bottom line. The workplace is starting to be seen as a key weapon in the corporate armory, and FM is being challenged like never before to provide innovative space tailored to and truly supporting the business.

Organizations across the spectrum, from large multinational corporations to SMEs in out-of-town business parks, from monolithic central government departments to service-focused local councils, are waking up to the need to change. They recognize the need to respond to economic forces, to make their space work more effectively, to drive innovation, increase collaboration, improve knowledge exchange, to facilitate knowledge creation, to do more with less. The drive to reduce costs, the advances in technology and the changing attitudes in society and the new generation of technologically savvy, socially minded workers present organizations with a perfect storm; one that has the potential to sweep away the old workplace. More importantly, it provides an opportunity to take the workplace to the next level of evolution. The new, innovation-driven, corporate world has to leave behind the factory-derived working environments of Taylor's day.

Organizations with visionary chief executives and boards are leading the way, prepared to experiment with new working models, to take risks and invest in innovative workspace. The vast majority of organizations, however, are in a dilemma. They often recognize the need to change, to innovate, to maintain a competitive advantage or improve value and service but cannot justify the funding to invest in a new working environment to facilitate this, especially in economically challenging times. Others are afraid of failure, they do not fully believe FM and the working environment can act as a catalyst for cultural change or deliver value to the bottom line. They see and admire the market leading few who have radically changed their cultures, but feel it is not for them, that they are somehow not worthy or different. This is often due to the failure to fully understand and define the benefits case for a change to the organizational structure, the working environment and the impact using these to drive change in employee behaviors will have on the bottom line. In this chapter I present a methodology and model for assessing the benefits of FM-driven workplace change, for analyzing the value delivered and its potential impact to the bottom line and for assessing return on investment periods.

UTILIZATION AND COST

As discussed earlier, organizations in the last few years were very focused on the cost of space. It is still important to be mindful of the cost, as especially in major cities the total occupancy cost can be high, typically in London this can be up to £14,500 per desk per annum.[1] With desk densities often exceeding 12 square meters per desk and desk-to-staff allocations often in excess of one to one, a considerable amount of space is being wasted. I have measured the utilization of a significant number of organizations both in the public and private sectors and, where no formal desk-sharing arrangements have been introduced, utilization rates very rarely exceed 55%. With midtown occupancy costs high, substantial cost savings can be made that can be partly reinvested back into the workplace, for example, for a business occupying 100,000 square feet in the City of London, the total occupancy cost of this space would probably be in the region of £10,000,000 per annum—with a utilization rate at a maximum of 55%, there is potentially £4,500,000 of space unused at any time!

This focus on utilization and cost has led to a reduction in the workplace footprint with an increase in desk density, uniformity and standardization. As part of the corresponding redesign of office facilities there have been collaboration improvements as workers are now in much closer proximity with one another and some saved space is often given over to team and social settings. However, it can also be counterproductive to simply take the reduced space occupied as a saving. With up to 50% of workers in the Western world categorized as "knowledge workers," a one-size-fits-all approach does not provide the catalysts for innovation FM needs to seek (Myerson, Bichard & Erlich, 2010).

It also ignores the size of the prize. A cost-focused approach to FM and the workplace delivers only a fraction of potential benefits. It does not deliver cultural and behavioral change; it does not deliver the fundamental mind-set change we need in staff and managers alike to fully unlock the human capital value.

HUMAN CAPITAL VALUE AND ITS IMPACT ON THE WORKPLACE

For the vast majority of organizations, their human capital (the inherent knowledge in their employees and value in their social networks) is their most valuable and important asset. As suggested by Vischer (Ch. 3), ideally an organization needs an active relationship with its accommodation, one in which workspace is viewed as a resource to support human capital. The workplace needs to be seen as an investment to unlock the value of this capital and to maximize its growth. Measuring the impact that unlocking human capital value has to an organization's bottom line gives us a framework within which we can prioritize investment of financial capital to areas with the greatest impact on the bottom line.

With any significant workplace change, move, restack or investment in a new or refurbished office, analyzing the benefit created by enhancing human capital value against the cost can give a totally different perspective on expenditure. Looking at the overall bottom line to the organization of a workplace project or other FM expenditure can often make the financial investment cost neutral or even cost negative over relatively short return periods. It has also led, in my experience, to the board making additional funding available for further value-creating enhancements to the workplace.

But how is the human capital value unlocked? Change to the workplace, if undertaken with the right focus on ultimate goals, can lead to fundamental changes to corporate culture and staff behaviors. Changing the culture of an organization and the corresponding changes to staff behaviors is the key to delivering increased value. But how do we set our goals? For Cameron and Quinn (2006) an organization's culture can broadly be measured using four traits; Clan (a friendly mentoring culture); Adhocracy (a dynamic, entrepreneurial and creative culture); Market (a results-oriented competitive culture); and Hierarchy (a formalized, structured and controlling place to work). Mapping where an organization currently sits on these axes against where they want to be provides a blueprint for the ultimate culture the workplace is trying to create. This blueprint can be further refined and developed into a benefits case using a series of measures to track the value created and targets set, often in terms of direct financial impact.

Using this blueprint and maintaining a focus on the endgame, the space subsequently designed and delivered, along with a structured training and change program, can and will deliver change in employee behaviors and corporate culture. This in turn acts to unlock human capital value and positively impacts on the organization's bottom line or delivery of service to its external stakeholders.

Measuring Value

How do you assess the financial impact of enhancing human capital value? What is the impact on the bottom line? Most CFOs or FDs have not got to their current positions by taking unnecessary risks. Most will agree that a new value-focused workplace will deliver benefits to the company, but for funding to be unlocked the benefits need to be compelling and quantified. It has become increasingly popular to measure benefit not just by the traditional financial bottom line, but also by its ethical and environmental performance—commonly known as the "Triple Bottom Line" (Elkington, 1998). However, for most organizations it is still important that the financial return is viable. We need to establish a series of credible measures that can be used to create a benefits case and assess the financial impact of a new FM and workplace model.

There is no refuting that new workplaces allied to well-conceived business change initiatives have a positive impact on the company overall. For instance, in the early 2000s Reuters was losing ground significantly to Bloomberg, both in terms of market position and share value; falling from a high of £16.20 in 2000 to a low in 2003 of just 95.5 pence. Reuters embarked on a consolidation project at their London headquarters, which saw six scattered buildings consolidated into one new facility on Canary Wharf. A new working environment was designed to enhance collaboration and interaction between different parts of the business, to introduce a more dynamic and vibrant culture, to celebrate Reuters themselves (and their heritage) and to act as a showcase for Reuters and their products. The new facility was intentionally located in the middle of most of their major customers, whose staff members passed it on their way to and from work.

Reuters share price soared to £4.29 (a 350% increase) within a year of the move. This was obviously dependent upon a number of both external and internal factors, such as new products, market conditions, new management team and a number of business change initiatives; however, the development of new products, the speed of bringing them to market and the customers' willingness to buy were all positively affected by the new culture at Reuters brought about in part by the new workplace. It would be impossible to claim that the share price improvement was all due to the new value-focused workplace, but it is undeniable that it had an impact.

Building the Business Case

In broad terms, a workplace lead business change initiative can have the organizational impacts summarized in Figure 11.1. For our model, we have found it practical to adopt the more easily quantifiable measures and attribute a financial value to them as follows:

	Financial	Non-Financial
Quantitative	• OPEX reduction via smaller portfolio footprint • CAPEX reduction due to longer workplace life cycles • Reduced churn costs • Reduced utilities consumption • Reduced staff attrition • Reduced absenteeism • CRC legislation & credits	• Improved staff satisfaction • Reduced carbon footprint
Qualitative / Subjective	• Improved productivity • Improved staff attraction • Greater workplace & portfolio flexibility • More efficient operating model	• Enhanced brand image • Effective & credible CSR • Greater staff mobility & flexibility • Enhanced collaboration • Greater level of innovation • Improved speed to market • Improved work / life balance for staff • Reduced commuter traffic

Figure 11.1   The benefits of a human-capital-value-focused workplace.

1. Reduction in cost of attrition.
2. Reduced absenteeism.
3. Reduced organizational expenditure (OPEX) costs.
4. Improved productivity.

Reduction in Cost of Attrition

The vast majority of HR departments will maintain reasonably accurate records of staff attrition; however, measuring the cost of that attrition on the organization is more complicated. The cost of the loss of an employee varies considerably, depending upon their level and role within the organization. The actual cost impact is likely to be made up of the following elements:

1. Cost of lost productivity—both in the individual role and the impact on the department overall.
2. Cost of lost knowledge and contacts.
3. Lost revenue, sales or goodwill.
4. Cost of covering the vacant position—this will be either the cost of a temporary member of staff or the lost productivity for another staff member to cover the role.
5. Internal cost of the staff loss and replacement—the time costs for both the line manager and HR personnel involved in the exit interview; the administration of the leaver process (payroll/finance admin, HR administration, etc.); drafting the job advertisement; initial review and sifting through CVs; any testing and interviews.
6. Lost cost of any training given to the staff member.
7. Cost of recruitment via an agency if applicable or referral fees—this is often as much as six months' salary.
8. Administration of the new starter process (HR, finance and departmental costs).
9. Training and induction of the new staff member.
10. Lost productivity whilst the new employee is learning the role. It can often take four to six months for the new employee to get up to full productivity. If the productivity goes from 0% to 100% over a six-month period the cost is equivalent to three months' salary.
11. Less the saving in salary cost while the vacancy is unfilled.

These costs can typically be equivalent to the annual salary of the person lost. Hence, for a company with a 20% attrition rate, the cost to the bottom line is 20% of total salary cost of the organization. The overall payroll burden can often account for anything from 20% to 50% of an organization's operating costs, depending upon the type of business and sector, so a reduction in attrition rate by 5% would have a 1% to 2.5% reduction on operating costs.

Cost of Absenteeism

Research has proven that staff members who are unhappy with their job are absent more often (Nelson & Quick, 2008). The psychological rationale is that an individual will withdraw from dissatisfying working conditions (Johns, 2007). Research by PricewaterhouseCoopers estimates that UK employees are taking off 10 unauthorized days per year and that this is costing UK business payroll £32 billion (PricewaterhouseCoopers, 2011). This rate compares to the European average of 9.7 days, but is a lot higher than 4.5 days in Asia and 5.5 days in the US. According to a new survey by Mercer (2010), the total cost of absence to US companies can equal as much as 36% of payroll. Of that figure, 9% is due to unplanned absences. Further, a survey conducted by the UK Office of National Statistics (Barham & Leonard, 2002) showed that absenteeism was higher in women than men, and that women with a dependent child aged 5–10 had the highest absence rate.

It is not difficult from these studies to surmise that improvements in the workplace leading to improved morale and job satisfaction combined with an adoption of more flexible working patterns will not only reduce absenteeism due to dissatisfaction with the workplace, but also absence caused by clashes between work and family life. The impact on the organization's bottom line is not insignificant. An absence rate of 10 working days represents approximately 4% of the working year. Using our earlier model, a reduction in absenteeism from 10 days to five days (i.e., 2% of the payroll costs) would represent, where payroll represents 20% to 50% of operating costs, a reduction in operating costs of between 0.4% and 1%.

Reduced OPEX Costs

Changing the workplace to a model more suited to the work styles of the individuals in the business and adopting more flexible working practices not only has positive benefit in terms of the increased value in the human capital of the organization, but also can significantly reduce the space required. Even with more space given over to both collaboration and individual contemplative space, savings in overall space terms of 30% to 50% are readily achievable.

Using the total occupancy costs measure of all property, hard and soft FM costs, a direct estimate in the reduced OPEX expenditure can be made specific to the organization, or using one of the benchmark surveys such as Actium Consults annual Total Operating Costs (TOC) survey. As discussed earlier, in a high-rent area such as London, the total occupancy costs can often exceed £100 per square foot per annum, making the potential space savings from a more flexible workplace financially very attractive. The following table is an example of a recent project undertaken in Central London.

Table 11.1 Example TOC Savings—Central London (Client confidential)

Current Floor Space Allocation	*15,036 m²*
Current Desk Count	*1,200*
Approximate saving of floor space (m²)	*5,250 m² (35%)*
Benchmark total occupancy cost	*£923 per m² per annum*
Current total occupancy cost of workspace	*£13,878,228 per annum*
Benchmark energy footprint	*0.21 tons CO_2 per m² per annum*
Potential OPEX saving	*£4,845,815 per annum*
Potential CO_2 reduction (energy only)	*1,103 tons CO_2 per annum*

Improved Productivity

The true measures of the human capital value lie in the improvements in productivity through greater knowledge sharing and knowledge development, an increased rate of innovation and increases in other measures such as speed to market. Getting an accurate and isolated measure of the effect that a human-capital-value-focused workplace has on the productivity of the employees affected, is very difficult for most organizations as so many other internal factors such as changes in management or external factors like changes in the economy, can also have an influence. How productivity is best measured varies greatly on the organization's type, outputs and size as well as on the job function of the employees affected. For call-center-type environments, measures of productivity are readily available using the CRM software to measure calls completed and speed to answer; for consultancies billable hours provide a fairly accurate measure. Other, broader measures can be tracked pre- and post project to give an indication of the impact of workplace change such as debtor days/cash flow improvement (potentially impacted by better communication), bid to win ratios (for sales-based businesses), net margin improvements, turnover, the level of customer complaints, customer satisfaction indices and the employees' own assessments of their productivity levels pre- and post project.

CASE STUDY: ECHQ

In 2005, EC Harris LLP was seen as a market-leading quantity surveying and project management consultancy. They saw the necessity of repositioning themselves as a multidisciplinary, built asset consultancy business at the high-value end of a competitive market that was increasingly being commoditized. They started a journey driven around a vision to deliver better value to their clients.

As a partnership, the corporate structure inherently encouraged the existence of a number of fiefdoms, often along discipline lines; this was further exasperated by the space itself. EC Harris's existing head office, occupied since the 1950s, was in a multi-tenant building that was badly in need of refurbishment. The firm had taken on leases at different times in different locations in the building as and when their steady expansion demanded, so their space had come to consist of a number of isolated insular floor plates that encouraged a silo culture not conducive to knowledge sharing or innovation.

EC Harris was also faced with a number of market drivers creating an overwhelming imperative for change. The consultancy market was becoming increasingly competitive, with the traditional high-end management consultancies offering a broader range of services, and a number of the traditional FM service providers were starting to offer consultancy services or buying consultancies to broaden portfolios. This was creating consolidation in the market with the creation of a number of major players with significant size, global reach and access to capital for expansion. Client buying patterns were also changing, with an increasing number awarding multidisciplinary global frameworks. Further, the firm faced a rising cost base; staff members had high expectations of reward, and there was an increasingly tough fight for talent in the marketplace, with few entrants into the market and a very high attrition rate.

EC Harris recognized it needed to improve its position in the value chain and be seen as a high-end, value-added consultancy, commanding premium fees. The value of human capital had to be unlocked with increased collaboration and knowledge sharing between previously isolated disciplines along sector lines. They launched a two-pronged initiative: a new headquarters (HQ), which was seen as a major catalyst to the delivery of this change, and a parallel program focused on business change to maximize the benefits. That program included a radical overhaul of their organization, structure and roles. A business case was developed and a series of key performance indicators (KPIs) were agreed on to deliver a return on investment of two years.

The key elements of the brief were that the new building should act as the London office, major European office and international HQ and that it should be a resource center for the whole of EC Harris, in its function as a business center. It should be a model for the organization as a whole: efficient, modern, technologically advanced. And it should instill a sense of pride in the whole organization. The design was tasked with promoting and supporting the new way of working that EC Harris was adopting, enabling better teamworking and allowing for expansion through flexibility. Further, clients visiting the space should gain a better understanding of what EC Harris offered as a leading provider of property service. Overall the new HQ should differentiate EC Harris from its competitors and be a factor in attracting and motivating employees.

Pre- and post-occupancy measures were taken to demonstrate delivery to the business case. The new building was occupied in December 2006 and the KPIs were reviewed against the business at strategic intervals. During the briefing and design process all major decisions about the content and style of the office space were tested against the benefits case, to ascertain whether the proposed element would deliver value. For instance, a bar was added to the scope after the benefits were assessed against the running costs and it was deemed that the financial benefits to improved collaboration, staff morale, client relationships, staff retention and staff attraction vastly outweighed the capital expenditure (CAPEX) and OPEX expenditure.

The results were significant and led to a fundamental change in EC Harris, its culture and its people. Six KPIs were used and the financial benefit of each was estimated to allow the impact to the bottom line to be modeled. Staff attrition was down 25% in a comparable economic climate, revenue growth was in excess of 17%, total support costs were reduced by 36%, carbon emissions due to utility use were down 28% per full-time equivalent and an improvement in communication between the front and back offices led to a significant cash flow improvement. Net margin was improved by over 20% and billable hours by 4%. Overall, the original return on investment prediction of two years was delivered in under eight months.

But what of the future? ECHQ represented a step change in the evolution of EC Harris as a business, but a step nonetheless. EC Harris recognized the need for continuous improvement and that the workplace would need to further evolve to continue to support the business and act as a catalyst for change. The workplace itself is still predominantly desk-based with a number of collaborative areas and one- to two-person quiet rooms within easy reach. There is further scope to redesign it to better balance the amount of space turned over to open-plan, desk-based working versus team space and quiet/contemplative space. With this in mind, the office furniture was leased over a five-year period to allow the workplace to be fundamentally redesigned should the partnership wish to drive further change. The design principles and working models established in ECHQ have been rolled out across all major locations and the company is moving towards a much more agile working model using a reduced portfolio of offices to act as business hubs for a mobile, client-focused workforce.

CONCLUSION

There will always be the need for the risk takers, the innovative CEO and board who are at the forefront of business thinking and change. Without these mould-breakers the FM and workplace design community would not be challenged to come up with new workplace and FM models. The majority of organizations are not, however, mould-breakers and are generally conservative and risk averse, especially in challenging economic climates. In such times the natural tendency is to be more cautious and stick with what is known and can be proven. By assessing potential business change initiatives by the value they unlock in terms of human capital and modeling this as a direct financial impact on the business bottom line with corresponding return on investment periods, a cautious board can move forward with more confidence and commit to adopting new, more flexible operating models.

We must also bear in mind that there is an inherent danger that, in seeking to measure the benefit of any change, we adapt the design to suit the process of measurement. Further, all measurement of human capital value has inherently a degree of subjectivity and can be influenced by many outside factors. If we remain mindful of that subjectivity and, if the measurement and models used and the methods of measurement are appropriate to the situation, there is significant benefit to using a human-capital-value focused approach and modeling the impact in financial terms on the business bottom line. This will assist the board in impartially assessing the value of workplace proposals to the business and help steer the organization to adopt practices that have wide-reaching and fundamental impact on culture and behaviors with significant benefits to the organization and its stakeholders.

NOTES

1. Data from Actium Consult, a proprietary service described at http://www.actiumconsult.co.uk/tocs.

REFERENCES

Barham, G., and Leonard, J. (2002). *Trends and sources of data on sickness absence*. London: Office for National Statistics. Retrieved August 29, 2011, from http://www.ons.gov.uk/ons/rel/lms/labour-market-trends—discontinued-/volume-110——no—4/trends-and-sources-of-data-on-sickness-absence.pdf

Cameron, K. S., & Quinn, R. E. (2006). *Diagnosing and changing organizational culture*. San Francisco: Jossey-Bass.

Elkington, J. (1998). *Cannibals with forks: The triple bottom line of 21st century business*. Oxford: Capstone.

Johns, G. (2007). Absenteeism. In G. Ritzer (Ed.), *The Blackwell encyclopeadia of sociology*. Oxford: Blackwell.

Myerson, J., Bichard J.-A., & Erlich, A. (2010). *New demographics, new workspace*. Aldershot, Hampshire: Gower.

Nelson, D. L., & Quick, J. C. (2008). *Understanding organizational behavior* (3rd ed.). Mason, OH: Thomson.

Mercer. (2010). *The survey on the total financial impact of employee absences*. Retrieved August 29, 2011, from http://www.mercer.com/press-releases/1383785

PricewaterhouseCoopers. (2011). *Absenteeism costing UK business . . .* Retrieved August 29, 2011, from http://www.ukmediacentre.pwc.com

12 Ecologies in Existence
Boundaries, Relationships and Dominant Narratives

Ian Ellison and John Flowers

Many professionals find themselves organizing, communicating and negotiating at the boundaries between organizations. Commercial and functional intended outcomes, whether measured in terms of cost reduction, efficiency, effectiveness (Akhlaghi, 1996), profitability or otherwise, can be tremendously challenging to achieve for the parties involved. We believe that the potential for success, or indeed failure, lies not in the rigid governance and procedural structures that provide the formal 'rules' for interaction but in an appreciation of the multifaceted, complex intra- and inter-woven ecology of organizations coexisting together, codependent upon mutual performance. Do the organizational cultures genuinely 'fit'? Do the protagonists and their actors salute similar flags? What affects the ability for complimentary and mutually beneficial interaction, and what might the professional and academic implications be for organizational management?

Consider for a moment a busy highway interchange, with multiple streams of traffic. These streams can be considered as fluid entities themselves, and also as groups of many individual vehicles of different sizes, shapes, compositions and capabilities. There is clear potential for chaos as the streams drive, literally, together toward their journey goals. Each stream, and indeed the resultant merging collective, has common group direction, yet possesses infinite individual complexity. Highway rules and regulations promote expected, conventional behavior, yet rule-breakers and unpredictable occurrences are common. Altruistic and selfish behavior can often be locally observed, alongside opportunities, mistakes and misjudgments as the vehicles vie for position. So what is the outcome? Usually the busy motorways merge, albeit with significant delays for all. Occasionally an unfortunate disaster befalls the system, and an accident results in even greater holdups for the majority and heartache and tragedy for those directly involved. Perhaps for transient periods the traffic just flows, as the streams merge smoothly without hitch.

Our point is that the image of multiple interfaces of merging traffic at an interchange is one possible metaphor to represent the boundaries of organizations working together. Organizations have collective aims and objectives, containing individuals and groups that may or may not, for whatever reasons, be in alignment with them. These interfaces can be seen from different perspectives: in advance, in the moment, in hindsight, amongst the milieu or from a protracted distance. The view also varies according to prejudices and perceptions of the observer. From a game theory perspective (Axelrod & Hamilton, 1981), do the altruistic and selfish acts pay off, at either an individual or collective level? Fundamentally, how can we make sense of such a complex, transient, dynamic systems—a highway interchange, or an ecology of organizations—to the extent that we are able to understand the forces at work, and perhaps even be able to affect them favorably?

CONSTRUCTS AND CONTRADICTIONS

We invite the reader to first pause and consider, as we did, the implications of these words. What is their significance here? On reflection, we interpret constructs to be the traditionally accepted, implemented and practiced frameworks that have come to be recognized as the norm—the 'conventional wisdoms' if you like—for how to govern and manage inter-organizational engagement. They are typically procedurally focused and structural-functional in their approach (Vischer, 2008; Price, Macdonald & Ellison, 2009), including recognized routes of procurement, service delivery and support. The implication is that if sufficient, capable resource is committed, following standard delivery processes, satisfactory outcomes will be achieved. However, as we shall see through the cases explored presently, following these conventional wisdoms creates no guarantee per se that the outcomes will be positive. They represent a constructed veneer that belies a far more influential complexity. So what else might be happening at and around these organizational boundaries?

In contrast, we see the contradiction to this approach in the way that, according to conventional wisdom, the softer people and cultural elements follow, if at all. And yet, if we revisit almost any organizational issue, dilemma or challenge faced, it is invariably 'people issues'—communication, emotion, change, culture, etc.—located at their heart, demanding the majority of time, resource and energy to address. From this perspective, what behaviors, beliefs, languages and stories permeate, influence—and are perhaps influenced by—the dominant narratives of those involved? What is the effect upon 'the way things are done around here,' the relative cultures and the organizational flags saluted? We believe some of the key indicators of, and routes to, more informed, potentially desirable interorganizational outcomes lie here.

To illustrate, we consider two different examples of such relationships from the UK corporate technology and National Health Service (NHS)[1]. For this chapter, then, the evolutionary organizational perspective (Weeks & Galunic, 2003) can be considered in terms of 'snapshots' of ecologies in stasis. Here, we are not exploring Darwinian evolutionary step changes in organizational relationship terms. We are observing the reality of operational coexistence and the day-to-day behavioral elements of these ecologies in practice.

As a final introductory note, some chapters in this volume discuss memes. We share Distin's (2010) view concerning the current acceptability of this term (cf. Price, Ch. 1). Whilst a growing academic minority is comfortable with its use, we have chosen broadly synonymous but potentially more palatable terminology of dominant narratives, where such discourses, akin to Ford's (1999) stories, are heavy with contextual meaning and cultural significance.

ETHNOGRAPHIC RESEARCH WINDOWS

As researchers we advocate an approach grounded in social construction, embracing the role of perceptions, sense-making and subjective 'truth' in organizational life. Our research sought to capture "the actual meanings and interpretations that actors subjectively ascribe to phenomena in order to describe and explain their behavior through investigating how they experience, sustain, articulate and share with others these socially constructed everyday realities" (Johnson, Buehring, Cassell & Symon, 2006, p. 132). We propose that subjectivity in social science is largely unavoidable, yet through critical reflection by the researcher, honest, powerful and robust 'real-world' research is achievable (cf. Cairns, Ch. 8). This phenomenological stance, accepting that humans attach meaning to events and phenomena that surround them, warrants a particular organizational lens.

To embrace subjectivity, and investigate the interdependency of narratives, language and culture, methods of social science research and information gathering are required that respectfully explore the 'lived experience' with authenticity and credibility. Ethnography is one such technique, which both authors independently employed to explore the dominant narratives existent within the organizational 'habitats' of the case studies. Traditionally, ethnography (ethno: 'folk'; graphy: 'description') is an anthropological approach employed to study people holistically and contextually in their natural settings. The existent, context-heavy, second-order realities (Ford, 1999) can therefore be recognized and explored. "Much like the social world that it seeks to portray, ethnographic writing is 'home' to multiple realities—the truths of our informants, the truths of the ethnographer's experience, and the disciplinary truths of concept and theory" (Grills, 1998, p. 200). Credible ethnography requires an appreciation of 'plurivocality'; situations contain multiple embedded meanings, as participants create their own interpretations (Boje, 1995). Indeed, Ward and Werner (1984) suggest seeking different and dissonant epistemological windows through which to gain insight.

The two cases that follow demonstrate the insights that an ethnographic form of inquiry can yield into declared second-order realities. We sought to embrace *verstehen*, or understanding, as opposed to outright *erklären*, declaring explanations (Johnson et al., 2006). The original studies are both examples of focused, critical ethnography, acknowledging that the researcher is inevitably a subjective participant throughout the process, which must be acknowledged and embraced. Information was collected over extended periods using a range of active and passive methods, including observation, discussion, interview and documentary review, alongside iterative, critical researcher reflection.

FM OUTSOURCING: PRELIMINARY CASE STUDY

Ellison explored the narratives of employees involved when a UK-based 'blue-chip' client began a first-generation outsourcing agreement with a major 'total FM' service provider (Ellison & Owen, 2010). The decision to outsource the hitherto in-house FM elements followed a protracted period of market testing, feasibility studies and negotiations. As is typical, the arrangement left a small 'intelligent client' contract management function on the client side. The majority of staff transferred under UK legislative protection[2]. Ethnographic research over a four-month period involved observation and interviews with individuals and groups. Participants included transferred client staff, personnel from preexisting client FM contracts, service provider staff involved with the contract (both existing and recruited for the new account) and from elsewhere within the business, and the new, in-house intelligent client.

Robust project mobilization and account management strategies were implemented. The service provider used these regularly as the rigorous procedural basis for outsourcing transition and performance management. Despite these constructs, a striking complexity of differing dominant narratives and related stories, beliefs, attitudes and behaviors existed within the affected population, effectively located around the client's organizational boundary. Whilst the incumbent workforce sought to make sense of this 'imposed' organizational change, and the management teams worked ceaselessly to achieve acceptable outcomes for both parties, the interpersonal engagements led to complex, unintended and often unpredictable operational situations (Ellison & Owen, 2010).

Unintended Outcomes

One reason cited for commencing the new contractual relationship was the 'blue-chipness' of both parties, implying they were well suited according to their international scope and reputation. Despite this expressed 'fit,' the flags they saluted were entirely different. The service provider favored risk-averse procedural control, protectionism and compliance, embedded within a dominant narrative of 'the [service provider[3]] way.' Success elsewhere promoted conventional wisdom that success would be achieved here through more of the same. Conversely, the client, with a more reactive, problem-solving, short-termist and personality-led culture, struggled to adapt to the new regime it had commissioned[4]. Locked within their contradictory narrative-influenced 'traps of success' (Nadler, Shaw & Walton, 1995), both parties found themselves spiraling away from their goals within an increasingly resource-intensive, accidently adversarial situation (Senge, Kleiner, Roberts, Ross & Smith, 1994). With evidence of myriad sense-making assertions and legitimized unwritten rules (Scott-Morgan, 1994), the actors strived to accomplish intended outcomes. Various achievements were recognized, although whether the engagement could ultimately be termed 'successful' is moot. Overall, the complex reaction of the actors to their environment created a richly subjective ecological dynamic. The constructs were part of a platform for this, but not the dynamic per se. Conversely, the following case study explores a largely successful boundary relationship, yet one with a similarly subjective, contextual ecological dynamic.

PFI HEALTHCARE: PRIMARY CASE STUDY

In the late 1990s Flowers was engaged as project director for the development and delivery of a Private Finance Initiative (PFI[5]) project in northern England, aiming to modernize the delivery of health services for older people with severe mental health problems. The scheme involved the successful development of an 80-bed unit over a period of approximately three years, from inception, including the selection of a preferred partner under PFI procurement rules, to design, financial sign-off, commissioning and occupation. The initiative was chosen as it afforded an opportunity to study interorganizational engagement at a human behavioral level. Similarly, various ethnographic research techniques were utilized. Flowers also used this project as a pilot for a further longitudinal study involving a larger PFI scheme in the south of England. Again that 'trust'[6] followed due PFI process; however, the perceived outcome fell short of that envisaged. This contrast in outcomes, despite similar, rigorous structural procurement inputs, catalyzed the research explored here.

Under the most common form of PFI, the private sector designs, builds, finances and operates facilities based on 'output' specifications decided by public sector managers and their departments. A 'Project Company' is often formed as a stand-alone 'Special Purpose Vehicle' to deliver the project. Trusts typically employ teams of external consultants, as 'category experts', to assist in the development and interpretation of the preferred scheme. Category experts include architects, engineers (structural, mechanical and electrical), FM, town planning, financial and legal advisors. Trusts also engage their own clinical staff to assist with planning and evaluating design options, supported by the trust's in-house business support teams (estates, facilities, finance and HR) with the overall intention of creating complimentary functional structures.

From the trust's perspective, the design process is considered complete once the designs and output specifications, according to core business requirements[7], have been signed off. Financial and legal arrangements and verifications then ensue. Within the NHS, the Department of Health Private Finance Unit undertakes governance checks to ensure best value, local economic affordability and appropriate risk transfer. Finally, the local district valuer verifies that due diligence has been followed, and approved actuaries confirm approval. Meanwhile, the preferred private sector bidder follows a similar path, culminating with the funder's actuaries and insurance brokers satisfying themselves that the agreed deal represents a viable business asset. Returning to our highways metaphor, here we can consider the sheer volume of different vehicles, and their passengers, streaming towards the intersection, all jostling to progress toward their destinations smoothly, yet with differing motivations and intent.

Enter the Protagonists

The principle organizations included a trust and a private sector firm (Timberco) whose history extended almost 100 years, where the originating family retained a viable influence. Timberco's core business was construction, but they regarded small-scale PFIs as an opportunity to broaden their strategic portfolio, and as such were proactively targeting sub-£10million investment opportunities. The endeavor was a significant component of their medium to long term operational strategy. The various actors representing Timberco displayed tight unity of purpose, which was also strikingly consistent amongst its employees. This 'taken for granted', unified approach contrasted hugely with the trust's approach, where actors involved tended to view the project through a local lens, seeking to interpret the scheme in terms of what it meant within their sub-ecologies. This was particularly obvious where the medical staff were concerned. There was also evidence of this somewhat disconnected ownership stance within the support and business service areas. For example, the trust's finance staff viewed this as a 'piece of finance work', quite remote from the project in its entirety.

This case was not unique or remarkable compared to other PFIs delivered throughout the late 1990s. Following completion the trust undertook a post-project evaluation exercise, assessing the project's output against the established 'benefits criteria' from the business case process[8]. The results demonstrated that the planned benefits were indeed being realized, both logistically and clinically, achieving decreased patient recovery times, reduced lengths of stay and increased patient throughput. Equally remarkable was the way in which this had been accomplished, not least through healthy communication established between the two principal organizations involved, which facilitated productive dialogue.

Against the aforementioned background, where criticism had been publicly leveled at a number of prominent PFI projects, Flowers began to consider why this particular venture had progressed relatively smoothly. Good progress continued to be made following financial close and occupation of the building, with no reported service failures or calls to invoke the contractual penalty system. The various teams appeared to be integrating and working productively. Indeed, where the protagonists are directed to follow such a detailed, protracted and precise construct, with meticulous, often independent, decision analysis and audit prior to signoff, how could a PFI endeavor possibly fail to deliver a scheme aligned with the desired outcomes? Considering the procurement methodology employed, the process focuses on an interorganizational system—part of the construct—that reflects the adversarial approach traditionally associated with the construction industry. Contracts within this industry echo the adversarial British judicial system. The evolution and development of these contracts has been predicated on relatively short contractual episodes, compared with the longitudinal agreements that underpin schemes procured through PFI, where secured contracts typically extend between 20 and 40 years. Flowers sought to understand the existent ecological dynamic, both in terms of what was working so well in this PFI arrangement—the contradiction—and also perhaps what might be flawed or missing from the conventional procurement framework. The key implications feature in the following section.

EXPLORING THE CONTRADICTIONS

From these two independent, contextually different cases, it is evident that there is something more subtle and complex at work within these interorganizational systems. If we frame the engagements ecologically, the diverse, subjective and interdependent nature of interaction becomes strikingly apparent (Figure 12.1). Furthermore, the formal structures and rules that are created both consciously and unconsciously, according to conventional wisdoms, do not govern these interactions per se. Instead, they create platforms for the development of dominant narratives that may influence behaviors within the ecology—from individual agents to the collective communities—far more fundamentally. What further insights might we gain from this perspective?

Self-sustaining Organizations

Are organizations goal-directed, socially constructed systems that both wittingly and unwittingly seek to safeguard their boundaries and internal 'know-how' (Aldrich, 1999)? Different organizational theories provide various insights regarding this. From the resource-based view of the firm (Prahalad & Hamel, 1990), for example, the inimitable aggregate of organizational competencies creates the potential for market differentiation and should be protected rather than disclosed. This protectionism drives self-policing and maintenance, and our case studies demonstrate examples of the resultant, socially constructed, 'unwritten' and potentially unanticipated outcomes. Consequently, organizations, or constituent elements, become sites for the genesis, reproduction and persistence of accepted cultural norms and practices; dominant narratives of accepted and acceptable activity. 'Culture,' therefore, constitutes an area of clarity—a clearing in the jungle of meaninglessness (Wuthnow, 1987). Furthermore, Welbourne's (1997) research suggests that large bureaucratically structured organizations—such as, potentially, an NHS trust—encouraged employees to work on their own jobs at the expense of 'working for the overall good of the company.' Timberco was goal directed around a common narrative. The trust was a more diverse and tangled interorganizational ecology. The FM involved had to manage the interface.

Ellison's accidentally adversarial client–service provider relationship displays organizational subunits struggling to cooperate for mutual gain, despite their declared 'partnership.' Conversely, Flowers's PFI dynamic illustrates just how well a complex 'tangled bank' of interdependence can function yet sustain the identities and values of different constituent units, ranging from private and public sector ideologies to the strong affinities to professional bodies, such as the medical Royal Societies.

Boundary Relationships

The next step of this discussion is to consider the nature of the relationships at these boundaries. We have already referenced the typically[9] adversarial governance structure of contractual arrangements and the 'partnership' rhetoric often espoused in interorganizational working. Given the intrinsic organizational self-preservation explored in the preceding section, it becomes clear how challenging partnerships may be to actually achieve. What is a partnership? A strategic alliance, a description of collaborative working, a statement of common understanding, maybe the activity of relationship management? Perhaps, from an ecological perspective, 'partnership' may erroneously represent a rational, linear, unitary construct, when a complex schema of iterated relationships actually exists, masquerading as a partnership.

Considering such relationships, it is evident from Flowers's case just how diverse these ecological links can be. This warrants further exploration. Umbilical, ephemeral, dominant, submissive and balanced relationships are all descriptors that facilitate greater interactional insight. Indeed, the adult-parent-child relational dynamics of Transactional Analysis also come to mind. Consideration of trust and game theory may additionally provide further

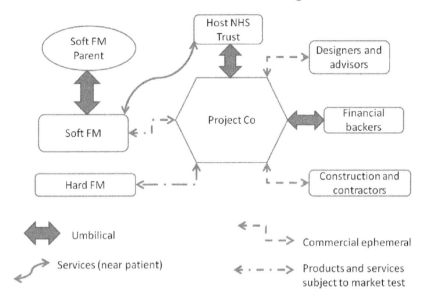

Figure 12.1 The relationship web adduced in the Flowers case.

insight. To fully realize the potential of an ecologies perspective, both functionally and theoretically, we therefore advocate a richer, more honest analysis of the nature of such relationships. To us, the current partnership rhetoric is woefully insufficient and is largely a misnomer; or even an oxymoron.

Fidelity and Information Transfer

What are these boundary relationships actually for? A primary function must be for information transfer. Again, we must not discount the influence of socially constructed realities. According to the dominant narratives embedded with the parties involved, information volunteered consciously or otherwise is decoded through subjective, second-order lenses. One consideration here is fidelity[10]. We conceive that the more rigid and guarded the organizational boundary, the greater the risk to both the fidelity of information and the subsequent likelihood of alternative, narrative-influenced reinterpretation. Information asymmetry and bounded rationality therefore feature, with significant detrimental relational risk. The role of metonymy must also be considered (Musson & Tietze, 2004) where culturally located stories (Ford, 1999) influence the labels given to significant constructs and the interpretation and assumed understanding given to the labels, according to the existent narratives.

Could a developing understanding of the different boundary relationships promote the conscious encouragement of more porous, perhaps 'osmotic' interfaces, facilitating more powerful interorganizational engagement? Aldrich (1999) considers boundary permeability, and Deacon (1997) stresses that it is impossible to gain information from a representation if you do not already understand the systems of which that representation is a part. Was an inherent appreciation of this element a key tool that enabled the private sector firm to engage successfully with the trust, wittingly working to soften potential boundary 'stuckness' (Price & Shaw, 1998) and protectionism? If this were the case, there is further evidence here for MacDonald's (Ch. 19) boundary management activities, creating integrated networks through relationship building, political awareness and management of conversational fidelity for shared cognition. In pursuing common language and understanding, perhaps reciprocal 'learning boundaries' should be sought for mutual benefit?

The Agency Dilemma

Ultimately, agency must be considered. If we regard language and conversations holistically as far more than words (Ford, 1999), accepting that there is socially constructed meaning in not just what others say, but in how they correspondingly talk and act, then we face a world of semiotics, permanently decoding and deconstructing meaning. Crucially, do we control the dominant narratives or do they control us? If we are striving to improve our boundary relationships as a route to accomplishing intended outcomes, this question is fundamental. Price and Shaw (1998) advocate the role of the change agent as capable of recognizing, and 'punctuating the equilibrium' of, conventional wisdom. This implies an acute, cultivatable ability to influence, rather than be slave to the narratives. Boundary managers require a similar reflexive awareness in order to navigate such relational interfaces, deconstructing and reframing the narratives at work.

CONCLUSION: TOWARDS 'TANGLED BANKS'

So how does our ecological perspective contribute to the organizational management arena? The studies explored promote insights regarding the activities occurring in and around interorganizational boundaries. Ethnography, and other social science research techniques, facilitate the unraveling and *verstehen* of the embedded, socially constructed meanings ever present in the 'lived-experience' of organizational reality. Both cases illustrate the value and potential of such studies in organizational management research and practice, and both researchers believe in the ethical value and position of such research, not just for pure observation and description, but also to potentially catalyze emancipatory change: "Do we have a duty to ensure that we leave the workplace in the state in which we found it? Or should we seek to bring about change and improvement, irrespective of whether this distorts the field during the research process itself, or later through publication?" (Brannan, Pearson & Worthington, 2007, p. 401). "Critical social researchers subscribe to the view that it is not enough merely to observe the world we live in, merely to understand it; the point is to change it. Otherwise, why be critical?" (Ferdinand, Pearson, Rowe & Worthington, 2007, p. 532).[11]

We believe that the evidence of influential, socially constructed dominant narratives provides a fresh perspective for practitioners and researchers alike. The role to which these narratives are shaped by, and shape, our interactions cannot be underestimated. Although we continue to debate the true impact and implication of agency, we believe critical decoding and reframing is possible by skilled, acutely aware protagonists. An appreciation of the 'softer' relational elements of interorganizational engagement from an ecologies perspective promotes a need to honestly focus on what flags are saluted, to truly gauge organizational capacity for interdependence, learning and genuine mutual benefit. Rather than adhering to the procedural structures and written rules that conventionally dictate the terms of engagement, seeking to advance these relationships should have an alternative initial focus far beyond 'due diligence' etc., commencing with some sort of 'litmus barometer' to appreciate exactly what nature the engagement is likely to be. As an aside, the recent proliferation of online dating agencies demonstrates clearly that for social relationships, it is entirely the 'softer' interpersonal elements that both mediate access and promote sustainability.

By recognizing the dominant narratives present within organizational ecologies, valuable cultural markers become apparent. Like stepping-stones from Schein's (1985) pattern of basic assumptions towards, conceivably, a representation of 'organizational DNA,' these dominant narratives act as blueprints that influence actions, provide and maintain a sense of identity. By being transmitted, and by transmitting, they instill meaning regarding how the world is organized, understood and inherited.

As a final comment, we are not suggesting conventional procurement and management structures are invalid. This is too radical. Well-constructed, robust mechanisms are valid; they have salience, value and constitute sound governance. But there is a missing dimension. These constructs cannot provide an entire awareness to predict, understand and manage complex boundary dynamics, and there is significant risk to desired organizational outcomes if this element remains dismissed or unconsidered. An ecological perspective and an appreciation of the contradictions—the socially constructed, dominant narratives at work—enable richer understanding.

NOTES

1. Editor's note: the case helped me recognize organizations as embedded within a complex, 'tangled bank' of interdependence rather than as singular organisms. Costly complicatedness is an emergent property of systems such as Flowers described.

2. Transfer of Undertakings (Protection of Employment) (TUPE) Regulations 2006; UK employment legislation that seeks to ensure transfer of employment with equitable terms and conditions.
3. In the sense of the service provider knowing best, the service orientation criticized by Vischer (Ch. 3), rather than being more responsive to changing client needs, the service orientation promoted by Coenen and von Felten (Ch. 10).
4. At the time of research, the contract was within year two of three. Subsequently, the client retendered it. The service provider was not awarded a second term, despite original, jointly declared intentions of a mutually beneficial, long-term relationship, underpinned by a partnership rhetoric.
5. PFI was then a relatively new concept. It has since become widespread and is adequately described in online sources. Word length prohibits a discussion here.
6. Macdonald (Ch. 19) clarifies the nomenclature.
7. An underlying tenet of PFI requires trusts to specify requirements in terms of 'output specifications'; in theory providing the bidding organizations with sufficient information to allow in-depth understanding of the trust's business, yet exploiting their ability to offer design and operational innovations.
8. A formal NHS process used to justify investment in new facilities, including an analysis of the anticipated benefits—both qualitative and quantitative—from the planned investment.
9. We assert that this is a descriptive, rather than judgmental statement. By their very nature, the majority of contracts are written from a dispute resolution perspective, as opposed to cooperation. All too often they primarily function as rules to be consulted in the event of an issue, legitimized by a mind-set of accountability and blame.
10. Fidelity, as in accuracy of reproduction. On balance, fidelity, as in 'loyalty' of information, is equally appropriate.
11. Editor's note: See Cairns (Ch. 6) on the same point.

REFERENCES

Akhlaghi, F. (1996). Ensuring value for money in FM contract services. *Facilities*, *14*(1/2), 26–33.

Aldrich, H. E. (1999). *Organisations evolving*. London: Sage.

Axelrod, R., & Hamilton, W. (1981). The evolution of cooperation. *Science*, *211*(4489), 1390–1396.

Boje, D. (1995). Stories of the storytelling organization: A postmodern analysis of Disney as "Tamara-Land." *Academy of Management Journal*, *38*(4), 997–1035.

Brannan, M., Pearson, G., & Worthington, F. (2007). Ethnographies of work and the work of ethnography. *Ethnography*, *8*(4), 395–402.

Deacon, T. W. (1997). *The symbolic species: The co-evolution of language and the human brain*. New York: Norton.

Distin, K. (2010). *Cultural evolution*. Cambridge: Cambridge University Press.

Ellison, I., & Owen, S. (2010). FM contract relationships: From mobilisation to sustainable partnership. In *European Facility Management conference: 9th Euro FM research symposium, Madrid, June 1–2*. Retrieved August 19, 2011, from http://shura.shu.ac.uk/1238/ unpaginated

Ferdinand, J., Pearson, G., Rowe, M., & Worthington, F. (2007). A different kind of ethics. *Ethnography*, *8*(4), 519–543.

Ford, J. (1999). Organizational change as shifting conversations. *Journal of Organizational Change Management, 12*(6), 480–500.

Grills, S. (1998). *Doing ethnographic research: Fieldwork settings.* Thousand Oaks, CA: Sage.

Johnson, P., Buehring, A., Cassell, C., & Symon, G. (2006). Evaluating qualitative management research: Towards a contingent criteriology. *International Journal of Management Reviews, 8*(3), 131–156.

Musson, G., & Tietze, S. (2004). Places and spaces: The role of metonymy in organizational talk. *Journal of Management Studies, 41*(8), 1301–1323.

Nadler, D., Shaw, R., & Walton, A. (1995). *Discontinuous change.* San Francisco: Jossey-Bass.

Prahalad, C., & Hamel, G. (1990). The core competence of the corporation. In D. Ulrich (Ed.), *Delivering results: A new mandate for human resource professionals* (pp. 45–68). Cambridge, MA: Harvard Business School Press.

Price, I., Ellison, I., & Macdonald, R. (2009). Practical post-modernism: FM and socially constructed realities. In *European Facility Management conference: 8th Euro FM research symposium, Amsterdam, June 16–17.* Retrieved August 19, 2011, from http://shura.shu.ac.uk/912/ unpaginated

Price, I., & Shaw, R. (1998). *Shifting the patterns.* Chalford, Gloucestershire: Management Books 2000.

Schein, E. H. (1985). *Organizational culture and leadership.* San Francisco: Jossey-Bass.

Scott-Morgan, P. (1994). *The unwritten rules of the game.* New York: McGraw-Hill.

Senge, P., Kleiner, A., Roberts, C., Ross, R., & Smith, B. (1994). *The fifth discipline fieldbook.* London: Nicolas Brearley.

Vischer, J. C. (2008). Towards a user-centred theory of the built environment. *Building Research & Information, 36*(3), 231–240.

Ward, J., & Werner, O. (1984). Difference and dissonance in ethnographic data. *Communication & Cognition, 17*(2/3), 219–243.

Weeks, J., & Galunic, C. (2003). A theory of the cultural evolution of the firm: The intra-organizational ecology of memes. *Organization Studies, 24*(8), 1309–1352.

Welbourne, T. M. (1997). Pay for what performance? Using the role-based performance scale. *Journal of Strategic Performance Measurement, 1*(5), 13–20.

Wuthnow, R. (1987). *Meaning and moral order; explorations in cultural analysis.* Berkeley: University of California Press.

Part III

Management Issues

13 Co-Creation of Value in FM

Keith Alexander

Leading FM practitioner Oliver Jones (2010) highlighted the uniquely challenging set of circumstances that characterizes the 'changing world' in which contemporary organizations operate. In a keynote presentation to the inaugural conference of the UK Government Property Unit, he outlined the global situation many believe creates an unprecedented context for contemporary business. He argued that a combination of the credit crisis, climate change, population growth, health epidemics and security threats presents opportunities for innovation and business advantage through FM.

Leadbeater (2008) investigated the opportunities and impact of information and communication technologies on personalization, mass creativity and open innovation. The electronic and interactive book *We-Think* broadly explored what Web technologies mean for our culture, work practices, government, science and business. Leadbeater argued that more people than ever can participate in culture. The Web allows them not just to publish ideas, views and information, but also to share and connect, to collaborate and create, together, at scale. The Web is a platform for mass creativity and innovation.

In response to the challenges presented by this climate of change and by such developments, there have been calls for FM to return to its roots in human ecology (Price, 2002; Price, Ellison & Macdonald, 2009), one of the central themes of this book, to become more demand driven, user centered and service oriented (Alexander, 2008a) and to identify and understand the added value of FM (Coenen, Jensen & van der Voort, forthcoming a). Here I explore the role that facilities play in creating the environment for social interaction and open innovation in a networked economy. I present practical examples from different sectors of the economy to highlight interrelated dimensions of an emerging community-based approach, each illustrating different facets of FM.

SYSTEMS THINKING

In an increasingly complex environment, understanding value and outcomes requires systems thinking, radically changing the way we address issues.

Components cannot be analyzed in isolation and should be considered holistically, interactions between them being the key to achieving system-level outcomes. All offerings are interconnected, and users contribute resources to the system, pay for different facets and derive different benefits. Interdependencies are accelerated by technologies, promoting convergence.

The service system interplay between processes and outcomes is nonlinear and multidirectional, making many current instruments of analysis ineffective. Miller and Page (2007 p.83) suggest it is like trying to "understand running water by catching it in a bucket." More dynamic system-level tools are needed.

During the industrial era, outcomes were achieved with inventions such as the steam engine (transportation) and TV (entertainment) designed and produced in a reductionist way. In the contemporary economy, systems-based outcomes such as community, sustainability, health and happiness are critical. However, knowledge to achieve these is still underdeveloped. Emergent properties such as community and health are now key outcomes to society. Design is not one of cause and effect or modularity (plug and play), creating the need to think differently.

Elsewhere, I have argued for consideration of built environment as a complex ecosystem (Alexander, 2011), and pioneering work by Price (2002) sought to understand organizations and the buildings they occupy as a complex adaptive system. This work provides a foundation for contributions to the book.

The Hub in King's Cross, London, is a workspace, a members club and business incubator and is described by its creators as "a unique ecosystem designed to enable people to thrive." Participants have co-created an enabling space for social innovation. It provides a series of flexible spaces for individual work, meetings and events, which are intensively utilized. Its designers call the process "place making for innovation"—a necessity for twenty-first-century entrepreneurialism (Beunderman & Johar, 2010). This place-making strategy, which seeks to create fertile conditions for different types of innovation, has been analyzed using qualitative interviews and roundtables with stakeholders, and emphasizes the importance of thinking both about physical parameters and about social and organizational tactics in order to succeed at fostering a different culture of daily behavior amongst the users.

Value-in-Use

Concepts of value co-creation have been developed in recognition of the collaborative role of customers as a key stakeholder in service organizations. Ng, Maull and Smith (2010) provide a commentary from a service marketing perspective and foresee a future for service systems of resources proposed and consumed and value co-created by a web of stakeholders, including customers themselves. They suggest that value drives everything we do—we buy products and services because we value them; we collaborate because there is value in the collaboration.

According to Ng et al. (2010), a business economist's interest in value lies in the way it can be captured in an exchange, monetarily or otherwise. They imply a belief in value as exchange value—value is always value-in-use. The business economist is interested in how use value translates to exchange value, a subtle but important difference.

They identify four dimensions of value—contextual, emotional, practical and logical—and describe each with reference to the use of consumer products—iPhone, watch, car and tape measure. They also distinguish between expected and perceived value. We seek to minimize costs and/or maximize net value (benefit minus costs), even if the benefit is in the future. In making purchasing decisions, the expected value in the future is weighed in the decision of how much to pay now. When we consume the service, we develop a perception of the value, compare that to what we expected when we purchased and then evaluate if we will repurchase.

A business economist's interest in these dimensions of value lies in an organization's perspective, in the design and delivery of all of them to the customer. They are often reduced to a six sigma of practical or logical value, but, to be able to deliver value to the customer, the organization must be able to deliver all dimensions of value. The design and provision of services often fails to deliver emotional value because the transformation required involves the customer themselves. A decade earlier, Pine and Gilmour (1999) considered experience as the ultimate form of economic offering and transformation as a final stage of the development of services to bring lasting benefit to customers. There is growing interest in applying this value-based, service-oriented thinking in the built environment and FM (e.g., Coenen & von Felten, Ch. 10).

In the United Kingdom, the public sector is facing an unprecedented challenge to make significant financial savings. After people, the most effective way to deliver targeted savings would be through the use of buildings and facilities—user perceptions and expectations will be the only constant. Users may be considered the key customers in FM relationships. Elsewhere I applied customer-oriented thinking to argue for user experience as the focus of provision for facilities and buildings (Alexander, 2006).

In research about the added value of design in the built environment, MacMillan (2006) defined use value (one of six value dimensions) as "that arising from the contribution of the building and associated services to organizational outcomes(Table 2, p.266)." Typical (business) outcomes were identified as productivity, profitability, competitiveness and repeat business. He suggests that use value arises from a working environment that is safe in use, promotes staff health, well-being and job satisfaction, encourages flexible working, teamwork and communication, and enhances recruitment and retention while reducing absenteeism.

The European Facility Management Network (EuroFM) and International Council for Research and Innovation in Building and Construction

(CIB) are working on collaborative research to consider the achievement of value in managing facilities. A EuroFM research project addresses the need for better understanding of the ways in which FM adds value (Coenen et al., forthcoming a). Two contrasting approaches have emerged, one focusing on a conventional built environment perspective and exchange value, the other on use value from a service perspective. Working groups seek to identify the components of the added value of FM and to account for economic, social and environmental value from the perspective of all stakeholders. The working group considering the value chain focuses on relationship value and co-creation of value in FM.

The CIB group (W111) has applied usability concepts and tools in the built environment with a focus on user experience (Alexander, 2005, 2008b, 2010). Amongst other objectives, this work has addressed the recognized discrepancy between user perceptions of the built environment and intentions for performance. The group see usability as "a cultural phenomenon that can only be improved through a better understanding of user experience, considered as situated action in a specific context" (Alexander, 2008b, p.1). The research has enabled a number of broad conclusions about the nature of usability as a concept and its application to the built environment and has challenged the basis of conventional approaches to briefing and post-occupancy evaluation. Usability is a contingent quality, depending upon the circumstances of users at a particular place and time. From this point of view, usability is not an inherent function of the built environment; a physical environment that works well for one set of users will not necessarily work well for another set. Moreover, as time passes new sets of circumstances will evolve so that a physical environment that was once supportive will no longer remain so. Lindahl, Hansen and I report (Ch. 9) on the state of the art of the usability research.

Maximizing use value was a prime consideration for the Catholic Agency for Overseas Development (CAFOD), an international aid charity running projects in 40 countries around the world; it created and managed a new headquarters (HQ) in London as an exemplar of an ethical workplace and balances social, economic and environmental criteria. The headquarters was intentionally developed as the heart of the organization to create a sense of community. As many members of staff work in disaster zones, it was essential that when they come together they feel a sense of belonging. CAFOD also wanted a new HQ building that touched "lightly upon the earth," reflected their charitable status and core values of social justice and "live simply" philosophy (Hayward, 2010). Users are engaged in all processes to ensure usability and achieve social sustainability.

Social Value

MacMillan's (2006) framework differentiates use value and social value. Social value is seen as that which arises from "the extent to which the working environment makes connections amongst people, enhancing opportunities for positive social interaction, reinforcing social identity and civic pride (Table 2, p. 266)." Social value also encourages inclusion and contributes towards health, prosperity, morale, goodwill, neighborly behavior, safety and security whilst reducing vandalism and crime.

This presents an organization as a closed system and only considers the social value achieved to the 'community of practice' within the workplace and the impact on the neighborhood. In contrast, in proposing a community-based FM approach, I see the organization as an open system in an urban and community context (Alexander & Brown, 2006) and as a social enterprise to create shared value (Porter & Kramer, 2011). For some, this means corporate social responsibility, but a community-based FM approach embeds responsibility for social and environmental sustainability in organizational strategies as part of its primary activities. Michell (Ch. 14) develops the concept of community-based FM in the context of townships in Cape Town, South Africa.

From this community perspective, and following Leadbeater, the emerging landscape for the networked society requires places that provide the social environment for interaction and creativity. Hoffman, Munthe-Kaas, and Elle (Ch. 5) consider creative environments in an urban context. Oldenburg (1989) introduced "third place" as a term used in the concept of community building to refer to social surroundings separate from the two usual environments of home and the workplace (cf. Beard, Ch. 6). He argued that they are important for civil society, democracy, civic engagement and establishing feelings of a sense of place. All societies already have informal meeting places; what is new in modern times is intentionality seeking them out as vital to current societal needs.

Creating social value drove the development of Stonebridge Hillside Hub. Completed in February 2009, this mixed-use development in Northwest London played a major part in transforming the area. It was the final phase of major regeneration in Harlesden as a replacement of rundown high-rise flats, together with significant upgrading of the local street scene and overall quality of the neighborhood.

Comprising 59 mixed-tenure apartments in an integrated public building, the scheme brings together residential, community and commercial use. A community center and café form the Hub's central axis, between a primary care center and a small supermarket, with apartments. Local residents were involved in the design of Stonebridge Hillside Hub from the outset and have continued management responsibility through the Housing Action Trust in a range of roles. The Stonebridge Housing Action Trust brought together a diverse range of people from the local community and has "strengthened community spirit and engagement in the process . . . the footfall greatly outperforms the original business plan (CABE, 2011)." It has been recognized for the provision of facilities that meets the aspirations of the community and the extent to which the project has improved social well-being and quality of life by reducing crime, improving public health, easing transport problems and increasing property values.

VALUE CO-CREATION

Prahalad and Ramaswamy (2004) first introduced value co-creation as a business strategy to emphasize the generation and ongoing realization of mutual organization/customer value. The concept of value co-creation views markets as forums for organizations and active customers to share, combine and renew each other's resources and capabilities to create value through new forms of interaction, service and learning mechanisms. It differs from the traditional active organization/passive consumer market construct.

They argued that value will be increasingly co-created by the organization and the customer, rather than being created entirely internally. In their view, co-creation also describes a movement away from customers buying products and services as transactions to their purchases being made as part of an experience. Consumers seek the freedom of choice to interact with the organization through a range of experiences and want to define choices in a manner that reflects their view of value, and to interact and transact in their preferred language and style.

To business economists, co-created value arises in the form of personalized, unique experiences for the customer (value-in-use) and achieves ongoing revenue, learning and improved market performance for the organization through loyalty, relationships and customer referrals. Value is co-created with customers if and when they are able to personalize their experience using an organization's product/service proposition—through a lifetime of its use—to a level that enables activities or tasks to be performed. This allows the organization to derive greater value from its product/service investment in the form of new knowledge, higher revenues/profitability and/or superior brand value/loyalty.

In this respect, Ng et al. (2010) distinguish between value co-creation and coproduction. Coproduction helps an organization shape its value proposition, for example, users helping Nokia with the next phone, or better software, or even a better café. Value co-creation uses a customer's own resource to achieve the beneficial outcomes with the organization at the point of consumption, to achieve value-in-use. They use the example of a café to illustrate the difference between attributes (features) and emotional and functional outcomes in creating the ambience and in turn the user experience and value-in-use derived.

People often ignore their own role in creating that experience, that they, as customers, co-create value with the café. They realize that for attributes to become outcomes, they unlock the value proposition of the café to achieve benefits. More importantly, they need to access their own resources to co-create that value, whether these are in choosing the right people to go to the café with or the basic resource of being able to see, hear and feel. In a sense, customers design themselves so that they can co-create value with the organization.

In essence, the best value proposition in the world is useless if customers don't know how to use it. For organizations this means that service designers should include the customer and the resources they need to co-create value, in order to achieve agreed outcomes. In Chapter 10 Coenen and von Felten extend the application of co-creation concepts to consideration of the value added by FM (see also Coenen et al., forthcoming b).

Recognition of co-creation led Kent County Council in Southeast England to develop a gateway concept combining principles of shared services and economies of scope with an understanding of the co-creation of services to achieve outcomes measured in terms of social benefit to citizens. The aims of project are to build services around customer needs rather than how the services are traditionally organized. Each gateway offers customers a mix of services, delivered by a range of partners including county and district councils, the National Health Service (NHS) and the voluntary sector. The project operates on the principle that customer needs determine both the location and mix of services provided in an area. The customer cares least about 'who is providing' the service, moreover, that the service is of a high quality and leads to an outcome or solution.

CO-LEARNING

The customer–provider relationship can also be seen as a process of co-learning. Every design process begins with developing an overview of the needs of those for whom the service is intended. Users may include individuals, groups and organizations, and the process of determining their needs in the UK is called *briefing*.

In a construction management context, considerable attention has been paid to the involvement of stakeholders in briefing processes. For example, Barrett, Kaya and Zeisel (2004) highlight the need for a robust briefing process in which there is mutual learning among all participants over a period of time including not only predesign, but also post-occupancy. They argued that briefing is most productive when it is an ongoing co-learning process centered on the organization as a whole, and including users, designers, professional advisors and other stakeholders. In a similar vein, Chandra and Loosemore (2010) have shown that knowledge exchanged during the briefing process is acquired not only explicitly, but implicitly through social processes whereby participants attempt to socially construct a common understanding of the project. This highlights the importance of providing the appropriate environment and enough time for culturally conducive social interaction and knowledge sharing amongst the many stakeholders involved.

Equivalent study of co-learning amongst stakeholders in FM is in its infancy. With Jensen and Fronczek-Munter (2010), I argue for *inclusive briefing* as an interactive, continuous process where the demand and supply sides are involved in a mutual dialogue. In exploratory work on briefing, Hudson (forthcoming) goes beyond a construction perspective to argue for usability as a contingent quality rather than as the inherent functionality of the physical environment. He argues that much of the existing work on briefing can be reduced to a rational process and is part of a finite project, the final outcomes of which are buildings or other physical facilities, and that user requirements have an external objective existence that can be captured in the briefing process. Usability research highlights the limitations of this approach and that a new approach to briefing may be necessary. This approach might be characterized by an emphasis of briefing as creative exploration of possibilities rather than requirements capture, a focus on the social construction of requirements and their evolution over time and a focus on human satisfaction rather than physical facilities.

A prototype social learning space at the University of Glasgow has highlighted the importance of co-learning. Incremental redevelopment of the University of Glasgow Library, one of the largest in Europe, has taken place over a period of 10 years, originally planned as an environmental improvement project. However, objectives have changed over time, driven by the changing environment for higher education and by technological advances.

University strategies envisaged a different mix of space to cater for changing demand and a need to enhance student experience. The library saw an opportunity to transform from "a warehouse for books to a study environment" and drove changes for space provision—from traditional to social learning. The aim of the redevelopment of the library annex was to transform the area into a more relaxed and informal space where students can meet and work in a social environment—a learning café.

Hospitality services, such as cleaning and catering, were fully engaged in the project and have direct involvement in planning. The catering offer has changed fundamentally, and the brand—"Food in Focus"—is continuously refreshed to offer a responsive service. The café continues to meet student needs and throughput and revenue have increased.

There is strong evidence of a positive impact of change on library staff and students. Introduction of the National Students Survey has put an emphasis on enhanced customer experience. University of Glasgow boasts the highest-rated library among Scottish universities. The estates team leading the project recognized the need for effective change management in a process of transformation. Continuity of involvement of clients, users and service providers enabled the development of strong relationships.

Value in Systems

The concept of value co-creation develops the idea that organizations do not really provide value, but merely value propositions, and it is the customer that determines value and co-creates it with the organization at a given time and context best for the customer to achieve the outcomes they want. So an organization's product offering, whether products or services, represents unrealized value. The proposition is a 'store of potential value' until the customer realizes it through co-creation and gains the benefit. Value co-creation implies customer resources to realize the value that becomes central towards achieving end benefits.

Value co-creation is gaining a more prominent role across the economy in healthcare, through greater customer empowerment; in mobile telecommunications and the Internet with user-generated content; and in education with self-study courses. In these situations, customer resources are central to value, benefits and outcomes. Value co-creation can be considered as a partnership with shared resources. As a 'customer/organization,' what are our resources? There is currency in our time, our insight, our effort, our loyalty and all kinds of resources accessible only to us, which we can trade off with money (price) and an organization's propositions—to co-create value. More knowhow is needed to measure this co-created value and to price it.

If an organization and the customer are in partnership, sharing resources and co-creating value, what price can the organization charge for a service that includes customer resources? How can we compute customer long-term value-in-use, including customer equity informed by value co-creation? When services are outsourced, an organization's value propositions are a network of propositional values, e.g., server farms from Amazon, social media from Facebook, search engine from Google, work together in one click, or on one Web page. In addition, content is sometimes provided by other customers. Consumption and the realization of value-in-use may be derived from multiple customers consuming and providing value propositions with organizations.

This is not restricted to online activity because, e.g., in airports, value is being co-created in systems by multiple stakeholders—customers, suppliers, organizations. In such systems, it is difficult to know the provider from the customer, who pays whom and for what is also unclear. In the future, organizations will operate in a service system of resources proposed and consumed and value co-created by a web of stakeholders, including customers themselves, all of whom have something to gain and something to give to the system. It will be more difficult to identify cause and effect, to manage relationships and to decide what technologies to use in these systems.

Cooperative organizations are often formed to transcend these divisions. Reddish Vale Technology College was the first school in England to become a cooperative trust school, with the Reddish Vale Cooperative Trust established in March 2008. Cooperative trusts allow all stakeholders greater participation in the running of schools and cooperative values offer schools an ethos that can lead to higher standards, aspirations and achievements. A trust offers not only the school, but a wide range of partners and stakeholders a way in which to continue to drive up standards and create a transformational platform to address wider issues of education, training, employability and regeneration.

Membership of the cooperative and co-ownership of the physical environment enable sustainability. The school's community has a continual throughput of potential new members and a strong connection within the community to bring stakeholder groups together at a grassroots level. Drawing on this, the school is able to grow support and capacity in and across the community for regeneration and transformation.

THE ADDED VALUE OF FM?

In the United Kingdom a civic economy is emerging, one that is more open and social, one that is fusing Web 2.0 technologies with civic purpose. Recent publication of a compendium of UK-based initiatives (Ahrensbach, Johar and Beunderman, 2011), comprising 25 case studies, provides a wealth of examples to stimulate social entrepreneurs. The projects are based on the initiatives of an increasingly wide range of civic-minded pioneers in the private, public and social enterprise sectors, and how they are built on local assets—whether existing or latent social networks, people's skills and aspirations or dormant physical assets.

In exploring the link between competitive advantage and corporate social responsibility, Porter and Kramer (2011) introduced the concept of creating shared value based on the idea that corporate success and social welfare are interdependent. A business needs a healthy, educated workforce, sustainable resources and adept government to compete effectively. For society to thrive, profitable and competitive businesses must be developed and supported to create income, wealth, tax revenues and opportunities for philanthropy.

Many approaches to corporate social responsibility pit businesses against society, emphasizing the costs and limitations of compliance with externally imposed social and environmental standards. Creating shared value focuses more on the opportunities for competitive advantage from building a social value proposition into corporate strategy. The concept of creating shared value can be extended beyond the service provider and customer relationships from which the original thinking about co-created value developed. Understanding the potential added value throughout a web of stakeholders, and identifying its components, will enable much greater shared value for all.

The examples, drawn from Centre for Facilities Management (CFM) case studies, were chosen to illustrate practical application of the concepts of value co-creation and represent a mixed group of enterprises from the social sector, all of whom have social objectives embedded in their business models. Rudimentary analysis of the cases reveals similarities in organizational form and a commitment to cooperative ways of working. Each provides an example of the engagement of stakeholders in social processes to create, adapt and manage facilities.

Further development of the cases will focus on the processes of change management, and on appropriate technologies to support these types of initiative. Early work has identified the need for further development of processes of change management, relationship management and benefits realization to enable value-based service systems. New standards for ethical workplaces are emerging to support the evaluation of value-in-use. Johar (2009), founder and director of the Hub movement, has suggested that it is time for the (built environment) profession(s) to move towards a model built on a qualitative and quantitative evidence base. Practice focused not just on building, but on creating conditions of use that make buildings' everyday value-generating assets in the use economy as opposed to the transactional economy.

REFERENCES

Ahrensbach, T, Johar, I and Beunderman, J. (2011). *Compendium for the civic society.* London: NESTA and CABE.

Alexander, K. (2005). *Usability of workplaces—report on case studies* (CIB Report 306). Rotterdam: CIB.

Alexander, K. (2006). The application of usability concepts in the built environment. *Journal of Facilities Management*, 4(4), 262–270.

Alexander, K. (2008a). *European Facilities Management futures.* Naarden, the Netherlands: EuroFM Research Report.

Alexander, K. (2008b). *Usability of workplaces—phase 2* (CIB Report 316). Rotterdam: CIB.

Alexander, K. (2010). *Usability of workplaces—phase 3* (CIB Report 330). Rotterdam: CIB.

Alexander, K. (2011). *Building performance and control: As if people and the planet matter.* Paper presented at the 2nd International Building Control Conference, July, Penang, Malaysia.

Alexander, K., & Brown, M. (2006). Community-based Facilities Management. *Facilities*, 24(7/8), 250–268.

Barrett, P. S., Kaya, S., & Zeisel, J. (2004). Briefing as a co-learning process. *Proceedings, CIB World Congress*, Toronto, Canada;

Beunderman, J., & Johar, I. (2010). The Hub: Creating a space to nurture innovation. In Mahroum, S., ed. *Local knowledge: Four case studies of innovative places (part 4)* (pp. 40–49). London: NESTA.

CABE, (2011), Stonebridge Hillside Hub, Case Study, Building for Life, Retrieved from National Archive, *http://webarchive.nationalarchives.gov.uk/20110107165544/http://www.buildingforlife.org/case-studies*, 7 January 2011.

Chandra, V., & Loosemore, M. (2010). Mapping stakeholders' cultural learning in the hospital briefing process. *Construction Management and Economics*, 28(7), 761–769.

Coenen, C., Jensen, P. A., & van der Voort, T. J. M. (Eds.). (Forthcoming a). *The added value of Facility Management.* Naarden, the Netherlands: EuroFM Research Report.

Coenen, C., Alexander, K., Kok, H., & Holzweber, M. (Forthcoming b). FM value network: Exploring relevant relations amongst key FM stakeholders. In C.

Coenen, P. A. Jensen & T. J. M. van der Voort (Eds.), *The added value of Facility Management*. Naarden, the Netherlands: EuroFM Research Report.

Hayward, C, (2010). Simply Cafod. Feature article, *FM World*, December 2010, London: BIFM

Hudson, J. (Forthcoming). Briefing for usability. In K. Alexander (Ed.), *Usability in the built environment*. CIB Report. Rotterdam: CIB.

Jensen, P. A., Alexander, K., & Fronczek-Munter, A. (2010). Towards an agenda for user oriented research in the built environment, in proceedings. In Haugbølle, K. ed. *Clients and Users, CIB W118 Workshop, Copenhagen, May 2010*. Rotterdam, CIB.

Johar, I. (2009). *Changing practice*. Paper presented at the RIBA Research Symposium, September, London.

Jones, O. (2010). *Winning strategies in a world of opportunity*. Keynote presentation, Smart Facilities Management Conference, September, London.

Leadbeater, C. (2008). *We-think: Mass innovation not mass production*. London: Profile Books.

MacMillan, S. (2006). Added value of good design. *Building Research & Information, 34*(3), 257–271.

Miller, J. H., & Page, S. E. (2007). Complex adaptive systems: An introduction to computational models of social life. Princeton, NJ: Princeton University Press.

Ng, I. C. L., Maull R. S., & Smith, L. (2010). *Embedding the new discipline of service science*. Discussion Papers in Management, University of Exeter Business School, 09/01.

Oldenburg, R. (1989). *The great good place*. New York: Marlowe and Company.

Pine, B. J., & Gilmore, J. H. (1999). *The experience economy*. Cambridge, MA: Harvard Business School Press.

Price, I (2002) The Complex Adaptive Workplace: A theoretical link between office design and productivity. In G T Frizelle and H Richards (eds.) *Tackling Industrial Complexity: the ideas that make a difference*. Cambridge: Institute for Manufacturing. Retrieved from http://www.ifm.eng.cam.ac.uk/mcn/pdf_files/part5_4.pdf on 25 August 2011

Price, I., Ellison, I., & Macdonald, R. (2009). *Practical post-modernism: FM and socially constructed realities*. Paper presented at EFMC2009, 8th EuroFM Research Symposium, May, Amsterdam.

Porter, M. E., & Kramer, M. R. (2011). Creating shared value: How to reinvent capitalism—and unleash a wave of innovation and growth. *Harvard Business Review, 89*(1), 62–77.

Prahalad, C. K., & Ramaswamy, V. (2004). *The future of competition: Co-creating unique value with customers*. Cambridge, MA: Harvard Business School Press.

14 FM as a Social Enterprise

Kathy Michell

It has been 17 years since South Africa's first democratic elections. Service delivery, infrastructure development and poverty alleviation remain some of the biggest challenges facing the South African local government (McLennan, 2009). Furthermore, the experience of the last 17 years has done little more than consolidate our understanding of the central role of local government in poverty alleviation and employment creation (Mufamadi, 2008). In this context, local government has a critical role to play in rebuilding local communities. It is widely acknowledged that government, at all three tiers, is the single largest property portfolio holder in the country. Hence it is appropriate to ask the question: to what extent does local government utilize an integrated approach to the maintenance, improvement and adaptation of the land and buildings within a community in order to support its social objectives? This contention requires an initial orientation towards the intrinsic social reality that is created in and around the use of public land and buildings and therefore the role that FM can play in the uplifting and empowerment of impoverished communities. In this chapter I explore this question in more depth. To this end, I use the findings from a grounded theory study into the role of FM as a social and community enterprise in the context of the townships of South Africa. I argue that the management, maintenance and operation of infrastructure and public facilities within the marginalized communities are essential to the success of township/urban regeneration initiatives.

GRASSROOTS PERSPECTIVE OF THE MANAGEMENT OF PUBLIC FACILITIES

South African cities continue to reflect the legacy of the apartheid government policies, which were founded on a racial separatist ideology and grounded in inequality (Southall, 2004; Turok & Parnell, 2009). This ideology resulted in cities being characterized by spatial separation of residential areas according to population group defined by race, urban sprawl, a lack of services to those marginalized residential areas and the concentration of the poor on the urban edge (Robinson, 2008). Moreover, these imbalances within the urban fabric resulted in unequal wealth-creation opportunities between different parts of urban areas (Parnell, 2005). Parnell contends that the political transition to democracy in 1994 laid the foundation for a commitment to a developmental state that is aimed at the reduction of both inequality and poverty amongst the urban poor. Patel (2004) argues that the biggest task facing the newly democratically elected South African government in 1994 was to ensure the transformation of the country as outlined in the Reconstruction and Development Programme (RDP; African National Congress [ANC], 1994). The ANC's primary objectives in the RDP were to meet the basic needs of the people, build the economy and the nation, develop human resources and entrench the democratization of the state and society. However, it should be noted that the execution of these policies was destabilized with the implementation of the Growth, Employment and Redistribution (GEAR) austerity policy in 1996 (Turok & Parnell, 2009).

It is clear that infrastructure development and service delivery remain some of the biggest challenges facing the South African local government (Mufamadi, 2008). Furthermore, the experience of the last two decades in South Africa has done little more than consolidate our understanding of the role of local government and its point of centrality in developmental processes in terms of effecting change in the nature of the urban landscape in South Africa. This period of time has also seen South African local government legislation in a state of transition. The aim of this evolution has been in fulfilling the constitutional rights of all South Africans, in order to provide greater accountability for the use of public resources. In this context there are growing demands for improved efficiency and value for money (Mufamadi, 2008). Local government has a critical role to play in rebuilding local communities and environments, as the basis for a democratic, integrated, prosperous and truly non-racial society (Department of Provincial and Local Government [DPLG], 1998). Moreover, it is clear that the current urban environment is in a state of flux as national government attempts to address the social imbalances of the past. To date, urban reformation in South Africa has primarily addressed the provision of infrastructure and housing to the urban poor (Robinson, 2008). It is within this urban landscape that the management of publicly owned property, and, more specifically, the management of public facilities, becomes of vital importance in the context of South Africa.

In beginning to examine a socially inclusive perspective of FM within a South African context, the starting point must be with the Constitution of South Africa (Republic of South Africa [RSA], 1996), which sets out the framework for local government. This includes, *inter alia*, the promotion of social and economic development and the promotion of a safe and healthy environment. Within the framework of the Constitution, the White Paper on Local Government (DPLG, 1998) established the basis for a new, developmental local government system. The primary commitment of the White Paper is to work with citizens, groups and communities to create sustainable human settlements that provide for a decent quality of life and meet the social, economic and material needs of communities in a holistic way. This White Paper requires local government to focus on the promotion of local economic development, social development and community empowerment. A number of pieces of enabling legislation have followed the Constitution that are intended to provide core principles, mechanisms and processes aimed at facilitating local government's endeavors in bringing about the social and economic upliftment of local communities. Huchzermeyer (2006) argues that the attainment of both social development and local economic development may be achieved through the development of municipal-level social amenities, community facilities and municipal-level economic infrastructure. Hence, it can be argued that FM, in terms of the management of these facilities, has a strategic role to play in the realization of social development and local economic development goals of local government.

THE ROLE OF FM AS A SOCIAL AND COMMUNITY ENTERPRISE

Traditionally the theory and practice of FM has focused on the strategic and operational dimensions to the alignment of the organization and its output via the provision of facilities and utilities (Alexander, 2003; Atkin & Brooks, 2005; Barrett & Baldry, 2003; McGregor & Then, 1999; Nutt & McLennan, 2000). Price (2002) argues that the FM research base to date has paid little or no attention to wider developments in social and organizational science. It is clear that the focus has been on the 'bottom line,' with the primary motive being profit-based. This begs the question: in what way is FM different when the 'bottom line' is not profit driven but singularly focused on the economic and social development of the community that the facility serves and the interrelationship between the two in the creation of 'sustainable human settlements'? Gordon (1993) argues that the primary focus for local government is not the 'bottom line,' but rather that emphasis is placed on the provision of services to the public. The South African legislation defines the objectives for local government in the country, i.e., social and local economic development, and the outcome/output of its performance is measurable. However, this performance is dependent on the creation, integration and management of facilities, utilities and infrastructure within their jurisdiction. Price (2003) argues that there is a direct relationship between the quality of the built facility and the perception within society with respect to living standards and overall economic development. In a discussion of their 'four trails to the future,' Nutt and McLennan (2000) highlight the role that facilities and infrastructure can play in the provision of a sustainable and supportive environment for business and social organizations.

To date, the FM response to this dichotomy has tended to continue to remain entrenched in the positivist paradigm of strategic and operational FM. Brackertz and Kenley (2002) point to a fundamental disparity in the goals and outcomes of strategic FM within the private sector and the public sector. Similarly, Heywood (2007), in a study of local government facilities in Australia, argues that local government facilities create a physical environment that has a direct influence on the behavior of the community in and around that facility.

There is some evidence of an orientation towards the sustainable cities agenda in the FM literature. Jones et al. (2004) argue that in order to achieve a sustainable urban environment, an improved understanding of the relationship between buildings, people and the environment is necessary. This is echoed by Elle et al. (2004), who argue for the need for FM to develop an increased awareness of sustainable facilities within the greater urban context (cf. Ch. 5). Manor (2004) develops this concept further, arguing that sustainable development can only be achieved by encouraging community participation in maintaining public facilities. The increasing awareness of the need to focus on the long-term sustainability of urban areas, and the role of management of facilities in this context, may be traced back to the 1990s. An early hint of the application of FM to urban management may be found in the work of Melvin (1992), where he raises the question as to the potential for the principles that underpin FM as a solution to filling a gap in urban management. Roberts (2004) takes this one step further by arguing that urban FM is a logical step towards the need to reinvest in community facilities, thereby achieving a social return for local government. It is in this context that Alexander (2006, p. 248) presents urban FM as the "integrated provision of public service accommodation and community support services." More importantly, urban FM has the potential to meet its objectives in terms of best value while 'putting people first.' Alexander and Brown (2006) further present an embryonic paradigm within the FM literature termed Community-based FM (CbFM). CbFM places the community as a key stakeholder in the planning, delivery, management and maintenance of the facility. The implication of placing the community as the key stakeholder in the FM process requires a reorientation from the organization and the workplace towards the community, neighborhood, community resources and the citizens in that community. Schriner (1993) argues for the creation of successful partnerships founded on a common set of expectation and beliefs within communities in order to create opportunities that are of benefit to both the community and the organization. For Alexander and Brown, these FM partnerships within the community could result in the creation of social enterprises specifically aimed at tackling social and environmental issues, thereby resulting in social and economic development within these communities.

Kasim and Hudson (2006) examine the extent to which the concept of a social enterprise fits with FM thinking and the manner in which it assists with the creation of community benefit. They call for the future direction of

FM to be explored in terms of the provision of services to support the local community needs and the local economy. In essence, they are calling for the alignment of FM away from its traditional focus on organizational interests to a more socially aligned focus on communities. Alexander (2008) echoes this view by emphasizing the role that community enterprise can play as a means of developing social capital and addressing issues inherent to social cohesion in areas of poverty.

The early roots of this more socially oriented view of FM may also be seen in the work of Becker (1990), Duffy (2000) and Grimshaw (2004). Grimshaw (p. 15) discusses the link between FM and social theory. More specifically, he explores the relationships between 'space, place and people' in terms of critical theory. In this context he argues that the physical infrastructure to be found in the work environment is a crucial aspect in the spatial experience of the users of that space and therefore has a direct impact on the social processes that occur between users of that said space. Price, Ellison and Macdonald (2009, p. 2) argue that strategic FM should begin to engage with the 'socially constructed realities' of organizations. Moreover, FM needs to embrace the power of organizational discourse in defining the environment within which the organization functions. If this concept were to be directly transferred to public sector FM, it may be argued that the physical infrastructure of an urban environment is a critical aspect of the spatial experience of the urban environment.

Clearly, the literature shows evidence of an increasing awareness of the need to invest in community facilities, community empowerment, community development and community control over the management and operation of facilities within their locale. The focus on the community may be seen as a means of achieving a 'social return' for local government and requires a more socially oriented view of FM that embraces these concepts.

FM SOCIAL ENTERPRISES IN ACTION: THE CASE OF THE SOUTH AFRICAN TOWNSHIPS

The fieldwork entailed seven case studies within the greater Cape Town metropolitan area. In total 60 face-to-face, unstructured interviews were undertaken with a variety of stakeholders, including local government officials, community persons and the private sector. The study revealed that, in the main, FM policy at a local government level is limited to a purely operational focus on the maintenance, cleaning and security of public facilities. Interestingly, it was further evident that local government does not lack the capital budget for the provision of assets for communities such as business centers, transport facilities, sports facilities, libraries and community centers. What they fail to do is to operationalize and manage the asset post the development phase. This failure can be attributed to departments within local government functioning in 'silos' with little or no cross-departmental responsibility for facilities. There is a generally acknowledged view in the field data that points to the lack of maintenance of public buildings as being a significant problem. Moreover, where maintenance is being undertaken, it is purely a 'reactive' form of maintenance management. It was clear from the fieldwork that the core of the problem lies in the lack of a coherent FM framework within which local government officials can manage and operate public facilities. During the evolution of the grounded theory of CbFM it became possible to visualize four scenarios with respect to the provision, management and maintenance of facilities in previously disadvantaged communities. The four scenarios are depicted in Figure 14.1.

The fieldwork identified that the core of the problem is local government's lack of an overarching FM policy and practice for the management of public facilities. Furthermore, the field data highlighted some problems that centered around the structure of local government and its associated policy. Hence, bisecting the FM policy and practice shown in Figure 14.1 is, on the one axis, the ability or not of local government to meet the communities' needs. The other axis represents the key barriers to implementation and operationalization on the one end, and the key enablers to implementation on the other end of the continuum. The core, i.e., the FM policy and practice, and the two axes, i.e., barriers and enablers, are bounded by the local context (the outer circle).

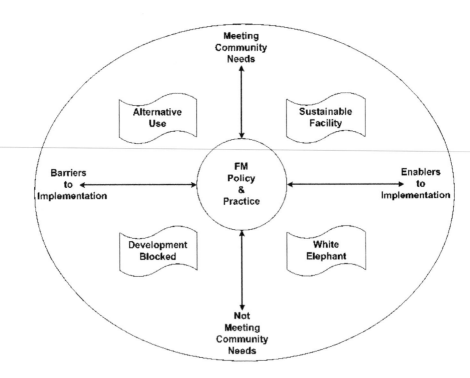

Figure 14.1 Scenario matrix.

In terms of this scenario matrix, the lower-left quadrant represents facilities that are viewed by the community as not meeting their needs and where there are a large number of barriers to implementation. In the case of a new development, this scenario will result in the development being blocked by the community. As a result local government are left with no choice but to abandon the development project altogether. Where this is an existing building, it usually stands vacant and is subjected to high levels of vandalism. This quadrant represents what may be seen as a 'classic disengagement' scenario.

The upper-left-hand quadrant of the matrix represents the scenario where there are still a number of barriers to implementation, but these are accompanied by a perception within the community that the facility meets their needs. What is important to note is that this quadrant usually represents a high level of community engagement in order for this perception exist. The result is that the facility is utilized by the community, but for an alternative use. Moreover, this is usually a result of local government's failure to manage and operationalize the facility post the development phase.

The lower-right quadrant is where the enablers to implementation are in place, but the facility is not what the community feel they need and/or want. This scenario usually results in 'white elephant'–type developments. These facilities stand vacant for years on end, are not utilized by the community and are unlikely to be used by the community in the near future.

The upper-right-hand quadrant represents a win-win scenario, i.e., the facility is perceived to meet the communities' needs and the enablers to implementation are in place. It is in this quadrant that evidence of the use of CbFM as a social enterprise was identified in the fieldwork. In facilities where local government has succeeded in terms of using CbFM to manage and operate a facility, there is evidence of a high level of community focus in terms of engagement, empowerment, participation and ownership. A key to the successful implementation and operationalization of a facility within this quadrant is the active participation of the community in the development and the subsequent management and operation of the facility. Embedded in this active community participation is the need to identify the key role-players within the community. Relationship building and a socially cohesive community, with well-defined democratically elected community structures, are seen as key elements in the relative success or failure in the implementation of CbFM. Moreover, there exists a direct relationship between this high level of community involvement, and the relative success or failure of a facility. The fieldwork clearly highlighted some evidence of a 'strategic intent' in terms of the management of the public facilities. In this regard, some departments within local government are making use of CbFM committees to manage the day-to-day operation and maintenance of public land and buildings. Coupled with the establishment of these FM committees is the clear need for training of community people involved in the committee. It was clear in the data that where the training of the community is taking place, it appears to be done by social enterprises and the private sector. In some instances, the FM committee is run and managed by a community trust. In essence, local government 'rent' the facility to a community trust. The trust then acts as both a property management and a Facility Management company. The trust takes responsibility for the leasing, operation and maintenance of the facility. More importantly, all profits generated by the trust remain with the trust and may be utilized for further development and uplifting within the community. The activities that are occurring within this quadrant represent what may be seen as a 'social enterprise' scenario. The use of FM committees and community trusts not only facilitates the active participation of the community in the management and operationalization of the facility, but also actively promotes local economic development and social development within that community.

As stated earlier, the legislation defining the activities of local government requires the active participation of the communities. The evidence at a grassroots level is that active participation is not usually happening. In the main, communities remain marginalized and disenfranchised, with the strong perception that local government is not directly focused on the community and their needs in terms of both the provision of public facilities and in promoting social development and local economic development.

What is clear is that where the 'trust' model outlined in the preceding section has been adopted, this has resulted in members of the community feeling consulted and are active participants in any intervention that is undertaken within their community. Moreover, the use of the community in the management and operation of the community facilities has resulted in some form of local economic development and social development back into the community. Hence, the establishment of an FM committee is seen by many as a viable vehicle for the management of public facilities in these communities.

The literature outlined earlier in the chapter highlighted the call from a variety of sources for a socially inclusive view of FM that embraces the 'socially constructed reality' of urban spaces. It is interesting to note at this point that the 'social enterprise' scenario and 'trust' model represent this change to a socially inclusive use of FM being implemented at a grassroots level. More importantly, this socially constructed reality of FM has created a conversation between local government and the community that has an increased focus on a number of the key objectives of local government. These conversations are concentrated on capacity and skills development, local economic development, community empowerment, community development and ultimately community control over the management and operation of the facilities within their locale.

CONCLUSION

The emergent themes from the grounded theory study identify a direct relationship between the facility and its surrounding area. Moreover, this relationship requires the application of CbFM to an urban precinct or community locale, as opposed to being singularly focused at the building level. The development of a CbFM approach offers a viable and contextually appropriate vehicle to assist local government in the attainment of their objectives. This approach requires local government to adopt a capacity-focused view of community assets and an increased focus on the well-being of communities and their capacity to self-manage. In addition, the application of CbFM provides a level of coherence to the management and operation of public facilities within local government. The use of FM as a social enterprise in the management, maintenance and operation of infrastructure and public facilities in impoverished communities provides a means of addressing the problems associated with these facilities, which were identified earlier in the chapter. At a broader level, the use of the community and FM as a social enterprise in the management and operation of community facilities enables the creation of a different set of narratives and constructs about the management of urban space. This allows for the formulation of a different social ecology within the urban locale, and therefore is more likely to result in the long-term sustainability of the facility and the urban precinct as a whole.

REFERENCES

African National Congress. (1994). *The Reconstruction and Development Programme: A policy framework.* Johannesburg: Umanyano Publications.

Alexander, K. (2003). A strategy for Facilities Management. *Facilities, 21*(11/12), 269–274.

Alexander, K. (2006). Editorial—new economics. *Facilities, 24*(7/8), 248–249.

Alexander, K. (2008). *Managing community assets for urban sustainability.* Paper presented at the International Conference on Urban Sustainability, Hong Kong, January.

Alexander, K., & Brown, M. (2006). Community-based Facilities Management. *Facilities, 24*(7/8), 250–268.

Atkin, B., & Brooks, A. (2005). *Total Facilities Management* (2nd ed.). Oxford: Blackwell.

Barrett, P., & Baldry, D. (2003). *Facilities Management: Towards best practice* (2nd ed.). Oxford: Blackwell.

Becker, F. (1990). *The total workplace: Facilities Management and the elastic organisation.* New York: Van Nostrand Reinhold.

Brackertz, N., & Kenley, R. (2002). Evaluating community facilities in local government: Managing for service enablement. *Journal of Facilities Management, 1*(3), 283–299.

Department of Provincial and Local Government. (1998). *The White Paper on local government.* Pretoria: Department of Provincial and Local Government, Republic of South Africa.

Duffy, F. (2000). Design and Facilities Management in a time of change. *Facilities, 18*(10/11/12), 371–375.

Elle, M., Engelmark, J., Jørgensen, B., Koch, C., Nielsen, S. B., & Vestergaard, F. (2004). Managing facilities in a Scandinavian manner: Creating a research agenda. *Facilities, 22*(11/12), 311–316.

Gordon, G. L. (1993). *Strategic planning for local government.* Washington, DC: International City/County Management Association.

Grimshaw, B. (2004). Space place and people: Facilities Management and critical theory. In K. Alexander, B. Atkin, J. Bröchner & T. Haugen (Eds.), *Facilities Management: Innovation and performance* (pp. 15–32). Abingdon: Spon Press.

Heywood, C. (2007). *The role of affect in local government corporate real estate management.* PhD dissertation, the University of Melbourne, Melbourne.

Huchzermeyer, M. (2006). The new instrument for upgrading informal settlements in South Africa: Contributions and constraints. In M. Huchzermeyer & A. Karam (Eds.), *Informal settlements: A perpetual challenge?* (pp. 41–61). Cape Town: UCT Press.

Jones, K., Clements-Croome, D., Bahaj, A., & Gann, D. (2004). *Achieving a sustainable urban environment: Working with existing buildings.* Paper presented at the CIB W70 International Symposium on "Human Elements in Facilities Management—Understanding the Needs of Our Customers", Hong Kong, 103–110. Retrieved August 30, 2011, from http://www.irbdirekt.de/daten/iconda/06089015806.pdf

Kasim, R., & Hudson, J. (2006). FM as a social enterprise. *Facilities, 24*(7/8), 292–299.

Manor, J. (2004). Democratisation with inclusion: Political reforms and people's empowerment at the grassroots. *Journal of Human Development, 5*(1), 5–29.

McGregor, W., & Then, D. (1999). *Facilities Management and the business of space.* London: Arnold.

McLennan, A. (2009). The delivery paradox. In A. McLennan & B. Munslow (Eds.), *The politics of service delivery* (pp. 19–42). Johannesburg: Wits University Press.

Melvin, J. (1992). Creating places. *Facilities, 10*(2), 14–18.

Mufamadi, S. (2008). Foreword. In M. van Donk, M. Swilling, E. Pieterse & S. Parnell (Eds.), *Consolidating developmental local government: Lessons from the South African experience* (pp. v–vii). Cape Town: UCT Press.

Nutt, B., & McLennan, P. (2000). *Facility Management risks and opportunities.* Oxford: Blackwell.

Parnell, S. (2005). Constructing a developmental nation—the challenge of including the poor in the post-apartheid city. *Transformation: Critical Perspectives on Southern Africa, 58,* 20–44.

Patel, Y. (2004). *New urban realities: Overview of urban challenges facing South Africa.* Paper presented at the World Urban Forum, Barcelona. Retrieved August 31, 2011, from http://www.dplg.gov.za/index.php/documents/doc_download/7–world-urban-forum-paper.html

Price, I. (2002). Can FM evolve? If not, what future? *Journal of Facilities Management, 1*(1), 56–69.

Price, I. (2003). The development of Facility Management. In R. Best, C. Langston & G. De Valence (Eds.), *Workplace strategies and Facilities Management: Building in value* (pp. 49–66). Oxford: Butterworth-Heinemann.

Price, I., Ellison, I., & Macdonald, R. (2009). *Practical post-modernism: FM and socially constructed realities.* Paper presented at the European Facility Management Conference, Amsterdam, 1–15. Retrieved August 30, 2011, from http://shura.shu.ac.uk/912/

Republic of South Africa. (1996). *Constitution of the Republic of South Africa Act No. 108.* Pretoria: Republic of South Africa.

Roberts, P. (2004). FM: New urban and community alignments. *Facilities, 22*(13/14), 349–352.

Robinson, J. (2008). Continuities and discontinuities in South African local government. In M. van Donk, M. Swilling, E. Pieterse & S. Parnell (Eds.),

Consolidating developmental local government: Lessons from the South African experience (pp. 27–49). Cape Town: UCT Press.

Schriner, J. A. (1993). Communities and companies. *Facilities, 11*(8), 7–11.

Southall, R. (2004). The ANC & black capitalism in South Africa. *Review of African Political Economy, 31*(100), 313–328.

Turok, I., & Parnell, S. (2009). Reshaping cities, rebuilding nations: The role of national urban policies. *Urban Forum, 20*(2), 157–174.

15 Strategies for Communication

Melanie Bull and Julie Kortens

Laframboise, Nelson and Schmaltz (2003) wrote a seminal piece around the need to develop a robust communication strategy in relation to change in workplace accommodation projects based on research carried out in government buildings in Canada. More recently, Bull and Brown (2011) have investigated whether the amount and frequency of communication impacts on the levels of satisfaction working for an organization following the implementation of an alternative workplace strategy in a large private organization. The different communication styles adopted by the line managers to disseminate information to staff resulted in a negative impact on the staff view of the company post change.

Here we further focus on the need to recognize the importance of communication within FM, drawing on practical examples from Channel 4,[1] sponsor of the Oscar-winning film *Slumdog Millionaire*, and also from further research investigating the impact of effective FM communication on the workplace (Bull and Brown, 2011), and the need to raise the profile of FM within organizations (Kaya, Heywood, Arge, Brawn & Alexander, 2004). The Channel 4 case evidences the need to ensure that the communication of projects is strategically aligned with the organization's values and strategy of keeping ahead of the competition and how the organization has also engaged the staff to actively encourage buy in to the project.

COMMUNICATION THEORY

To further explore business communication and strategies for communicating with other human beings, there is some need to understand communication theory and how communication is engaged with by individuals. Clampitt (2001) in Hartley and Bruckman (2002) discusses management communication as using three different approaches. Here we suggest that there is use for all three, but perhaps there needs to be more consideration on when each style is appropriate.

The arrow—one-way communication or "firing the arrow"—is arguably information giving as opposed to communication (Quirke, 1995). The firing of the arrow assumes that the listener or receiver is a passive processor of information. Quirke (1995, 2000) further suggests that information giving may be appropriate when there is little chance of misunderstanding the message and a lean medium such as posters or information on an intranet site would suit this style of communication. The overall scope of this volume is to appreciate that words can signify different meanings to different groups, and using this approach to communication ignores this.

The circuit—two-way communication—places a higher emphasis on the importance of receiving feedback and therefore engaging in more listening skills and trust in relationships. However, there can be weaknesses in this style in that the circuit manager may believe that disagreement or non–buy in is due to the need for more communication and that more communication will automatically lead to buy in. Quirke would also suggest that this is effective when there is chance of misunderstanding and refers to this style of communication as a "rich medium," which could be verbal discussions either face-to-face or on the telephone.

The dance metaphor suggests that communication can be used in relation to the speaker and the listener engaging in coordination of meaning. It suggests an understanding that individuals will create their own meanings due to their subjective view of the world, and therefore there is a need, sometimes, to stand in the receiver's shoes; to engage in empathy. The metaphor of dance also relates to the fact that we can dance to impress or express ourselves to others, and in the same way we can communicate to inform or express our thoughts and ideas. Both dance and communication are governed by rules such as turn taking in speech or recognition of nonverbal signs.

Following on from this concept there is also a need to understand basic communication theory in that our communication is not just the words that are being spoken but also our nonverbal communication. Dr. Albert Mahrabian (1971) suggested that from our communication the receiver takes away 55% of our body language and facial expressions; 38% of vocal characteristics—tone, volume, inflection—and only 7% of our words. So considering organizational communication, whilst we would argue that the statistics may not be perfect, there is some evidence that these nonverbal signals are important to our understanding of the meaning of the messages being delivered (cf. Myerson's 'narrative space,' Ch. 2).

As we continue to evolve, and perhaps referring back to Darwin (1871), are we starting to rely on different needs in our communication? Do we rely so much on the nonverbal signals? In our world of technology and e-mail, how do we ensure that our messages are being communicated effectively? How many times are e-mails misconstrued or the tone of the e-mail misunderstood? As human beings do we still rely on the nonverbal communication signals to form a fuller picture or are animals, as Darwin suggested, able to evolve over time to meet the changing needs of their environment (cf. Price, Ch. 1; Beard, Ch. 6)? From a social constructionist point of view, in any conversation the receiver and the listener are drawing their own conclusions on the basis of their *a priori*, their previous knowledge; therefore, is the medium as important as being able to use empathy to understand the message, standing in the other person's shoes? We would argue that this is not necessarily considered when individuals communicate and could also be a factor in misunderstanding of communication.

CHANGE AND ORGANIZATIONAL COMMUNICATION

Quirke (1995) suggests that communication is a two-way process; Holm (2006) suggests that communication is the process that enables individuals to share meaning through a transactional process between two or more parties. However, in times of organizational change, and in particular changes to the working environment, this is very often forgotten. The Channel 4 case study discusses the benefit of engaging staff in two-way communication, and in comparison the case study, as discussed in Bull and Brown (2011), recognized the potential dangers in relation to staff satisfaction when this communication need is ignored.

During any period of change, and as Laframboise et al. (2003) discussed, there is a need to engage the business (or end users) in some form of communication process to ensure they understand the implications of the change and also have a chance to feedback their own thoughts. In relation to space change, there is a tendency to make the decisions based on a need to reduce asset portfolios, or a belief by a chosen few that their ideas of space are what are needed. However, if the business is not engaged or asked to be involved and business requirements are not heard, then this can lead to dissatisfaction amongst employees (Bull & Brown, 2011). The concept of changing the workspace to engage in greater collaboration and actively encourage the organization to change their conversations should be the priority focus. Stuart (Ch. 11) shows that changing the conversation can actually reduce costs more dramatically than traditional approaches do.

Quirke (1995) suggests that communication has the pivotal role in relation to any change programs, and the need to explain the "why" is essential. Communication should be regular, timely, honest, clear, easy to follow and interactive to allow for feedback (Smith, 2006). There is also a need to ensure the communication has meaning to the recipient; it therefore needs to be personally relevant to the receiver (Klein, 1996; Goodman, Holihan & Willis, 1996), reinforcing Quirke's ideas that there is not a one-size-fits-all when it comes to communication. We now explore the concept of communication in an organizational setting, discussing Channel 4's communication in relation to a change of organizational space and how the organization engaged employees in the change.

CASE STUDY

As noted earlier, Channel 4 Television Corporation is a UK-based media broadcaster and film production company. It is funded by advertising revenue, and, with no shareholders, the bulk of its income is directed back into the program and content budget. Unusually the FM function and hence the responsibility for the workspace reports to the director of HR,[2] which ensures that people-related issues remain at the forefront of strategic decision-making. Kortens, as the head of facilities, is a qualified HR practitioner who was previously responsible for providing a generalist HR service to the staff in the organization. With that background she states:

> I believe passionately that the built environment impacts on the health, well-being and performance of staff, and that collaborative workspaces are essential for ideas generation in a creative organization. The senior management structure at Channel 4 is nonhierarchical, meaning I have the autonomy to introduce innovative workplace solutions.

In 2009, Channel 4 made a strategic decision to outsource its broadcast facility.[3] This significant decision involved the outsourcing of more than 100 staff members and relocation of their transmission-related technical facilities from the lower ground floor of its London headquarters (HQ) building to a third-party location. The building is a landmark with a striking and distinctive exterior. However, internally there is little to reflect the corporation's values. There is a relatively corporate feel with little color, and the workplace design is very "safe" and uninspiring. The outsourcing of the technical broadcast facility gives the organization an opportunity to refurbish the space and to convert it to office accommodation. This would enable Channel 4 to consolidate staff from other buildings into the HQ, improving overall organizational design and, at the same time, reducing its property costs significantly. The HQ was designed by Lord Richard Rogers and, as part of the original build (1994), measures were put in place to future proof the building and its investment value. In August 2010 transmission vacated the space, which was stripped back to its shell pending the refurbishment.

COMMUNICATING CHANNEL 4'S VALUES

An integral part of the design brief was to ensure that the project reflected Channel 4's values, which are "to inspire change; to do it first; and to cause trouble." Those core values and purposes are integral to everything it does and underpin its culture. This meant that the design needed to be innovative and reflect Channel 4's on-screen content. The brief to the FM team was that the working environment should reflect those values— the aim being to embrace both connectivity and convergence in the new digital world, to be distinctive, challenging and innovative. Collaboration is at the heart of Channel 4 and by creating an environment where Channel 4 staff members can have "serious fun" and collaborate more in creative surroundings they aimed to stimulate creativity and ensure that new screen content was communicated to staff. As the bulk of the exterior walls are glazed, the aim was to introduce branding via the new meeting room concept. The rooms were color coded to match the different television channels in the Channel 4 family and contained artwork from on-screen content such as *Slumdog Millionaire.*

When commissioning the new project, it was essential that the client brief made clear that the new design reflected the core values, and, at each stage of the design process, the designers have been challenged to demonstrate that those values are being embraced. Key design concepts have then been presented to the executive board for ratification on a regular basis. The new design provides a socially vibrant, collaborative space, in line with the CEO's 2011 declared wish for the organization to "adapt to the exciting opportunities of the digital world."

PROJECT BACKGROUND

The HQ building was originally designed to accommodate 650 people. Pre-2010, several projects had increased the capacity. The most significant was the 2003 conversion of cellular offices to open-plan accommodation. Channel 4's very flat organizational structure is reflected in the design of its workplace. All staff members sit in the open-plan area at the same bench-style furniture system with access to the same technology and communal facilities. Likewise, the ethos is that everyone matters and has a contribution to make.

In leading the current project, the FM team have engaged with the business and ensured that the building is planned efficiently. Advice has been sought to ensure that there are appropriate facilities for the number of people accommodated. Meeting room facilities have been benchmarked against similar organizations and reviewed with Channel 4 staff to ensure that the complement of large versus small meeting rooms and formal versus informal space reflects the profile of the Channel 4 working day. This reinforces the proposition that the needs of the business must be understood to enable any alternative workplace strategies to engage staff and management.

Central building-related facilities have been enhanced to ensure that Channel 4 operates in a more economical and sustainable way, and the innovative designs have included an increase in branding throughout the building. This is a daily reminder to staff of the values and output (cf. Myerson's 'narrative space,' Ch. 2). New furniture is provided by up–and-coming designers, in line with Channel 4's key purpose of nurturing and supporting emerging talent.

As well as improving the working environment and general facilities, the project consolidates everyone into the HQ (1,000 desks) and has given Channel 4 an opportunity to future proof the building infrastructure (minimizing disruption to staff and the business by undertaking the work in one step). Technology changes are enablers of different forms of communication, allowing staff to carry out jobs in a more effective way, for example, the installation of wireless "reference points" in the ceilings to support future wireless networks/mobility and other technology to ensure that Channel 4 is able to provide mobile and flexible working solutions in line with their strategy of keeping ahead of the competition. This joined-up thinking, merging the physical, virtual and psychological factors within the Channel 4 workspace, delivers a workplace that reflects the values, purposes and ethos of the organization. "Joined up thinking between HR, IS and FM drives cultural change" (Dixon & Ross, 2011 p. 7).

COMMUNICATIONS PLAN

Channel 4 is a media organization, and any communication must be appropriate to the internal audience, visual and interactive wherever possible. All presentations included 3-D graphics, mood boards and furniture samples and whenever practicable meetings or presentations occurred in the space to be refurbished. All communication had to be timely, honest and open (Smith, 2006). Some high-level communication was sent to the internal communications manager, who was responsible for the intranet, but the bulk was managed internally by the FM team.

Various means were used to communicate the changes with the staff and stakeholders, as discussed in the following, correlating with Quirke's (1995) advocacy of using mixed methods of communication without a one-size-fits-all approach. Firstly the head of FM attended the main Channel 4 board meeting to present the accommodation strategy. This presentation included financials, return on investment (ROI) and visuals. Following the opening of the new refurbished floor (ex-transmission) there was general communication to all staff (via employee representatives, intranet publicity and a "Message of the Day") advising that there was a four-week review period. Any feedback received from staff was reviewed and incorporated into the ongoing scheme. During the four-week review the help desk coordinated all feedback. This was then discussed by the design team (architect, Quantity Surveyor, FM) and formally presented to employee representatives. The process ensured that staff members were aware that their feedback had not only been taken seriously, but had been built into the project rollout across upper floors. The approach ensured that staff members felt that they were playing a part in the design process and their buy in was secured. This again reinforces the views of Quirke (1995, 2000), Laframboise et al. (2003) and Bull and Brown (2011).

To further enhance the joined-up approach, the head of FM had a regular slot on the agenda of the Channel 4 employee forum. This forum has representatives from all departments across the business and is organized by the head of HR operations. Additional attendees include the CEO, COO and the director of HR. Presentations were made at each meeting (quarterly fixed meetings and ad hoc as required), ensuring that employee representatives understood the project from a strategic overview, that expectations were managed and that the investment the organization was making was understood by all. Areas of concern raised at previous meetings were incorporated into the design; for example, the employee representatives were tasked with getting feedback from their areas on the future design of communal facilities. To get buy in from the FM team, operational staff were also consulted in this way, with particular success when the cleaning team members were asked for their suggestions on the design of the new toilet facilities, the brief being to make them as easy to clean as possible and to make the cleaning staff more effective.

Liaison with the senior management was prevalent throughout this change and the head of FM presented to the chief executive and also to the weekly meeting of executive directors. The overall design concept of each phase was presented and departmental adjacencies discussed for final sign-off. Meetings were also organized between the head of FM, the FM space planner and individual heads of department to discuss their teams' specific needs.

Staff Engagement

To ensure full staff engagement with the process, the CEO made reference to the accommodation project at an all-staff, end-of-year roundup. These sessions were high profile as they were for all employees and were held off-site; an opportunity for everyone to hear the corporate message simultaneously and to have an open question–and-answer session with executive directors. There was also a display stand showing images of the forthcoming changes.

In March 2011 the head of FM presented details of the project to all staff members, including changes to the way everyone would be working at the end of the project. The phased approach to the moves was also presented to staff so that they were aware of their involvement and their expectations were managed as early in the process as possible. The open approach to sharing the scheme with staff at all levels has ensured that staff members have had ample opportunity to raise concerns and for those concerns to be allayed as swiftly as possible or, alternatively, the rationale for the changes explained up front.

A small working group was established to create a leaflet to be distributed to staff members when they arrived in their new location. As each phase of the project has been planned, the FM team have held relaunch events, such as the reopening of the staff restaurant, and have encouraged staff participation wherever possible. This was particularly important as the in-house catering facility needed to retain its clientele in order to ensure it is sustainable going forward.

Tours of the LG space were advertised on the intranet and arranged with the principal contractor. The head of FM took staff members around the floor and introduced the project, furniture samples and an overview of the various phases. A competition on the intranet encouraged staff to visit and to suggest a new name. Again it raised interest. There were numerous suggestions put to a vote to find the winner. Going forward the floor will be called "Base Camp." To further enhance the staff engagement process there was an ad on the intranet for anyone interested in joining focus groups. The first was a furniture team that helped to select from a small range of final samples, including furniture for all communal areas. The range was already approved in terms of overall look and feel, as well as practical suitability, in terms of being portable, stackable, durable, cleanable and within budget. Designers attended these sign-off meetings so that they could hear feedback directly from staff members.

THE FINAL STAGES

As the project extended into deciding departmental adjacencies, the team began to look at the final locations of respective business units and their critical adjacencies, and a brainstorming session was organized to discuss where the seven executive directors should be located. The CEO was relatively new to the organization, and one of his priorities had been to develop a cohesive and collaborative senior team. The initial suggestion was for the team to be colocated. Word soon spread across the organization and the general feedback was that this was not in line with Channel 4's culture as it would create an executive "enclave" that staff would be reticent to visit; something that was alien to Channel 4's culture of collaboration and open communication.

After further discussion, the designers proposed a central "hub" that would extend upwards through the building, making the collaborative and executive spaces central to the whole organization. In the heart of the basement there are welfare facilities, and on the lower ground a meeting room complex, which includes the boardroom. There is a staff restaurant in the center of the ground floor and, following this pattern, the executives are located in the center of the first, second and third floors. Whilst the executives have their own meeting rooms (and they are the only staff members to have dedicated rooms), they are seen as "team rooms," used by their individual directorates. All executives sit in the open-plan area and their rooms are in the middle of the floor plate—central and visible but also not the prime space with natural light—this is given to staff. The net result of these proposals is an acknowledgment that the executives and CEO understood the necessity for them to be visible across the organization and by their own teams, and for there to be a feeling of equality across the business.

A BRIEF COMPARISON

Channel 4's approach focused on two-way communication and staff engagement. In contrast, Bull and Brown (2011) discussed another case, where a 'blue-chip' organization (Finance Co.) engaged in delivering an alternative workspace strategy without engaging its staff. Most communication was one-way (information giving) with little context about why the changes were happening. The company's focus was on reducing overheads as opposed to creating a more collaborative environment. The research focused on the hypothesis that a lack of communication strategy had led to reduced staff satisfaction in the workplace and therefore negatively impacted on the change. In contrast to the Channel 4 approach, the chief executive did not engage with staff members to discuss the changes; therefore, the message of change was delivered by the FM department as opposed by the executive.

The research, via an electronic survey, found that there was little opportunity to offer feedback and therefore the communication was predominantly seen as one-way. As one member of staff noted, "The whole communication process from the FM team was very poor. There should have been consultation about its implementation; instead it was a 'tell' session and the needs of the business were not listened to or taken on board."[4] The survey indicated that 43% of the respondents' satisfaction levels were worse or much worse after the change, compared to only 7% seeing any improvement.

Whilst both Channel 4 and Finance Co. engaged in communication, there was little focus on the latter in relation to staff engagement, to enable them to feel part of the change or to encourage great buy in to the new ideas. Phillips and Addicks (2010) and Wagner and Harter (2006) believe that engaged employees demonstrate virtuous qualities, such as innovation and creativity, taking personal responsibility when things happen and an authentic desire to make the team and the organization successful. They also have an emotional bond to the organization, its mission and vision. This was also reinforced by Hedicker (2010) in her research into management communication to housekeeping staff within the National Health Service (NHS).

CONCLUSION

From a communications perspective encouraging information sharing and two-way communication between staff and management cannot be improved whilst doors are closed; however, perhaps facilities teams need to learn and be empowered by the business to advise on how best organizational space can be utilized to encourage collaborative working environments. Quirke (2000) suggests that we need to consider the following in relation to developing a robust communications plan. We need to ensure we match our communication in relation to need: to create awareness we can use bulletin boards, advertising campaigns, direct mails, e-mail, etc based on a one-way distribution to a passive audience. If there is a need to create understanding then this must allow for feedback and active participation needing face-to-face communication. This could include interactive road shows and feedback fora. Creating support can be gained through training events and clear explanations behind the rationale for change, for example. Involvement requires active encouragement to share objections and concerns and again to ensure the management thinking behind the change has been clearly understood by the staff. At this stage FMs need to ensure they are using active listening skills and perhaps also listening for what is not being said. If commitment is required, then be honest (Smith, 2006). Explain if the change is required to enable the safety of jobs, for example; let staff understand that there has been consideration for other strategic options and why the organization has chosen the particular route. Don't forget to measure how effective the communication has been after the change/project and evaluate want went wrong and what went well. And don't forget contingency. With any good communications plan, things can go wrong and there may be unexpected employee responses. Be prepared to flex the communication to the needs of the business!

There is no doubt that open and timely communication with staff is a contributory factor to ensuring that an FM team is regarded as integral to the strategic performance of an organization. As Kaya et al. (2004) discussed, in some organizations FM is seen as an operational role and it is necessary for the FM team to evidence how they support and enable the business in relation to the organization's strategic directions. The Channel 4 project has helped to raise the profile of the FM team across all departments; they are seen as strategic, proactive and supportive but, most fundamentally, as an open and collaborative team underpinning the values of the organization.

NOTES

1. Channel 4 is a UK-based public service broadcaster. It was established by an Act of Parliament in 1982 and is a not-for profit-organization. It is funded by advertising revenue and has no shareholders. The bulk of its income is directed back into the program and content budget.
2. Editor's note: is this where FM should sit in organizations that want to manage their ecology via space (cf. Green, foreword; Myerson, Ch. 2; Vischer, Ch. 3)?
3. Channel 4 has transmitted programs from its HQ building since 1994. Following an open market tender, a third-party organization was appointed to provide this service and the on-site facility was decommissioned.
4. Editor's note: Yet another example of the authoritative approach parodied by Hudson (Ch. 6) or lacking the sensitivity suggested by Cairns (Ch. 8).

REFERENCES

Bull, M., & Brown, T. (2011). Implementing change. In E. Finch (Ed.), *Facilities change management* (pp. 108–122). Oxford: Blackwell.

Darwin, C. R. (1871). *The descent of man, and selection in relation to sex.* London: John Murray.

Dixon, M., and Ross, P. (2011). *Measuring the benefits of agility at work: A research study.* London: Regus and Unwired Ventures Limited.

Goodman, M. B., Holihan, V. C., & Willis, K. E. (1996). Communication and change: Effective communication is personal, global and continuous. *Journal of Communication Management, 1*(2), 115–133.

Hartley, P., & Bruckman, C. G. (2002). *Business communication.* London: Routledge.

Hedicker, H. (2010). *Can improved communications enhance staff engagement within housekeeping services?* Unpublished MBA thesis, Sheffield Business School.

Holm, F. (2006). Communication processes in critical systems: Dialogues concerning communications. *Marketing and Intelligence and Planning, 24*(5), 493–504.

Kaya, S., Heywood, C. A., Arge, K., Brawn, G., & Alexander, K. (2004). Raising Facilities Management's profile in organizations: Developing a world-class framework. *Journal of Facilities Management, 3*(1), 65–82.

Klein, S. M. (1996). A management communication strategy for change. *Journal of Organizational Change Management, 9*(2), 32–46.

Laframboise, D., Nelson, R. L., & Schmaltz, J. (2003). Managing resistance to change in workplace accommodation projects. *Journal of Facilities Management, 1*(4), 306–321.

Mahrabian, A. (1971). *Silent messages.* Belmont, CA: Wadsworth.

Phillips, D. R., & Addicks, L. K. (2010). Engaging a multi-generational workforce—a strategic framework for success. *International Journal of Facilities Management, 1*(1), 1–10.

Quirke, B. (1995). *Communicating change.* Aldershot, Hampshire: Gower.

Quirke, B. (2000). *Internal communications.* Aldershot, Hampshire: Gower.

Smith, I. (2006). Continuing professional development and workplace learning—15: Achieving successful organisational change—do's and don'ts of change management. *Library Management, 27*(4/5), 300–306.

Wagner, R., & Harter, J. K. (2006). *12: The elements of great managing.* Washington, DC: Gallup.

16 Educational Implications of an FM Social Constructionist View

Kathy Roper

The practice of FM has existed practically forever. Someone cleaned the castle and redesigned the rooms after fires, attack or even to subdivide spaces for new occupants. Only since the late 1970s have the terms "Facility Management" or "Facilities Management" come into popular usage (Price, Ch. 7). Education in the realm of FM traditionally came from existing programs of engineering, architecture or more recently business, but in the last 20 years, FM educational programs have come into being and are now rapidly expanding as more and more organizations recognize the importance of well-managed buildings and the benefits of workplaces that support workers in more productive ways.

Acknowledging that social construction is a key element of the reality of FM, education in the field is in need of improvements. As FM programs developed in building sciences, building engineering, architecture, construction or business management, the traditional elements of these fields have been emphasized, with a focus on the physical aspects of the building, facility and workplace. These programs typically retain the technical elements of their origins, and in most cases have not expanded to include broader considerations of organizational psychology and how the building impacts the users and occupants.

To successfully accommodate the social constructionist needs of workspaces, FM education requires specific coursework in social construction theory and the appropriate applications to successfully transition the field of FM from technical and aesthetic focus on the building, per se, to one focusing on the organizations' use of facilities as tools in support of the work required to productively improve an organization. As Dale and Burrell state (2006, p. 11), "Our social world is built through interactions between things and people and, as such, space is a neglected but highly significant part of this world." This viewpoint is rare in current FM education.

DEVELOPMENT OF FM EDUCATION

The first programs to provide courses in higher education specific to FM were those developed in the US after formation of the National Facility

Management Association in 1980 and then International Facility Management Association (IFMA) in 1981 (IFMA, 2011). United Kingdom universities quickly embraced FM education and the spread of university-level educational programs has grown dramatically around the globe since 2005. Currently, the IFMA Foundation has accredited 17 university programs at the associate, baccalaureate and master's levels (IFMA Foundation, 2011), and many other programs exist around the world. As the value of the built environment becomes more widely recognized in the general business environment through sustainability and other lean and efficiency methods, the growth of professional FM is expected to grow substantially. These business-focused demands also require that the FM education bring value, not only to technical requirements, but to benefit the organization overall. A strong understanding of organizational culture is primary to this professional education in FM and a key element missing from many of the current domain-focused programs.

Engineering programs developing FM degrees have included basic courses in management, finance and other business degree courses to bring the Facility/Facilities Manager closer to the management qualifications required in the workplace. These programs provide great technical expertise but lack the occupant viewpoint of the facility as a tool to produce work. Architectural programs with FM degrees provide user needs analysis and often include post-occupancy studies within the curriculum. But these programs typically focus on the aesthetic expectations of buildings rather than the interactive needs of workers within the workplace. Human Ecology is one branch of architecture that has some applicability with FM as taught at Cornell University; however, generally Human Ecology focuses on a broader area than just the built environment and in many schools does not specifically relate directly to workplace issues but the larger societal issues humans face.

ISSUES IN CURRENT FM EDUCATION

As the development of FM in the late 1970s was driven by two major changes in the workplace, the use of computers and the development of open planning concepts and the cubicle, similarly, two major changes are influencing the current need for realignment of FM education. First, the development of mobile computing enables workers to work "anytime, anywhere." Workers are no longer tied to the desk as they were with the invention of the computer and personal computing in the later twentieth century. This mobility has changed the concept of the workplace, such that work is often successfully accomplished in the coffee shop, a bookstore or in a park. Second, the progression from industrialized thinking in the modern organization to an appreciation of "knowledge work" requires that FM adapt and support the knowledge age worker, rather than provide an industrialized view of workers all convening to conduct work with the equipment and support formerly required of industrialized workplaces. No longer are the majority of today's workers tied to a specific piece of equipment; most can access needed information virtually anywhere. Rather than assembly and physical handoff of paperwork in one specific work setting, today's workers share information, ideas, drawings, databases, electronic files and all manner of digitized matter across the globe in real time. A construction project in Beijing may have an architect in London, a construction management company working out of Amsterdam and specialty consultants in Los Angeles, Rio de Janeiro and Kuala Lumpur, who all share documents, files and information via the Internet and meet in telepresence for project meetings on a weekly basis. The workplace is not always the "place" where work is conducted.[1]

This understanding of the new ways of working and how the demands of worker interactions influence the work that is accomplished is a key factor of social constructivism. This understanding is also at the heart of FM, requiring knowledgeable facility professionals to be educated in social issues to meet these demands. The FM today and into the future is required to provide value to the organization. This value stems from technical understanding, but also from knowledge of the complex social impacts that the workplace has on the worker and that the workers impart on the workspaces and the interactions of users and space.

FM EDUCATION WITH SOCIAL CONSTRUCTION KNOWLEDGE

A new, clearer focus on users and outcomes is needed in the education of FMs. While technical and aesthetic education is required, this no longer is the requisite focus for FM; rather, there is a base with more complex social issues surpassing the technical skills, which are often "hired" for the organization, either on staff or through contracts. Interpretive research and organizational psychology courses are needed to allow the FM to adequately evaluate the organization and provide support that will match the organizational needs with the provision of workplaces and workplace policies enhancing productivity anytime, anywhere.

TEACHING TOOLS INCORPORATING
SOCIAL CONSTRUCTIONISM

As Beard (Ch. 6) summarizes a number of theories of learning involve social construction, so the use of these methods in teaching social constructivist viewpoints for FM is natural. One primary instructional method is the use of problem-based instruction whereby students must analyze and use prior and shared knowledge to resolve issues. The teaching is focused on reinforcing the collaborative nature of this methodology and is a practical example of how facility professionals often resolve real world issues (Lave & Wenger, 1991). Peer collaboration is another similar instructional method that uses students' interactions to resolve problems presented in the course. Group projects, team tests and similar course elements help to give students experience with group dynamics. A part of the instruction in these courses includes team, group and personal dynamics instructions or, for more advanced classes, resources to find and utilize these methodologies.

Initially students need a cognitive tools perspective, which is based on a participative process producing an end product in which their own meaning has been imposed to arrive at the final product. This perspective is the foundation for understanding cognitive strategies. Later idea-based constructivism is required to deliver traditional concepts and common language such as technical knowledge from engineering, architecture or business management (McMahon, 1997). Finally, transactional cognitive perspectives emerge as the relationships of people, environments and their interaction and dependency become understood by students (Gredler, 1997). They eventually understand in this perspective that learning and the environment are merged and one cannot effectively take place without the influence of the other. Figure 16.1 shows this developmental relationship.

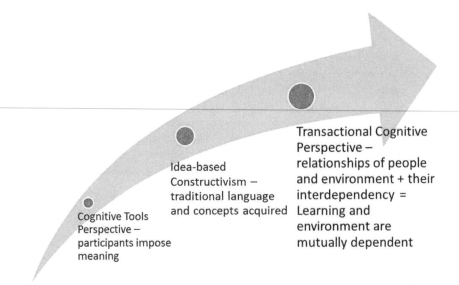

Figure 16.1   Developmental relationship of social construction learning.

Developed during World War I for improvements in training and morale, organizational psychology, or industrial and organizational psychology, crystallized as a specific branch within psychology dealing with workplace issues such as assessment, coaching and performance management (Society for Industrial and Organizational Psychology, 2011). The focus for applied organizational psychology has been stated by Donaldson and Bligh (2006) to include the following goals:

- Maximize person-job-organization fit and optimal functioning through rigorous selection, socialization and training programs.
- Build optimal team performance.
- Develop organizational leaders.
- Provide effective mentoring and coaching.
- Support career development and planning.
- Foster and capitalize on diversity and cross-cultural relationships.
- Optimize work and family balance.
- Create healthful work environments through comprehensive wellness programs.
- Promote organizational learning and continuous improvement.
- Inspire and facilitate positive organization development and strategic change.

These are all goals that are used throughout FM. Team performance, mentoring, continuous improvement and strategic focus are all required elements of effective FM and should be included in FM education. Courses in organizational psychology may already be taught at many universities and incorporating them into the curriculum for FM degrees is a needed aspect to fulfill the constructionist education.

Teaching Tools Summary

The transactional cognitive perspective is the basis of social constructivism and of effective FM, enabling the facility professional to interact and understand the environment and people utilizing it in tandem. Problem-based learning, collaborative projects and specific instruction in organization psychology help to make FM a true support organization to any company. Without these courses in the FM curriculum at all levels, baccalaureate and graduate, the chances of incorporation of collaborative learning, complete understanding of the environment and people interdependencies key to social constructivist viewpoints and management of the workplaces to satisfy user requirements will be missed. This missing element is critical to effective understanding for development and operations of facilities as workplaces and to avoid suboptimization of the FM's role to that of twentieth-century responder, rather than knowledgeable twenty-first-century advisor and supporter of the organization.

INCORPORATING TEACHING TOOLS
AT APPROPRIATE LEVELS

The abilities of students will vary depending on the level and experience in which the FM course is taught. Obviously, those students at the lower-level undergraduate level will need much more detailed explanations, examples and practice than graduate students who may already be working and have on-the-job experience, as well as educational degrees already under their belts. At all levels, however, the social construction skills will need to be incorporated into an excellent FM curriculum since traditional technical education has not provided those skills to any significant degree.

It is recommended that baccalaureate programs initiate students with problem-based learning from introductory courses, through to the final capstone experiences. Building off of the developmental relationship of social construction learning described in Figure 16.1, students would begin their exposure with development of terms and experiences that have them grasp the importance of how participants in any process impose their own meaning. The primary cognitive tools useful in FM education include information seeking, information presentation, knowledge organization, knowledge integration and knowledge generation (Elliot, Washington & Robertson, 2007).

Information Seeking

Information seeking is a skill most university students have at least some rudimentary knowledge of; yet experience can be enhanced by helping them to find new sources beyond the obvious Google and Internet searches. Often students need assistance with library search skills or they may be unfamiliar with scholarly research journals. Information seeking allows students to expand beyond the limits of their memory to incorporate new materials and refer to these when solving problems. This basic knowledge is fundamental for successful continuing education beyond the basic university education. All baccalaureate students need this fundamental information-seeking skills knowledge in order to progress to more advanced cognitive tools.

Information Presentation

The presentation of information that has been gathered, requires students to assimilate, organize and format the material gained in information seeking, so that their unique viewpoint can be effectively shared with others. Various formats for presentation of materials will be the primary instructional vehicle in this phase of learning cognitive tools. Verbal, graphic and electronic tools such as databases or maps are all tools that students may need to learn. As one of the purportedly most frightening activities identified by adults, presenting before others is a helpful tool for students to practice in order to overcome fear and to hone skills of clarity, confidence and proper speech. Formal instruction in this skill is helpful to both undergraduate and graduate students, especially since it is not a natural skill for most people. Resources abound for presentation skills tips, exercises and training.

Graphic tools are extremely helpful for FMs and teaching appropriate uses in higher education is often ignored. Students need to learn from abundant research that demonstrates which tools are most helpful in specific settings. For example, most FM professionals work daily with architectural drawings, floor plans and building drawings. Initially, students may need to learn the symbols and anatomy of architectural drawing, but they then forget that their customers and clients, the users of the building, are not so familiar with floor plans. Therefore, it is essential that students understand the value of three-dimensional drawings, electronic "fly-through" technologies and other graphics to aid in their presentation of information to others. Even the simple use of pie charts and other graphics are often unknown tools to help explain numerical data for many students.

Knowledge Organization and Integration

A deeper step into cognitive tools is the use of tools to help organize and better understand information. The proper organization of information can lead to knowledge. Students will need to learn how to best organize data. For example, when comparing costs for buildings, should only the rental costs be included? What additional costs would provide meaningful information to fully understand the total costs involved in the use of a building? Tools such as spreadsheets are helpful to organize data and provide meaningful knowledge. Relationships can be found; data can be compared to provide meaning to meaningless numbers.

The integration of knowledge is a higher-level cognitive tool that allows aggregation of previously learned information with additional knowledge. Assessing, verifying, reorganizing and eventually making decisions with information and knowledge are the goals of knowledge integration. Education up to the progression of integration is needed so that students have the appropriate skills to effectively progress with cognitive tools rather than assumptions, guesses or unsubstantiated claims. Demonstrating these skills in the FM working environment will further differentiate the knowledgeable Facility/Facilities Manager and validate their educational skills.

Knowledge Generation

The ultimate level of student performance with cognitive tools is the interaction with information and the ability to represent knowledge in a meaningful format that mirrors cognitive skills and strategies employed through the interaction with the information. Further, the creation of unique learning artifacts is, as Iiyoshi, Hannafin and Wang (2005) point out, important in constructivist-inspired views of learning. This skill is often not expected until the graduate level of study, but it can be a valuable tool to carry to the workplace, as new information, changing technologies and a changing workplace requires that FMs adapt and learn throughout their careers. Generating the knowledge to lead the organization's physical requirements and gain approval by senior management is crucial to FM success.

As with other cognitive tools, knowledge generation is difficult to assess from a grading standpoint. Effective knowledge generation is often not fully clear until it has been proven in practice, but the ability to educate FMs in cognitive tools including knowledge generation is the path toward a constructionist viewpoint. It is worthwhile to negotiate the grading difficulties to provide improved education for the profession. FM education is still evolving and agreement across the world will help to advance the profession and help it to achieve the status it deserves as a senior advisor within the organization.

SUMMARY

Cognitive tools to enable students learning throughout their educational experience and into their FM careers are the key change needed to provide for the FM professional into the future. No longer are only technical skills needed; in addition to technical knowledge, FM education is moving to the social constructionist viewpoint. Just as FM has evolved over its short life, FM education is evolving even more rapidly. The social constructionist viewpoint in FM education can be seen as part of the evolution of FM to a mature discipline that considers not only basic, but more elaborate and thoughtful approaches to educating the fully rounded professional.

NOTES

1. Editors' note: The point is made by this very book. We produced it "in the cloud" using a shared contributors' folder at www.dropbox.com. Pages 247 through 249 give a small example of the dialogue thus enabled

REFERENCES

Dale, K., & Burrell, G. (2006). Working space. *LE1—The Magazine of the University of Leicester, Autumn*, 11.

Donaldson, S., & Bligh, M. (2006). Rewarding careers applying positive psychological science to improve quality of work life and organizational effectiveness. In S. I. Donaldson, D. E. Berger & K. Pezdek (Eds.), *Applied psychology: New frontiers and rewarding careers* (pp. 277–296). Mahwah, NJ: Lawrence Erlbaum Associates.

Elliot, L., Washington, D., & Robertson, B. (2007). Cognitive tools. In M. Orey (Ed.), *Emerging perspectives on learning, teaching, and technology*, unpaginated. Retrieved May 16, 2011, from http://projects.coe.uga.edu/epltt/

Gredler, M. (1997). *Learning and instruction: Theory into practice* (3rd ed.). Upper Saddle River, NJ: Prentice Hall.

Iiyoshi, T., Hannafin, M., & Wang, F. (2005). Cognitive tools and student-centered learning: rethinking tools, functions and applications. *Educational Media International, 42*(4), 281–296.

International Facility Management Association. (2011). Retrieved April 26, 2011, from http://www.ifma.org/events/media-info.htm#history

International Facility Management Association Foundation. (2011). Retrieved June 18, 2011, from http://www.ifmafoundation.org/scholarships/degree.cfm

Lave, J., & Wenger, E. (1991). *Situated learning: Legitimate peripheral participation.* Cambridge: Cambridge University Press.

McMahon, M. (1997). *Social constructivism and the World Wide Web—a paradigm for learning.* Paper presentation to ASCILITE annual conference, December, Perth, Australia.

Society for Industrial and Organizational Psychology. (2011) Retrieved June 18, 2011, from http://www.siop.org/

Part IV

Applications in Practice

17 Conversational Networks in Knowledge Offices

Barry Haynes

The office environment has been a subject of constant debate and evaluation over the years. This constant reevaluation of the office environment has been required because of the changing nature of working practices. Identifying the real purpose of the office requires an understanding of what actually takes place in the office environment (Haynes & Nunnington, 2010).

A simple distinction of the types of office work undertaken would be process work or knowledge work (Laing, Duffy, Jaunzens & Willis, 1998). Initial office working practices consisted of individuals largely undertaking routine and repetitive tasks that replicated the mechanistic way of thinking from the manufacturing sector (Greene & Myerson, 2011; Haynes & Nunnington, 2010). More recently there has been a shift in office working practices to support the knowledge economy (Greene & Myerson, 2011). The design of innovative and creative workplaces has a pivotal role to play in the development of the knowledge economy (Duffy, Craig & Gillian, 2011). However, there is the suggestion that there is an emergence of a new economic cycle called the *creative economy*, which means that the modern office environment needs to stimulate creativity and innovation as well as enable knowledge creation and knowledge transfer (Oseland, Marmot, Swaffer & Ceneda, 2011).

Developments in technology have allowed virtual working to be considered as a viable alternative to working in the office environment. In addition, virtual working has the potential to minimize the need for travel thereby reducing an organization's carbon footprint. However, face-to-face interactions still have a great benefit as they allow nonverbal communications, such as body language, to be used as a means of enhancing the effectiveness of the interaction (Oseland, 2009). Offices that stimulate creative thought and enable innovation through productive working will require workspaces that facilitate face-to-face interaction (Oseland et al., 2011).

KNOWLEDGE AND CREATIVITY

Knowledge work can be undertaken at an individual level or with others in the form of collaborative working. The interaction with others can be planned or can be ad hoc. Whilst planned interactions need structure and time allocations in people's diaries, informal interactions can take place anywhere and at any time. The types of places where these informal inter-actions take place can be tea points, refreshment areas and places where equipment is located, such as printers and copiers (Fayard & Weeks, 2007; Haynes, 2007, 2008a, 2008b). These parts of the office environment can be called *informal interaction points*.

Results from research that identifies the components of office productiv-ity indicate that interactions in the office environment can have the most positive effect on office occupiers' productivity (Haynes, 2007, 2008a, 2008b). One way of making the knowledge stored in peoples' heads (tacit knowledge) into more shared knowledge (explicit knowledge) is through informal social networks. It is through social networks that people develop personal relationships, leading to informal learning, which can form the basis of an organization's social capital (Becker, 2007). Increasing the num-ber of social interactions can lead to a development in knowledge creation and knowledge transfer, leading to accelerated innovation (Oseland, 2009). Using social interactions as a way of increasing knowledge creation can be particularly useful for dynamic firms that have to have a high degree of organizational agility to respond to the rate of change within their sector (Becker, 2007). Identifying ways that social interactions facilitate the transfer of knowledge is an integral part of the design of the modern office environment (Heerwagen, Kampschroer, Powell & Loftness, 2004; Haynes,2008a; Oseland et al., 2011). Interactions within an office environ-ment can be seen as the conduit for knowledge creation and transfer (Heer-wagen et al.; Haynes,2008a) and also creativity and innovation (Sailer, 2011; Oseland et al.).

Sailer acknowledges that creativity is a social process that is difficult to measure. The complexity of establishing a relationship between creativity and the physical space leads her to propose the use of interaction patterns and spatial configuration as a surrogate measure. She adopts a UK media company as a case study and applies a range of research methods to collect data, including a Space Syntax analysis of the floor plans. One of the main findings of this research was that the move into a shared building increased the opportunity for interaction and cross-fertilization of ideas with people in different business units. She argues that the move from six different office locations across London into one shared building has allowed staff to be exposed to other people's ideas, thereby increasing the potential for higher creativity levels.

The significance of an interaction in the creative process is very much dependent on the timing of the interaction. Whilst it would be too sim-plistic to view the creative process as merely a linear continuum (Martens, 2011), it is useful to consider the various phases of creativity and innova-tion (Oseland et al., 2011; Martens; Sailer, 2011). Wallas (1926) identified four stages in the creative process:

1. Preparation: this stage of the process pulls together current facts and data and then organizes them into some form of structure.
2. Incubation: this stage requires time for reflection. Consideration is given to the data and information previously gathered.
3. Illumination: it is at this point in the creative process when a new idea or concept suddenly appears. This could be classified as the "Eureka" moment.
4. Verification: this stage tests the idea to ensure that it can be successfully implemented. It could be argued that the stages preparation and verification could be the stages that may benefit most from collaboration and knowledge sharing.

Allen (1997) proposes that it is this type of creative communication that is most unpredictable and tends to occur in spontaneous encounters that are most affected by architecture. In contrast, the stages incubation and illumination may best be achieved through individual solo working and are therefore undertaken in private spaces (Sailer, 2011). This is partly supported by research undertaken by Oseland et al. (2011)[1], who identified that much creative thought takes place alone. This finding indicates the need for space provision in the office environment for solo working (cf. Beard, Ch. 6). Ultimately, the complex relationship between individual and collaborative working throughout the creative process will be very much dependent upon the problem at hand, the individual's own capabilities and the work settings available.

COLLABORATION AND INDIVIDUAL WORKING

To ensure that the office environment is creative and productive a balance has to be achieved between individual working and collaborative working. Another way of looking at this would be to consider the balance between positive interactions in the office environment and negative distractions (Heerwagen et al., 2004; Haynes, 2007, 2008a, 2008b). My research identifies the impact of positive interactions and negative distractions on office occupiers' productivity. The initial 27 evaluative variables used in the analysis were reduced to four distinct components using factor analysis. Two of the components related to the physical environment and its impact on perceived productivity (comfort and layout). The other two components related to the social dynamics within an office and therefore can be considered to be the behavioral environment (interaction and distraction). The four components of office productivity were subsequently used to form a scale against which the results could be measured. The results revealed that it was the behavioral components of interaction and distraction that were having the most impact on office occupiers' perceived productivity.

The interaction component was perceived to be having the most positive impact on office occupiers' productivity with the main variables loading onto this component being social interaction, work interaction and creative physical environment. The results indicate that office occupiers value both work and social interactions and also the process of creativity as means of enhancing their productivity. The distraction component was perceived to have the most negative impact on perceived productivity with the main variables loading onto this component being interruptions, crowding and noise. These results indicate the need for individual, distraction-free solo working.

In an open-plan office environment it can be difficult for office occupiers to identify if their interaction with a colleague will have a positive or negative impact on their productivity. This can be encapsulated in the term *one person's interaction is another person's distraction*. This highlights the need for designated collaborative working areas and individual private work areas. Establishing the right balance of office space for interactive collaborative working and individual distraction-free working is a complex problem. However, part of the solution would be the provision of a range of different workplace settings specifically designed for different work activities (Sailer, 2011). A research project entitled the *Welcoming Workplace* identified that there was a need to support different work styles (Smith, 2008). The three workspaces proposed were as follows:

- Spaces to concentrate: these would be designated private areas that would allow distraction-free working. These areas allow office workers to totally concentrate on the problem. This deep level of thinking is sometimes referred to as the "flow state" (DeMarco & Lister, 1987; Martens, 2011).
- Space to collaborate: spaces included in this category are spaces that allow working to be undertaken with another person or a group of people. An essential component of collaborative work areas is the fact that people can feel comfortable talking without being conscious that they may be distracting other people.
- Spaces to contemplate: these spaces allow people time away from the normal everyday activities of the office environment so that they can refresh and recuperate.

Parkin, Austin, Pinder and Baguley (2011) used case study analysis to evaluate the difference between two different academic environments with regard to support for collaboration and privacy. The first case used in the evaluation adopted an open-plan office design and provided academics with a desk in a shared/open area of the office with some facilities for individual working. In the second a combi-office design was adopted and academics were provided with an individual study office (10.2 square meters) and access to shared/social work settings. The findings of this research identified that when it comes to office environments that provide the best support for collaboration and privacy, academics reported a higher level of satisfaction with the combi-office design than the open-plan office design.

Whilst individual working may be a solitary exercise allowing incubation of ideas, the collaborative working process is more dynamic. The means to achieving collaboration can be both informal and formal. The formal approach would be that a meeting room is booked at a certain time and an agenda is sent out before the meeting including all the matters to be discussed during the meeting. An informal approach would include the chance conversation by the photocopier (Fayard & Weeks, 2007).

Hua, Loftness, Kraut and Powell (2010) undertook a two-year multisite field study of workplace settings in an attempt to evaluate both formal and informal collaborative spaces. They identified that office occupiers preferred a range of places for casual conversations and collaborative work. When it came to casual conversations, most respondents (82.3%) identified the individual workstation as the preferred place for this type of interaction. In addition, 32.8% of participants reported kitchen and coffee areas as the preferred places for casual conversations. In contrast, meeting rooms are the preferred place for collaborative work (88.6%) and individual workstations are the next preferred place for collaborative work (52.8%).

However, unplanned interactions can have a significant impact on the knowledge sharing and knowledge transfer and productivity within an office environment (Haynes, 2007, 2008a, 2008b). Therefore, rather than these interactions occurring by chance they could be facilitated by the inclusion of more informal interaction points, which would create more possibilities for ad hoc conversations. This means that there is a need to understand how these interaction points work, and consideration should be given to their location to maximize these acts of serendipity.

INTERACTION AND MOBILITY

The concepts of office worker interaction and mobility need to be ingrained into the office building design. Mobility and interaction could be increased by the inclusion of a main connecting pathway throughout the office building. This main pathway is usually referred to as the *street*. One way of understanding how interactions occur in the workplace would be through the consideration of office worker movement within the office building. Therefore, mobility can be a useful way of categorizing different types of office workers (Greene & Myerson, 2011). Mobility will now be used to classify office worker activity.

Low-Level Mobility

This is where the office worker tends to stay at their desk for the majority of the working day. This type of worker is relatively static in the office and so can potentially act as a form of anchor within the office environment. This means that people know that they will always be there and therefore are seen as a constant within the office environment. The low-mobility worker will probably be the type of person that will have a good overview of what is happening within the office. This makes them a very good resource with useful information about everyday office activities.

The low-mobility office worker acts as a form of glue within the office environment. They not only act as an anchor, but can also act as an attractor within the office environment. This means that by acting as an attractor the low-level mobility worker attracts other office workers to their desk. The type of interactions and conversations that occur at the low-mobility workers desk could be either social interactions or work interactions. The balance of social interactions to work interactions will be largely dependent on the worker's personality type and their level of authority within the organization. It is the social interactions that can potentially enhance the office worker productivity (Haynes, 2007, 2008a, 2008b). It is through the development of working relationships that common bonds and values can be developed that could be classified as the social capital of the office environment (Gensler, 2008).

Medium-Level Mobility

These are office workers that have a higher degree of flexibility than the low-level mobility workers. The increased flexibility means that medium-level mobility workers can work in a range of different types of office space either within the office environment or throughout the office building. Medium-level mobility workers can be classified as the people who leave their jackets over their chairs but are not always at their desks (Greene & Myerson, 2011). The frequency of movement of this kind of office worker will be dependent on the types of attractors in the office and the building. The attractors cause people to move around the office, and the building can take a number of different forms. An attractor can be a person, a place or an activity.

- People attractors: medium-level mobility workers will be drawn to people attractors for either one of two reasons. The interaction will be work related and therefore will be some form of knowledge exchange. The other type of interaction will be social interaction that may not be directly work-related but will help to develop relationships that could be the basis for future work collaborations (Gensler, 2008).
- Workplace attractors: these will relate to office facilities that are generally required by an office worker. They will include such things as post room, printer/photocopier room, resources room, breakout area, café bar, restaurant, etc.

- Activity attractors: in this situation, it will be the actual activity that will determine the purpose of the attractor. Therefore, this will relate to all kinds of meetings including: one-to-ones, staff/group meetings, departmental meetings and informal social get-togethers.

The frequency of interactions of people can be considered to be dependent on the distance traveled to facilitate the interaction (Allen, 1977). People who sit in close proximity are more likely to bump into each other than with people who are situated at the opposite ends of the office environment. The implications are that the location of office workers (co-presence) can have an impact on the amount and frequency of knowledge sharing (Allen, 1977; Appel-Meulenbroek 2010).

High-Level Mobility

The high-level mobility worker will spend most of their working day outside the office environment. This type of office worker can be best classified as a worker who visits the office rather than a worker that is constantly in the office (Greene & Myerson, 2011). Since this type of office worker is not always in the office environment it would be inefficient to allocate them a dedicated desk. This means that high-level mobility workers will tend to adopt a nonterritorial work practice when in the office. The very fact that high-level mobility workers will not tend to have a dedicated desk means that they will be required to either share a desk or find an appropriate work area somewhere within the office environment or even elsewhere in the building. The nature of high-level mobility working means that this type of worker will probably work within a wide range of office settings and will have to move around the office or the building to get to those work settings. It is this act of movement that creates the possibility of chance interactions with other colleagues that can lead to new opportunities for knowledge sharing and knowledge creation (Becker, 2007).

OFFICE NODES AND NETWORKS

The office environment can be considered as consisting of a number of different nodes. A node could be a person such as the low-level mobility worker who acts as an anchor within the office environment. Alternatively, a node could be a specific work setting designated for a particular activity such as printer room, breakout area, etc. A knowledge worker that is predominantly out of the office environment may view the office itself as a node in their network (Greene & Myerson, 2011). Whilst the positioning of the nodes within the office environment will give an office its structure, it will be the nodes' use, and the movement to and from the nodes, that will determine whether the office environment works or not.

It is the movement of office workers to the office nodes that establishes office networks.

The possibility of interactions with other colleagues is increased as office worker movement around the office and the building increases (Becker, 2007). Therefore, strategic positioning of nodes can be a useful strategy to try to maximize office worker movement. Informal interactions caused by movement tend to be ad hoc and usually turn into conversations by bumping into people in places such as the corridor, the coffee/tea area or by the watercooler (Fayard & Weeks, 2007; Haynes, 2007, 2008a, 2008b; Appel-Meulenbroek, 2010). Becker terms these informal interaction points as *neutral zones*. Since these neutral areas are not actually owned by anyone, they may allow an employee who has a lower status in the organization to interact and challenge the ideas of an employee who has a higher status within the organization. These types of interaction can potentially allow a more open and honest discussion, leading to the free flow of ideas.

Appel-Meulenbroek's research indicates that knowledge sharing occurs simply because people bump into each other. In addition, coincidental meetings that are undertaken in the hallway and at the coffee machine take place significantly more often than intentional meetings. Since these informal interactions can create situations for knowledge sharing, it makes sense that nodes are strategically positioned to maximize positive interactions rather than these interactions being left to chance or serendipity. Increased office worker mobility can lead to enhanced informal interactions, which could potentially lead to increased productivity and creativity.

The nodes within the office environment can act as interaction points. One obvious node that has the great potential to increase interactions and conversations is the photocopier/printer room (Fayard & Weeks, 2007). If a large open-plan office environment shares the photocopier/printer room then there is the possibility for people to interact informally whilst in the photocopier/printer room (Fayard & Weeks; Haynes, 2007, 2008a, 2008b). It is this type of informal interaction that can lead to the development of the organization's social capital.

Nodes can be strategically positioned around the office environment to enhance the possibility of interactions with the other work colleagues. They can also be positioned around an office building to actually get people to move around the building. This increases the chance of interaction not only with their usual work colleagues, but also with members of the organization that they do not normally meet (Becker, 2007). This could be one way of developing cross-selling opportunities as well as enabling a cross-fertilization of ideas within an organization (Sailer, 2011).

A node that could create office worker movement around the building is the post room, since individuals will need to visit it on a fairly regular basis to pick up their post. The post room has the potential to bring together office workers from different parts of the organization and therefore could facilitate interactions between members of different departments. In this way there is the possibility that informal conversations could foster the development of the organization's social capital. It is these kinds of conversations that could lead to product developments and cross-selling. These kinds of informal interactions and conversations can be encouraged with the creation of spaces that enable people to connect in the workplace. In addition, an organization's culture can be supported and enhanced through workplace connectivity (Haynes, 2008b).

The probability of a positive informal interaction in an office node could be improved by the manipulation of a number of factors. The number of times that the office node is visited (frequency), the amount of time spent in the office node (duration) and the quality of the office node (quality).

- Office node frequency: the number of times an office node is visited can be increased by the use of attractors. Using the printer/photocopier room as an example, the attractor in this instance would be the requirement to pick up printed documents or undertake copying. This means that the office worker is probably attracted to the printer/photocopier room on a number of occasions throughout the day.
- Office node duration: the longer the office worker spends in the node, the more opportunity to engage in informal interaction with other colleagues. It is therefore important that the office worker has a reason to dwell in the node. Again, using the printer/photocopier room as an example, the kinds of things that would keep an office worker in the printer/photocopier room could be a notice board that contains both organizational information as well as information about social activities. In addition, a table and some chairs could be placed either in or near the printer/photocopier room for the possibility that an informal interaction could turn into a more meaningful conversation.
- Office node quality: Oseland et al. (2011) established that the number of interactions undertaken in an interaction space was dependent on the quality of the space provided. They propose that the meeting space quality could be improved by paying attention to the physical space and facilities such as: temperature and air quality, lighting, flexible furniture, IT and audio visual equipment, room size, seamless technology, color and clear labeling.

If office nodes are to act as informal interaction points, then there is a need to consider their location. Two factors that should be considered with regards to the location of interaction points are accessibility and privacy. The accessibility factor can be addressed by locating informal interaction points near primary circulation routes. However, to ensure a level of privacy is achieved the informal interaction points will need a certain level of screening (Oseland, 2009).

One way of facilitating and enhancing the number of interactions in an office environment would be the inclusion of a range of different work settings in which different work styles can be undertaken. As Becker (2007) identified, increasing the variety and range of different work settings increases the possible interactions leading to informal learning. Similarly, Oseland et al. (2011) identified that more meetings take place in office buildings that have more meeting space available. However, they also identified that on average meeting rooms were only used 37% of the time.

CONCLUSIONS

The office environment still has a vital role to play in today's business world. It enables and facilitates face-to-face interaction, which allows the development of social networks. Social networks in the office can play an instrumental part in the creating and transferring of knowledge. In addition, workspaces that enable and enhance collaboration can lead to the development of social capital, which is increasingly becoming a highly valued asset. However, the social dynamics of the office need to be understood and a balance has to be struck between workspaces that allow collaborative working and workspaces that allow private, distraction-free work.

Informal interactions can add value to an organization either through cross-fertilization of ideas or cross-selling. Unfortunately, informal interactions tend to occur through serendipity. Therefore, a more strategic approach would be to create office environments that actively facilitate informal interactions. A way of encouraging informal interactions is through the movement of office workers around the office workplace or office building. Office worker movement could be facilitated by the number, and location, of different work settings (nodes). Increasing the number of different work settings (nodes) encourages movement and the possibility of informal interaction. In essence, the development of an organization's social capital can be influenced and enhanced through the use of office nodes. Each office worker will develop his or her own unique social network when working in the office environment. It is the collective social networks of office workers that form an integral part of the *connected workplace*.

NOTES

1. Editors note: With modern ICT private space need not equate with having a dedicated office.

REFERENCES

Allen, T. (1977). *Managing the flow of technology.* Cambridge, MA: MIT Press.
Allen, T. (1997). *Architecture and communications among product development engineers* (Working papers 165–97. Sloan School of Management). Cambridge,

MA: MIT Press. Retrieved June 6, 2011, from http://www.enpiprocess.com/doc/Colocation%20on%20Communication.htm

Appel-Meulenbroek, R. (2010). Knowledge sharing through co-presence: Added value of facilities. *Facilities, 28*(3/4), 189–205.

Becker, F. (2007). Organizational ecology and knowledge networks. *California Management Review, 49*(2), 42–61.

DeMarco, T., & Lister, T. (1987). *Peopleware: Productive projects and teams.* New York: Dorset House.

Duffy, F., Craig, D., & Gillian, N. (2011). Purpose, process, place: Design as a research tool. *Facilities, 29*(3/4), 97–113.

Fayard, A.-L., & Weeks, J. (2007). Photocopiers and water-coolers. *Organization Studies, 28*(5), 605–634.

Gensler. (2008). *2008 workplace survey: United States.* Retrieved May 26, 2011, from http://www.gensler.com/uploads/documents/2008_Gensler_Workplace_Survey_US_09_30_2009.pdf

Greene, C., & Myerson, J. (2011). Space for thought: Designing for knowledge workers. *Facilities, 29*(1/2), 19–30.

Haynes, B. P. (2007). Office productivity: A theoretical framework. *Journal of Corporate Real Estate, 9*(2), 97–110.

Haynes, B. P. (2008a). An evaluation of the impact of office environment on productivity. *Facilities, 26*(5/6), 178–195.

Haynes, B. P. (2008b). Impact of workplace connectivity on office productivity. *Journal of Corporate Real Estate, 10*(4), 286–302.

Haynes, B. P., & Nunnington, N. (2010). *Corporate real estate asset management.* Oxford: Elsevier.

Heerwagen, J., Kampschroer, K., Powell, K., & Loftness, V. (2004). Collaborative knowledge work environments. *Building Research & Information, 32*(6), 510–528.

Hua, Y., Loftness, V., Kraut, R., & Powell, K. (2010). Workplace collaborative space layout typology and occupant perception of collaboration environment. *Environment and Planning B: Planning and Design, 37*(3), 429–448.

Laing, A., Duffy, F., Jaunzens, D., & Willis, S. (1998). *New environments for working: The redesign of offices and environmental systems for new ways of working.* London: Construction Research Communication.

Martens, Y. (2011). Creative workplace: Instrumental and symbolic support for creativity. *Facilities, 29*(1/2), 63–79.

Oseland, N. (2009). Enhancing interaction. *Facilities Management, November,* 22–23.

Oseland, N., Marmot, A., Swaffer, F., & Ceneda, S. (2011). Environments for successful interactions. *Facilities, 29*(1/2), 50–62.

Parkin, J. K., Austin, S., Pinder, J., & Baguley, T. S. (2011). Balancing collaboration and privacy in academic workplaces. *Facilities, 29*(1/2), 31–49.

Sailer, K. (2011). Creativity as a social and spatial process. *Facilities, 29*(1/2), 6–18.

Smith, J. (2008). *Welcoming workplace: Designing office space for an ageing workforce in the 21st century knowledge economy.* Retrieved May 26, 2011, from http://www.hhc.rca.ac.uk/cms/files/welcomingworkplaceguidance.pdf

Wallas, G. (1926). *The art of thought.* New York: Harcourt, Brace and Company.

18 Creating Effective Learning Environments
Meeting the Challenges

Jenny Thomas

In the creation of an effective learning environment there are two issues that require careful thought. The first is what actually makes an effective learning environment, and the second is how we measure this effectiveness. These were thoughts preoccupying School X when they were granted Building Schools for the Future[1] (BSF) funding. A secondary school north of Manchester, they were learning in buildings that were in a poor state of repair and not fit for purpose. With a strong leadership team and an understanding of what they wanted to be able to do in the new building, the school wanted an effective learning environment that would help them achieve their educational aims and provide a positive learner experience. But how could the school influence the design to ensure that the learning environment created was effective once in use?

The learning environment has long been thought of as a static, fixed entity that can be evaluated deterministically, primarily in terms of quality. Little consideration has been given to usability; the impact of the building upon people and people upon the building. The users themselves seem to be the forgotten element in understanding the effectiveness of the learning environment, but their experience of the learning environment needs to be taken into account.

Price, Clark, Holland, Emerton and Wolstenholme (2009 p. 19) argue, "Facilities Management, as an activity, still suffers from a tendency to concern itself with the physical building rather than with that building's intended influence on those who use it and the purpose for which it was constructed." Evaluations of schools by FMs, and other professionals from the design industry, tend to focus upon very specific aspects of the building that can be objectively measured, such as the temperature or size of classrooms, and they are used solely to inform future design rather than effective use of the environment.

An increased interest in creating environments that perform sustainably, particularly in an environmental sense, has prompted greater interest in considering the operation and use of an environment as well as the design. Soft Landings[2] is a process that focuses upon the operation and performance of an environment in use. It encourages consideration of the building in operation right from the briefing and design phases to ensure it meets users' needs through to aftercare once the building has been handed over. *Soft Landings for Schools: Case Studies* (Buckley, Bordass & Bunn, 2010) explores the effectiveness of the framework when applied to learning environments. The findings begin to demonstrate how the operation of the building can, and should, be considered to shape the design and use of school facilities, making them more effective. However, Soft Landings is still heavily focused upon the building fabric and mechanical and electrical (M&E) systems. There is little emphasis placed upon impact of the school environment in terms of the user experience and no consideration of education outcomes. What appears to be required is an evaluation process centered on the users and their experience rather than simply the building fabric.

Effective engagement with users early on in the process has had a positive impact upon the designs developed (Woolner, Hall, Wall & Dennison, 2007). However, few research studies have demonstrated the impact of true participation of students. Where users of the learning environment have been involved, there is a much greater and in-depth understanding of the impact of the learning environment obtained. In one such study, Maxwell (2000) discovered that there was a difference between the staff and parent perceptions and the perceptions of students in relation to health and safety in their school. Areas such as the classrooms and toilets influenced students' perceptions of whether the school was welcoming and safe, whereas for adults these spaces were less significant. The staff and parents tended to consider the cleanliness of public areas such as the main entrance as being a more important influence. This highlights the difference between users' experiences and the importance of considering the effectiveness of the learning environment from their point of view. So there is evidence that the effectiveness of the environment can be measured and the usability of that environment understood. But does the learning environment really make a difference?

THE IMPACT OF THE LEARNING ENVIRONMENT

Headlines based upon studies taking a very broad, high-level view of the capital investment in the BSF program decried the lack of a significant relationship between investment in these schools and improved exam results (Durbin & Yeshanew, 2010). But more in-depth research suggests a link between the learning environment and the user experience. This is being used to develop a greater understanding of what makes an effective learning environment.

At a theoretical level, the premise of the Third Teacher has been developed by a team of designers to clarify the impact of the learning environment (O'Donnell et al., 2010). It is based upon the work of Loris Malaguzzi in the 1940s; he founded the Reggio Emilia approach. He argued that children develop through various interactions at different levels. The first level is their interaction with adults, which include parents and teachers. The second is their peers. The third level is the interaction between children and their environment. Thus, the learning environment became classified as the Third Teacher.

Other work supports the Third Teacher concept. Higgins, Hall, Wall, Woolner and McCaughey (2005) reviewed literature to find evidence of the impact of learning environments. Their research revealed not only the impact of certain aspects of the environment, but also the nature and complexity of the relationship between users and the learning environment. One of the main findings was that the multifaceted nature of environments made it difficult to draw clear and direct links between a learning environment and educational outcomes. The researchers note that much of the reviewed research focused upon a specific aspect of the environment, such as temperature. However, the potential relationships between aspects of the environment and the combined impact that they might have are less well researched. From their review Higgins et al. also warn against architectural determinism and advocate the benefits of engaging users in the design and operation of buildings. They noted that various users have different perceptions and needs and that the attitude and behavior of staff were vitally important to the use made of the space, which supports the argument of Soft Landings but in a much more holistic way.

Further research into the impact of real-life learning environments supports the review's findings. Barrett and Zhang (2009) evaluated a number of primary schools. They concluded (p. iv), "Considerable evidence shows that there is an explicit relationship between the physical characteristics of school buildings, and the spaces within them, and educational outcomes." Thus, at a theoretical level it is reasonable to accept that the environment has some impact upon users' experience of the environment and education outcomes. However, the impact is complex, and in measuring effectiveness it will not always be easy to draw direct correlations between the environment and education outcomes. Others have reached similar conclusions. Price et al. (2009) considered the influences on attainment and categorized them as: social characteristics, economic characteristics, school organizational characteristics and pupil physical factors, alongside environmental physical factors. This again supports the Third Teacher concept. However, they also include a category of environment intangibles such as condition as an indicator of worth, symbolism of the environment, social behaviors controlled by space, etc. These are the indirect impacts of the environment upon users and contribute to the effectiveness of the environment as much as the tangible, physical factors.

The British Council for School Environments (BCSE) reached a similar conclusion as part of their Great Schools Inquiry, aspects of which are summarized in their publication *School Environments Charter: A Blueprint for British Schools* (BCSE, 2010). Based upon a meta-analysis of the factors that affect attainment in education (Hattie, 2008) BCSE developed a three-

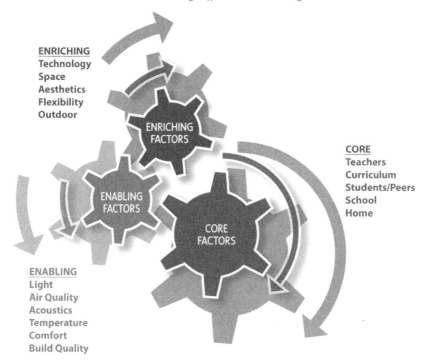

ENRICHING
Technology
Space
Aesthetics
Flexibility
Outdoor

CORE
Teachers
Curriculum
Students/Peers
School
Home

ENABLING
Light
Air Quality
Acoustics
Temperature
Comfort
Build Quality

Figure 18.1   Blueprint for a school (BCSE, 2010).

level model to illustrate the impact that the learning environment has upon users and educational outcomes (Figure 18.1).

At the heart the core factors, identified by Hattie, refer to things in their lives that have the greatest, direct impact upon education. BCSE have taken these core factors and identified how the learning environment enables and enriches them. The enabling factors are those that have a primarily physiological impact upon users and a direct impact upon educational outcomes, e.g., attainment. Failure at a basic level to get these factors right has been found to have a negative impact upon users and the occupying educational organization.

The enriching factors are those that have a practical, psychological or emotional impact upon people. Their presence or absence does not necessarily affect people's ability to teach or learn, but they may motivate or stimulate them indirectly through impact upon self-esteem, mood, etc. BCSE recognizes that Figure 18.1 does not contain an exhaustive list, but argues that these are the aspects of the environment that have been researched with evidence to demonstrate that they are linked to educational outcomes.

Taken together, these theories of the learning environment support an effect upon the user experience and reveal that the relationship is both direct and indirect. It is also important to realize that the effectiveness of the environment is not purely the result of the design of the environment; actual use plays a significant role in effectiveness. The need to understand the impact of the environment is clear, but if users are the ones who will benefit from a greater understanding of effectiveness, should students and school staff be taking more ownership of their environment and demanding to know the impact that it is having upon educational outcomes?

DETERMINING THE EFFECTIVENESS OF THE ENVIRONMENT

Before further considering the responsibility of evaluations, let us look in more detail at the process of evaluation. The first thing to recognize is that an evaluation needs to be holistic, including performance data, user perceptions and objective measures of the environment. Performance data include objective measures of educational outcomes such as attainment, behavior, attendance, etc., and those more specific to a particular school such as community use of their facilities. The most common way for user perceptions to be gathered is through the use of questionnaires and/or workshops. The perceptions of a large cross section of people who use the learning environment can be gathered using questionnaires. Patterns can be established to demonstrate in what ways the majority of users are satisfied and dissatisfied. Workshops allow the reasons for collective responses from the questionnaires to be explored and links between the learning environment and educational outcomes to be established. Through discussions with a representative sample of users of the learning environment, large quantities of qualitative information can be gathered and analyzed. Objective measures of the environment are usually taken by an industry expert, such as an FM specialist, engineer or architect, who makes an objective assessment of the building fabric and performance such as energy bills and required maintenance, etc.

An evaluation of learning environments should be conducted at least one year after moving into a new building. This is to allow people to settle into the building and for any novelty factor to wear off. People will have settled into a pattern of teaching and learning and the ongoing, longer-term impact of the environment will be easier to measure.

The people involved in the evaluation from the educational organization should be representatives of a range of user groups, including students, teaching staff, nonteaching staff, governors, community users, parents, etc. This is because each of the users will have a different perception of the learning environment. This can be illustrated with an example of the toilets provided within a learning environment as the priorities of user groups will differ. Students want a pleasant environment they perceive to be safe to use with no risk of bullying. For teaching staff supervision is a priority. For cleaning and maintenance staff, ease of cleaning and keeping the facilities in a good state of repair are cited as being important. A positive user experience of the learning environment or aspects of it, for example, the toilets, will be obtained when the provision satisfies the requirements of all users. Therefore, to be effective the evaluation needs to be holistic in terms of incorporating the perceptions of a diverse range of users, including all aspects of the environment from enabling to enriching factors and based upon both quantitative and qualitative data.

BARRIERS TO EVALUATIONS

The importance and benefits of evaluation are clear. And the need for users to be intrinsically involved is key. Despite this, there are few systematic post-occupancy evaluations of learning environments published for economic and practical reasons. However, by exploring the barriers to post-occupancy evaluation we can establish a potential solution working with the schools and students, expanding upon the work of Price et al. (2009) and the BCSE (2010).

One of the practical barriers is that design teams are concerned about negative results reflecting badly upon them and their work. By adjusting the focus and outcomes of the evaluation to address usability and management of the space the positive results of an evaluation can be emphasized. This links with a common user perception and second barrier that once a building is completed and handed over it is a fait accompli. Again, adjusting the focus to usability ensures that ongoing benefits from a learning environment can be realized through evaluation.

A further practical barrier is having the appropriate resources, in terms of time, participants and expertise, to carry out an evaluation. As discussed earlier, the most effective evaluations involved a wide, diverse range of users. However, the time required to conduct an in-depth, user-centered evaluation, rather than building centered, requires participants to contribute a significant amount of their time. Thus, there need to be benefits to them. Additionally, where possible, it needs to be linked to the curriculum to give it ongoing relevance. On the issue of expertise, to set up and coordinate an evaluation requires an independent facilitator to ensure that the information collected is useful, high quality and accurately analyzed. This allows unbiased information to be collected from a wide range of people and the impact of the building and user experience to be fully understood.

These practical barriers contribute to a significant economic barrier. Involving an independent facilitator and the other resources required such as the time given by the participants all has a cost. It is therefore essential that the benefit derived from the evaluation is great enough to justify the expenditure. By providing the school with information about how they use the environment and the impact that the learning environment is having upon education outcomes allows them to benefit by making changes and creating an even more effective learning environment.

With the practical and economic barriers removed through understanding the benefits of evaluation, the question of responsibility can be addressed. Traditionally, architects had responsibility for carrying out evaluations of their completed buildings. In 1965 it was included as Stage M: Feedback in the Royal Institute of British Architects (RIBA) Plan of Work (RIBA, 1965). However, it was omitted in future editions (Hughes, 2003). More recently there has been an increased interest in evaluation from the building services industry as engineers and FMs recognize the importance of understanding how a building is performing from an environmental sustainability perspective. However, as found with Soft Landings, the focus of these evaluations is the building itself rather than a holistic approach including usability. Therefore, if users recognize the benefits of evaluating the effectiveness of the learning environment, have the methods and resource and take some of the responsibility to ensure that the environment is understood, this may lead to a greater understanding of what makes an effective learning environment.

EFFECTIVE LEARNING ENVIRONMENTS IN PRACTICE

Although the research has tended to be building focused, there are examples of user-centered evaluations giving students an understanding of their environment and the opportunity to ensure it is effective. A number of post-occupancy evaluations were conducted by the BCSE of completed BSF schools. The focus of these evaluations was the user experience and the impact of the learning environment on educational outcomes. The evaluations followed the methodology described earlier and the results were analyzed to begin to determine what constituted an effective learning environment. A small sample of just 5 schools precludes drawing definitive conclusions applicable to all learning environments. However, some anecdotal examples of the findings will demonstrate the importance of evaluation and the impact of gaining a more holistic understanding of the environment.

One aspect of the learning environment that was highlighted by the evaluations of all the schools participating was the external landscape. Typically the students and staff from the schools liked the landscaping but used it very little for learning other than sport. Knowing that users liked the space but didn't use it raised the question of why. Exploring the user experience of outside spaces revealed that there was an issue of restrictions, with students believing that there were many aspects of the external landscape that they could not access at break times. However, these restrictions appeared to be inconsistent; students were confused about the rules and their beliefs differed from the actual, or lack of, restrictions revealed by the head teacher. This was a matter of recognizing the desire to use the external landscape and developing effective communication to ensure that everyone knew the official terms of use to provide a more positive user experience.

Another example that clearly highlights how understanding the effectiveness of the learning environment can have a positive impact is that of the staff room. In some of the schools evaluated there were large, centralized staff rooms for both socializing and working. In other schools there were dispersed staff bases located in the different departments. Evaluations revealed both 'positives' and 'negatives' with each design that need to be recognized so the way in which the learning environment is managed can mitigate against negatives. Centralized staff rooms were found to bring staff together from different departments, which facilitated cross-departmental working. The staff had a better understanding of their students as they were able to discuss them informally during breaks and recognize patterns of working or behavior across a day or week rather than a single lesson period. However a centralized staffroom was naturally a fair distance from some teachers' rooms, and they therefore found that much of the break was spent traveling to and from the staff room.

More dispersed staff bases were much easier for staff to get to at break times and staff often felt they were easier environments to work in as there were fewer distractions. However, the evaluation also highlighted that with dispersed staffrooms there was less interaction on a daily basis between departments and this had an impact upon a broader understanding of students. Newly qualified teachers also raised the issue of finding it harder to settle into the school as their level of interaction with other staff was relatively low. Understanding the impact of the design of the learning environment meant that changes to management could be put in place to increase the effectiveness. With centralized staffrooms this might be providing tea points around the school and in schools with dispersed staff bases it might be ensuring gatherings are arranged to ensure all staff members are meeting regularly and sharing knowledge.

The work of the BCSE is supported by Price et al. (2009), who conducted an evaluation with students in two schools. Their aim was to develop and refine a research instrument to encourage user-centered evaluations. With only two schools in the sample, Price et al. accept that much like the BCSE work there are not enough data to draw strong conclusions. However, there were some indications of what made a positive learning environment, including the importance of social learning spaces; availability of space throughout the day, such as dining halls; condition of the building and fixtures; and maintenance and cleanliness. What was of significant interest was the benefit of the pupil-centered evaluation that they developed and their recognition that the environment had both direct, tangible effects and indirect, psychological effects upon the users.

The method of evaluation developed by Price et al. (2009) evolved as they began working with the students. Finding a focus group in the head teachers' office a little stilted, they invited the students to lead them on a tour of the school, identifying both the positive and negative aspects of the learning environment. Insightful discussions led to valuable qualitative data being obtained, which was used to inform the development of a survey so that a wider group of students could rate their perceptions of the learning environment. The results support many of the findings from previous research, including the BCSE post-occupancy evaluations in terms of what makes a learning environment effective. The findings also highlighted the existence of both tangible and intangible factors in relation to the learning environment. From the data gathered it appeared that the intangible factors such as it being a motivational environment were more important than single, tangible aspects like the temperature.

Thus, it can be understood that FMs need to start considering the way in which an environment impacts upon those who use it and educational outcomes rather than focusing on the building fabric. Taking this into account, and the importance of involving the users, brings us to an interesting proposition. Could the students and staff take on some responsibility for managing their facilities if they had an understanding of the effectiveness of the learning environment?

SUMMARY AND CONCLUSIONS

In this chapter I have explored the notion that a learning environment is more than just the building fabric, and that how it is used is an important contributor to its effectiveness. Thus, the focus needs to be upon users, including the students and staff, and their interaction with the built environment. This will provide an understanding of the user experience and the impact of the learning environment upon educational outcomes. The complexity of understanding the effectiveness of the environment has been highlighted and the direct and indirect relationships between users and their learning environment discussed. The process of evaluation and the gathering of both quantitative and qualitative information (cf. Cairns, Ch. 8) highlighted the need to ensure that an evaluation was student and staff centered and that the understanding gained could influence a school's use of their space. Adopting this approach, and removing the usual barriers to evaluation such as use of resources, has produced positive results. The BCSE (2010) and Price et al. (2009) have conducted user-centered evaluations, and a much more in-depth and greater understanding of the effectiveness of the environment has been obtained.

Evaluating how a building can facilitate effective use will help designers in the future create environments that can have a positive impact upon users. At the same time, users need to understand how their environment affects them and vice versa to make the most effective use of their space. With an interest but a lack of systematic and widespread uptake of evaluations by those designing learning environments, it might be time for users to recognize the importance of understanding the impact of the learning environment and encourage evaluations.

So, what does this mean for School X? How can they build upon their participation in the design development to ensure that they create an effective learning environment? Firstly, they need to understand and recognize their own needs and aspirations, from the perspective of all users. This needs to be explored in the context of the learning environment and incorporated within the design to support the way in which the school will operate. Once completed, the school can evaluate the effectiveness of its environment to gain a greater understanding of usability in terms of the user experience and the link between the learning environment and educational outcomes. Taking this approach, School X will have the knowledge to create a truly effective learning environment to support the vision of their school.

NOTES

1. A program to renew schools across the UK via public–private partnerships.
2. For much more detailed information on the process, see *The Soft Landings Framework* (Usable Building Trust, 2009).

REFERENCES

Barrett, P., & Zhang, Y. (2009). *Optimal learning spaces: Design implications for primary schools* (SCRI Report No. 2). Salford: SCRI.

British Council for School Environments. (2010). *School environments charter: A blueprint for British schools.* London: BCSE.

Buckley, M., Bordass, B., & Bunn, R. (Eds.). (2010). *Soft landings for schools: Case studies.* Berkshire: BSRIA.

Durbin, B., & Yeshanew, T. (2010). *BSF school report.* Berkshire: National Foundation for Education Research.

Hattie, J. (2008). *Visible learning: A synthesis of over 800 meta-analyses relating to achievement.* London: Routledge.

Higgins, S., Hall, E., Wall, K., Woolner, P., & McCaughey, C. (2005). *The impact of school environments: A literature review.* London: Design Council.

Hughes, W. P. (2003). A comparison of two editions of the RIBA plan of work. *Engineering, Construction and Architectural Management, 10*(5), 302–311.

Maxwell, L. E. (2000). A safe and welcoming school: What student, teachers and parents think. *Journal of Architectural and Planning Research, 17*(4), 271–282.

O'Donnell, Wicklund, Pigozzi and Peterson, Architects Inc., VS Furniture & Bruce Mau Design. (2010). *The third teacher.* New York: Harry N. Abrams.

Price, I., Clark, E., Holland, M., Emerton, C., & Wolstenholme, C. (2009). *Condition matters: Pupil voices on the design and condition of secondary schools.* Reading, Berkshire: CfBT Education Trust.

Royal Institute of British Architects. (1965). *The architect's handbook of professional practice.* London: RIBA.

Usable Buildings Trust. (2009). *The soft landings framework.* Berkshire: BSRIA.

Woolner, P., Hall, E., Wall, K., & Dennison, D. (2007). Getting together to improve the school environment: User consultation, participatory design and student voice. *Improving Schools, 10*, 233–248.

19 Dense Networks and Managed Dialogue
The Impact on the Patient Environment

Rachel Macdonald

The United Kingdom's National Health Service (NHS) provides an interesting test bed for comparative managerial research. Despite being national, it is far from homogenous; standards of service vary widely. For nearly 20 years delivery of care has been managed at local level by semiautonomous units known as 'trusts' that deliver a range of hospital services. In the last 10 years political responsibility for services in Wales, Scotland and Northern Ireland has been devolved, with the services becoming more centrally managed by each province. The English NHS has seen the financial autonomy of trusts increase even though the dominant discourse has been one of nationally managed standards with a number of mandated change initiatives.

Most acute hospital services in England are provided by circa 168 trusts, within which there are teaching hospital trusts and trusts offering specialized clinical services (e.g., children's services). The balance provides the most publicly recognized services, general acute care. These trusts are responsible for anywhere between one and six individual hospitals and offer a very similar service portfolio, but respond in a varied way despite the same national guidance and public expectation. I examine one instance of this variation: the differences achieved in the standard of patient environment that resulted in only 15 (12%) of the trusts achieving consistently high standards at all their hospitals (23 in total) over a four-year period, despite working to the same set of nationally accepted standards and being assessed using the same criteria. I set out to identify what characteristics these 15 trusts shared.

THE PATIENT ENVIRONMENT ACTION TEAM INITIATIVE

The NHS Plan (Department of Health, 2000) was a major attempt to introduce standardization to the English NHS. It set out to increase funding to redress inequalities and bring service standards to agreed levels, with improved performance being demonstrated through a rigorous system of performance measurement. The impact and importance of the hospital environment on the health of the patient had gained political recognition, resulting in the inclusion in the plan of two measures for the patient environment. The first, the Estates Returns Information Collection, contains some 2,000 individual data and seeks to establish a cost per square meter; the second, the Patient Environment Action Team initiative (PEAT), assesses the quality of the patient environment.

At the inception of PEAT each trust nominated a board member to take responsibility for the hospitals' patient environment and the associated improvement plan that focused on the elements covered by the initiative (including car parking; entrances and reception areas; visitors' and ward toilets; decoration, maintenance and cleanliness of wards and public areas; and the condition and cleanliness of linen). Patient food was assessed against separate criteria and is not considered in this study. Originally, external multidisciplinary teams assessed every inpatient healthcare facility of 10 or more beds, while the inclusion of patients, their representatives and members of the public in the team ensured involvement of service users. Each hospital was awarded a color to denote a Good (Green), Acceptable (Amber) or Poor (Red) performance, changing to Excellent, Good, Acceptable, Poor or Unacceptable as the program developed into self-assessment.

PEAT results are a useful research tool as they are nationwide, include standards for each element of the patient environment as drawn up in consultation with NHS trusts and do not recognize differences in organizational structures. The PEAT results I used were interpreted by multidisciplinary teams using an objective standard scoring mechanism that was audited and verified. My study was a rare opportunity to assess how 15, out of a total set of 168 similar organizations, managed to provide a better standard of patient environment for their users.

THE RESEARCH

It is intuitively logical to suggest that a number of external influences might offer an advantage to those providing a high standard of patient environment. To test whether such an advantage existed, I undertook a high-level investigation of the main trust characteristics and external drivers that might have influenced the 15 trusts. I compared those characteristics traditionally employed by the NHS to categorize acute trusts: type of trust, size of the trust, geographical area, number of hospital sites in the trust and the age of the trust. In order to understand whether a single point of responsibility for the patient environment allowed for better results, I considered two additional criteria: integrated/split responsibility for the patient environment and contract/in-house services (i.e., responsibility split between organizations).

When it became evident that there were no common characteristics between the trusts and therefore no advantage to the 15 trusts, I considered whether the advantage might lie in the catchment population. I studied accepted indicators of health (e.g., age, poverty, isolation, density of population, unemployment). These factors were interpreted as: population size and density, age profile of the population, economic activity and affluence and health profiles of the population. Again I found nothing to distinguish the 15 trusts from a random set of trusts, other than their ability to achieve a high standard of patient environment on a consistent basis (Macdonald, Price & Askham, 2009a). My study did not attempt to explain why the majority of acute trusts in England did *not* consistently achieve high levels of PEAT scores, and arguably, therefore, does not totally exclude the possibility of some external influences making the environment more difficult to sustain.

Ethnographical Study

Given the lack of commonality in external influences and trust characteristics, the question remained as to why these trusts had consistently delivered high standards of patient environment. Of the 15 trusts, six agreed to participate in further research using an ethnographic approach: observing and speaking with the managers responsible for the patient environment (usually within FM directorates) in their own contexts, through interviews that allowed open exploration and that might show common attributes/ characteristics/behaviors. In this way, 22 managers (hereafter, the group) who operated at director, senior manager and operational manager levels, and were responsible for the patient environment, contributed to the research through 16 interviews, with some being interviewed individually and others in groups of two or more. The interviews were conversations, not in the colloquial sense but rather as complex, information-rich mixes of auditory, visual, olfactory and tactile events that included not only what was spoken, but the full range of symbols, artifacts, theatrics, etc., that were used together with, or as substitutes for, what was spoken. I chose this method because listening is more than hearing and includes all the ways in which people become aware and conscious of, or present to, the world (Ford & Ford, 1995).

During the interviews I asked the group members about their organization and how their services were structured, and then invited them to discuss how they achieved consistent high standards of patient environment. I also observed the physical environment in order to understand the full conversational apparatus and allow a match to be made between the rhetoric and the reality.

The Outcomes

The phrasing used during the interviews and the observations of the physical environment were grouped by coding each comment made by each member of the group; eight themes emerged (Macdonald, Price & Askham, 2009b). These were:

1. Pride and commitment.
2. Personal style.
3. Luck.
4. Personal development.
5. Maximizing the contribution from the team.
6. Change, stability and experience.
7. External perspective.
8. Integration.

Themes one to seven resonated with the plethora of literature and rhetoric regarding leadership in the public sector, and, other than indicating that the group took up a leadership role, raised nothing of significance worthy of further study. The group exhibited the leadership behaviors and characteristics generally attributed to the quiet leaders (Yukl, 1993), who are not interested in bureaucratic structures, status and power. They had pride in their work and their organization, believed they were in a lucky position, enjoyed working as part of a winning team, embraced change and enjoyed working with experienced and skilled people. They invested time and energy in their people and created a learning environment, whether staff members were directly employed or employed by contractors. The good reputation of the organization was seen as key, and the group proactively sought to protect and enhance this. Theme eight, *integration*, was more developed and emphatic than I anticipated from the literature or my *a priori* assumptions and was clearly worthy of further study. In the rest of this chapter I seek to show how this emphasis on integration enabled the group to use their leadership skills to develop their role within the organization, thus creating and sustaining the high standard of patient environment.

INTEGRATION

The group saw the patient environment as an essential part of the hospital's *raison d'être*, and by integrating with the clinical and executive teams, they ensured that their services were not isolated or sidelined by competing priorities on the corporate agenda. In order to achieve this the members acquired financial investment and top team support through the formal route of strong, robust business cases and funding bids that clearly demonstrated how the corporate agenda would benefit.

Dense Networks

My study showed that the group was concerned not with bureaucratic structures, but with the forming of dense networks where relationships were informal and intense, and lively interaction enhanced performance (Henttonen, Janhonen, Johanson & Puumalainen, 2010). Furthermore, as

Matinez and Aldrich (2011) contend, these dense networks created opportunities for boundary-scanning activities, thus addressing the 'structural holes' that form the gaps in an organization's formal structure through which problems fall or are allowed to pass around. Boundary-scanning activities are those that enable a team to work across boundaries: e.g., representing the team to outsiders, getting divergent ideas and knowledge from outside the team and facilitating their use in service development and delivery and buffering the team from outsider demands (Ancona, 1990; Rosenthal, 1997) to allow a focus on priorities.

Breslin (Ch. 20) describes how the co-evolution of components of knowledge can be achieved through continual communication. In order to achieve this co-evolution within a complex organization such as the NHS the strong ties seen in the group's dense networks are needed to ensure that sophisticated knowledge and intricate information is exchanged regularly and frequently. Knowledge and information cannot be seen as neutral or objective as they are shaped and linked by personal understanding, which in turn is governed by our values, norms, beliefs and understanding of power. As a consequence of these multiple viewpoints, transference of knowledge and information one to another is not simple, with Bergenholtz (2011) calling for the personal familiarity that can only be obtained by frequent face-to-face interaction. This was evidenced by the group's investing deliberate time and effort to achieve the strong interface that would allow a transference culture to flourish. They recognized that not only did the networks facilitate the transference, but they also generated the necessary creative tension that catalyzed and fed teamwork to achieve timely delivery of resources and allowed service improvements. Because of this the group felt justified in contributing the most effort in the initial stages of building the networks. These networks forged the difficult connection between the micro-departmental agenda and the macro-organizational agenda by using relationships already built by the network in the tentative, constantly shifting adaptive middle region of the organization (Ford, 2010), which I term structural holes. As the group networked across structural holes, they would found themselves working consistently in the adaptive middle region, meaning that the networks had little formal recognition and accountability, taking a diagonal slice across organizational structures. The networks were multilayered and predominately made up of collaborating peers (Lipnack & Stamps, 1990) of whom only a few had responsibility for delivering the objective. There was evidence of Goodwin, Peck, Freeman and Posaner's (2004) model of risk management as a hybrid of networks was created, such as to include enclave[1] networks that had flat internal structures with no central authority but high levels of personal commitment between the group and the executive. A further result was hierarchical networks that are found to be more successful in coordinating and controlling predefined tasks, tasks that involve complex divisions of labor, as they have an organizational core and the authority to regulate the work of members. This was evidenced by multidisciplinary inspection for the PEAT inspection team, where status and acknowledgment of technical or clinical skills would impress observers and convince them of the necessity of the agenda. The group did not use networks to drive people towards an organizational vision shared from the top, but loosened hierarchical controls to allow networks to flourish and a more consultative approach to be used; although they recognized this would weaken the organization's power to mandate from the top (Schmidt, 1992). The creation of the networks was not undertaken in a cynical or self-interested way, but for the good of the organization.

The dense networks spun by the group were webs of quiet, consistent dialogues, reinforced with the tantalizing glitter of symbols (e.g., models of integration that gave nurses control), decorations (e.g., long service and training awards), stories related to others (e.g., about their own experiences and difficulties) and legends (e.g., stories of senior staff who had performed badly and the fate that had befallen them). These dialogues took place between leaders (e.g., managers and senior nurses) and between leaders and followers (e.g., managers and their staff). The group spoke of time and effort being spent capturing the hearts and minds of others, both laterally and vertically across the organization. I believe they did this by spinning their visionary webs in advantageous places (e.g., with clinical teams) at advantageous times (e.g., in meetings to discuss others agendas) to catch the juiciest of flies (e.g., senior staff who had great influence). When they were sure of having created an advantage they moved into practical implementation. Alongside successful implementation, mutual adaptation occurred, the services offered improved and the interdependence, and thus the bonds, of the network members (Awuah, 2001) were enhanced, creating trust, rapport and cooperation. Barrett (2000) points out that relationship building takes time and is a slow process. A focus on establishing and maintaining the bonds between members is paramount in building and developing dense networks. The group's efforts in this area paid off by ensuring patient environment issues became part of the corporate agendas, which in turn led to overt support by their chief executives, thereby giving them credibility and standing within the organization. The integration between the patient environment and the corporate agenda was also strengthened by ensuring that the sharing of objectives was reciprocated by all members of the network; this sometimes happened by means of allocation through the chief executive, but not necessarily so. I believe that healthy networks often result in objectives being agreed on among peers, and indeed in organizations where a more consultative leadership style is used, peer-agreed objectives are often encouraged.

Managed Dialogue

The group's focus on dense networks could be construed simply as having a vision and ensuring that followers from all parts of the organization were recruited to help deliver this vision. However, a vision is a compelling, attractive shared view of the future; it creates a picture of a better world, but is little more than a dream until it is widely shared and accepted and implementation commences. Hearts and minds have to be won for a vision to be effectively implemented in the complex world of the NHS with its hybrid ecology of stakeholders and conflicting agendas (cf. Ellison & Flowers, Ch. 12) and that is something only achieved through strong relationship-building skills and high levels of political awareness. Much of the leadership material suggests that communication is at the heart of the matter, but I contend that communication is only one part of the issue and managed dialogue is where the true leadership skill lies. Managed dialogue is a deconstruction of individual meaning and a shared creation of meaning (Grill, Ahlborg & Lindgren, 2011). The dense network is an ideal vehicle to allow managed dialogue during which a leader can build relationships where openness, reciprocity, authenticity and trust exist between all parties. As true dialogue slowly develops over time the quality of interaction changes, it allows others minds to enter a new space, to see things with fresh eyes, taking them into a deep level of collective wisdom (Varney, 1996). Reflection through 'listening to yourself' can help leaders examine their own underlying assumptions and alter their mental models, allowing them to untangle and represent information and knowledge in a format others can use. Managing dialogue in this way creates a pool of common meaning that is then capable of constant development and change.

This shows how vital the sharing of knowledge and information is to an organization's future. A leader must be able, by making a vital choice regarding the media vehicle, to present knowledge and information in the language of the listener, who will then in turn suspend their assumptions and self-importance and start to listen and talk, following the flow. As we discussed earlier, those receiving knowledge and information shape and link it in particular ways that reflect their own values, norms, beliefs and relations of power. They also take on board additional signs that are made available through their other senses, such as body language unconsciously noted by sight. Dialogue is not a simple case of communication (talking and listening), but a far more complicated issue of body language, symbols, artifacts, storytelling and theatrics. Musson, Cohen and Tietze (2007) suggest that dialogue frames our understanding because our interpretations are culturally situated. The signs contained in dialogue take their meaning from our established and shared understanding and familiar contexts—what we know (or think we know) about the signs, their contents and contexts and other similar things. When presented with a new dialogue we turn, without conscious thought, to our existing stocks of knowledge, drawing unconsciously on deep-rooted assumptions that become the lens through which we view things. As such, it is imperative for a leader to ensure that not only is their conversation congruent with their vision, but that the signs and symbols fit as well. For example, a member of the group spoke of a need for a nonhierarchical, open style of leadership to support his/her vision. S/he was seen to enact the vertical and horizontal integration s/he articulated through the office door, which needed to stand open, the complementary artifacts (the photographs of the time-out when all status was laid to one side), and the informal, public walkabout. Indeed, in earlier chapters (Myerson, Ch. 2; Alexander, Ch. 13; Hoffman, Munthe-Kaas & Elle, Ch. 5) the case has been made that the space that FMs create should facilitate dialogue. When this happens the organization's symbols will not only evidence the culture required, but will help develop and sustain that culture.

I observed the group using storytelling, which is rife in all organizations, to assist in the creation of the common understanding necessary for dialogue to take place. Every member had stories to tell about their organization's history, including those about key people who were either seen as successes or failures. Organizational stories include tales of mutual relations, heroes, villains, higher powers, glorious victories and tragic defeats that have created episodes in the history of an organization (Basten, 2011). These stories then become formalized in organizational language and start to appear in the mission statements, brochures, business reports and narrative texts, which allows others to learn about the behaviors and work practices that their organization expects. Price (Ch. 1) makes the case for seeing an organization as a system of 'conversations,' talking of how an organization's language shapes what is real to it and how the organization evolves through using this language.

Ford and Ford (1995) and April (1999) contend that, if change is to be real, it is not something that is decided upon and then communicated, but must be an interactive process of social construction in which new realities are created, sustained and modified during the process of dialogue. The networks created by the group were fertile ground for this type of working, making the group's abilities to manage dialogue a key skill in the change management process and illustrating their engagement with social construction (cf. Roper, Ch. 16).

There were two levels to the group's activities; not only were the members concerned with building and maintaining integration in their own work, but they strove for this to be mirrored at all levels throughout their organization. Some strengthened their ability to offer the best service by transferring day-to-day control of their workforce to the wards, accepting all the challenges this would bring, while some managed structural holes by implementing geographical zoning of services and implementing joint FM/nursing cleaning and maintenance schedules. Thus they evidenced through their actions (i.e., the language of symbols) that which they believed, offering solutions to problems and showing interest in and support of others' agendas, which in turn elicited reciprocal collaboration.

As a subsidiary, but highly relevant, comment to my main theme, Thomas discusses the use of staff bases in education and how the geographical positioning of these facilitated cross-departmental discussion that had an impact on business results—in this particular case pupil behavior. This echoes the business impact of geographical zoning of services that this group chose to implement in order to obtain improved integration (cf. Thomas, Ch. 18).

Leaders are results-oriented people. They know what they want, and they are committed to, and focused on, outcomes. The group used formal systems and feedback mechanisms that worked both laterally across the organization and vertically from top to bottom of the organization to inform all of the service outcomes. The members spoke of the mechanisms for reporting outcomes, saying that they saw performance measurement to be one of the essentials in effective implementation of their patient environment strategy. They knew that the issues important to organizational success could be determined from the information drawn from these measures (Shohet & Levy, 2004). In a world of competing agendas, the group used information on outcomes to create a focus on their vision, thus limiting distractions and driving meaningful action throughout their teams and networks. The intensity of a leader's vision, coupled with the high levels of commitment to making it happen, creates a powerful force of momentum that draws people into the flow. It is this passion and commitment that grabs attention (Bennis & Nannus, 1985) and maintains focus.

As has been shown, the group displayed the skills necessary to build and maintain good relationships with all types of people at all levels in the organization. They relentlessly focused on delivering their vision, through developing services and by addressing difficult issues nondefensively. Personal credibility generated respect and allowed a robust relationship with open dialogue among teams of all types and at all levels. Again, these dialogues were underpinned by focused action, including allowing wards to take control over day-to-day coordination of FM staff so that services could follow patient needs more closely, proactively seeking regular input from clinical staff over improvements to services and promoting ownership of the patient environment.

The Role of the Broker

In 2005, Heng, McGeorge and Loosemore argued for a strategic broker within FM who would forge networks across FM departments that enabled support services to exceed the conventional expectations of their customer by constantly looking to drive new ideas and attempting to convert them into value-adding opportunities. I contend that the group enhanced this brokerage model to a truly strategic role at the corporate level, working within dense networks to gain support from the different types of expertise scattered over the organization, thereby improving collaboration and enhancing knowledge and information transference right across the organization and creating a dynamism that maximized added value.

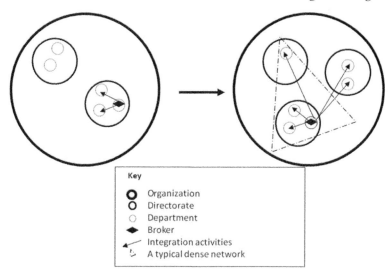

Figure 19.1 Development of Heng et al.'s (2005) concept into the truly strategic broker.

The members were not only looking to enhance the delivery of their own services as depicted in the role described by Heng et al. (2005), but were delivering significant parts of the organizational agenda. The examples offered by the group included working with clinical teams to build patient environments that delivered new clinical services or supported new technologies and ways of working and jointly developing services that allowed maximum throughput of patients by agreeing on new ways of using and servicing clinical space. Reduced length of stay was another organizational objective jointly addressed by the group. Through their dense networks, they facilitated this objective by introducing measures that appear simple but challenge culture and historic practices, such as working with wards to reduce the cross infection that lengthens patient stays and speeding up bed turnover following use by infectious patients, thus increasing throughput. By making the organizational agendas their own in this way, the group developed the brokerage role to work across the organization and moved their services from operational to strategic: from shop floor to boardroom.

CONCLUSION

My desk study found that the 15 trusts had nothing in common other than their ability to achieve a high standard of patient environment on a consistent basis. I then carried out a series of interviews with 22 FMs at director, senior management and operational levels at six trusts. I established that they adopted a leadership role that could be summarized into eight themes. I found that many of the themes resonated with the literature and *a priori* knowledge; however, what had not been previously explored was the theme of integration where the group took up the role of a truly strategic broker, creating cross-organizational dense networks developed through managed dialogue.

The group had the capacity to deliver the organization's agenda through using managed dialogues to create high-density networks. These networks involved lively interaction that addressed structural holes and allowed difficult issues and complex problems to be resolved. This facilitated the delivery of service improvements that in turn gained the respect and trust of colleagues and ensured the delivery of consistently high standards. It was this ability to use managed dialogues to create dense networks—thereby facilitating knowledge and information transference—that resulted in the group creating a truly strategic broker role at the organizational and board levels. I see this as a development of Heng et al.'s (2005) model of the strategic broker, a model that worked across all FM departments regardless of traditional or structural boundaries (Figure 19.1). Members integrated multiple agendas to drive the organization's strategic objectives by working across the whole organization, not only between FM departments.

The wider engagement allowed the group to use their more commonly recognized leadership characteristics and attributes both laterally and vertically, and to the best possible advantage within their organizations. They achieved this through their ability to manage dialogue in such a way that their vision caught and focused the attention of all, at every level. This ensured a place for the FM agenda within both the operational and strategic arenas. I believe that it was the more traditional leadership skills identified in the themes, enhanced with the integrating attributes, that enabled the group to achieve a great deal. These achievements are reflected in consistently high PEAT scores over the years.

NOTES

1. Defined in summary as close knit groups with high levels of social cohesion sustained through common bonds, equality, shared commitment, trust and egalitarianism. A flat structure, with little inclination to accept central or mandated authority and a strong sense of group membership.

REFERENCES

Ancona, D. G. (1990). Outward bound: Strategies for team survival in an organization. *Academy of Management Journal, 33*(2), 234–365.

April, K. A. (1999). Leading through communication, conversation and dialogue. *Leadership and Organization Development Journal, 20*(5), 231–242.

Awuah, G. B. (2001). A firm's competence development through its network of exchange relationships. *Journal of Business and Industrial Marketing, 16*(7), 547–599.

Barrett, P. (2000). Achieving strategic Facilities Management through strong relationships. *Facilities, 18*(10/11/12), 421–426.

Basten, F. M. R. (2011). Narrating around. *Journal of Management Development, 30*(3), 260–269.

Bennis, W. G., & Nannus, B. (1985). *Leaders.* New York: Harper and Row.

Bergenholtz, C. (2011). Knowledge brokering: Spanning technological and network boundaries. *European Journal of Innovation Management, 14*(1), 74–92.

Department of Health. (2000). *The NHS plan.* Retrieved February 2, 2007, from www.dh.gov.uk /PolicyandGuidance/Organisational Policy/Modernisation/ NHSPlan

Ford, J. D., & Ford, L. W. (1995). The role of conversations in producing intentional change in organizations. *Academy of Management Review, 20*(3), 541–570.

Ford, R. (2010). Complex adapting leading-ship and open processional change processes. *Leadership and Organizational Development Journal, 31*(5), 420–435.

Goodwin, P., Peck, E., Freeman, T., & Posaner, R. (2004). *Managing across diverse networks of care: Lessons from other sectors* (Final Report to the NHS SDO R&D Program, Health Services Management Centre). Birmingham: University of Birmingham.

Grill, C., Ahlborg, G., & Lindgren, E. C. (2011). Valuation and handling of dialogue in leadership: A grounded theory study in Swedish Hospitals. *Journal of Health Organization and Management, 25*(1), 34–54.

Heng, H. K. S., McGeorge, W. D., & Loosemore, M. (2005). Beyond strategy: Exploring the brokerage role of Facilities Manager in hospitals. *Journal of Health Organization and Management, 19*(1), 16–31.

Henttonen, K., Janhonen, M., Johanson, J., & Puumalainen, K. (2010). The democratic antecedents and performance consequences of the social-network structure in work teams. *Team Performance Management, 16*(7/8), 388–412.

Lipnack, J., & Stamps, J. (1990). *The architecture of complexity. The Seybold.* Newton, M.A. U.S.A., NetAge Inc. Retrieved May 15, 2011, from http://www.netage.com/pub/articles/Publications/Seybold/Seybold9_2–90.html.

Macdonald, R., Price, I., & Askham, P. (2009a). Excellent patient environments within acute NHS trusts: External influences & trust characteristics. *Journal of Facilities Management, 7*(1), 7–23.

Macdonald, R., Price, I., & Askham, P. (2009b). Leadership conversations: The impact on patient environments. *Leadership in Health Services, 22*(2), 140–160.

Martinez, M., & Aldrich, H. (2011). Networking strategies for entrepreneurs: Balancing cohesion and diversity. *International Journal of Entrepreneurial Behaviour and Research, 17*(1), 7–38.

Musson, G., Cohen, L., & Tietze, S. (2007). Pedagogy and the 'linguistic turn': Developing understanding through semiotics. *Management Learning, 38*(1), 45–60.

Rosenthal, E. (1997). Social networks and team performance. *Team Performance Management, 3*(4), 288–294.

Schmidt, D. P. (1992). Integrating ethics into organizational networks. *Journal of Management Development, 11*(4), 34–44.

Shohet, I. M., & Levy, S. (2004). Development of an integrated healthcare Facilities Management model. *Facilities, 22*(5/6), 129–140.

Varney, J. (1996). The power of dialogue. *Management Development Review, 9*(2), 30–32.

Yukl, G. (1993). *Leadership in organizations.* Upper Saddle River, NJ: Prentice Hall.

20 Spaces and the Coevolution of Practices within a UK Metallurgical Equipment Supplier

Dermot Breslin

In the last 30 years a number of researchers have studied coevolutionary processes within organizations, drawing in their approach on the variation-selection-retention framework of evolutionary studies. Notable amongst these were Burgelman's (1991) account of the coevolution of the computer memory chip business at Intel in the 1980s and Murmann's (2003) account of the coevolution of the global synthetic dye industry in the nineteenth century. These accounts are rich in detail and describe the interrelationship between the evolution of practices, rules, cognitive and behavioral patterns, strategic initiatives and organizational structures and forms at various hierarchical levels within the organizations and industries. Others have argued that the coevolution of elements of culture can be facilitated or hindered by the management of spaces within these organizations (Price, 2009), and in this chapter I seek to develop this line of inquiry by using an evolutionary approach to describe the multilevel coevolution of practices and spaces within a UK metallurgical equipment supplier during the 1990s. Throughout this chapter I shall refer to this company as Steelco. Drawing on extensive firsthand experience, I examine the coevolution of discrete components of knowledge at multiple levels within Steelco in light of the management of spaces within the organization. However, before putting forward an approach that describes the coevolution of practices at different levels, I must make the case for the existence of discrete evolutionary systems at each hierarchical level. In addition to these discrete evolutionary systems, discrete units of analysis must be identified for each of these levels.

MULTILEVEL COEVOLUTION

In the biological world evolution occurs over time through the key evolutionary mechanisms of variation (of genotypes), selection (of the consequent phenotype) and retention (of the underlying genotype), where the genotype is defined as the material inherited by an individual from its parents, which has the potential to be transmitted to future generations. The phenotype, on the other hand, represents the developmental expression of the genotype in the physical characteristics of the organism. Some authors argue that at a sufficiently general level of abstraction the principles of variation, selection and retention can be used to describe evolution within a variety of domains (Breslin, 2011b; Hodgson & Knudsen, 2010; Price, Ch. 1). To distinguish general from genetic evolution, the concepts of "replicator" (Dawkins, 1976) and "interactor" (Hull, 1988) are substituted for the genotype and phenotype. The replicator is thus defined as a component of knowledge or information of which copies are made such as genes in the biological world. These replicators interact with their environment through interactors, which Hull defined as entities that interact as a cohesive whole with their environment in a way that causes differential replication.

A number of authors who have used an evolutionary approach to study organizations have identified the routine as a candidate for the replicator (Aldrich, 1999; Nelson & Winter, 1982), where the routine is defined in a number of ways including "regular and predictable behavioral patterns" (Nelson & Winter, 1982, p.14); "if–then" rules, heuristics, rules of thumb (Becker, 2004), standard operating procedures (Cyert & March, 1963) and dispositions to express certain behavior (Hodgson & Knudsen, 2010). Whilst most authors agree that routines are collective phenomena and involve multiple actors (Becker, 2004), ambiguity exists as to whether the routine refers to cognitive- and/or behavioral-level knowledge and/or the complex of actions that result from the enactment of this knowledge. With a view towards unpacking this relationship, I argue (Breslin, 2011a) that separate and distinct representations of cognitive and behavioral knowledge should be included in the concept of the replicator at the level of the group, through the concepts of cognitive frameworks and a more narrowly define "behavioral routine."

In order to consider the coevolution between levels within an organization's hierarchy, we must first define the units of analysis and evolutionary processes at each level. Clearly, individuals, whilst manifesting degrees of heterogeneity, also exhibit homogeneous collective behavior by participating in group routines. This degree of heterogeneity, despite the homogenizing influence of routines, can be captured by representing the behavioral and cognitive knowledge mentioned in the preceding at the level of the individual. In this manner, individual cognitive frameworks and behavioral habits (Hodgson & Knudsen, 2010) can be said to represent the replicators when studying the evolution of individuals within organizations (Breslin, 2011a). The definition of the interactor will depend on the level at which selection occurs, with individual actions, group actions or firm actions representing the interactor (or developmental expression of this knowledge) at the level of the individual, group or organization respectively (Breslin, 2011b). For example, at the level of the group, the interactor is represented by the group's actions and is the expression of the group's routines and frameworks.

COEVOLUTION OF PRACTICES WITHIN STEELCO

Using the definitions of replicator and interactor at the various levels within an organization's hierarchy, I shall now present a coevolutionary account of evolving practices within Steelco during the 1990s. I draw the account from my extensive firsthand experience of Steelco, including the design, sales and projects operations. During this period I took part in meetings; participated in a number of key operations, tasks and group activities; and had extensive discussions with design engineers, design managers, commissioning engineers, sales managers and project managers. In the process I gained firsthand experience of the practices in each department, not only within Steelco, but the wider network of suppliers, competitors and customers. The structure of this account will begin at the level of the individual and move to include the group and broader organization. Steelco supplied plant and equipment to the global steel industry throughout the 1990s and indeed had dominated the UK industry in the preceding decades. However, the global steel market experienced difficulties in the 1990s, with steel production exceeding consumption throughout the decade, resulting in lower levels of capital investment in new plant and equipment. This made it increasingly difficult for the organization to secure orders within this very challenging and competitive global market.

Coevolution of Individuals and Groups

Within Steelco, there were three key operational activities, namely, design, sales and projects. The main activity, design, was divided into subactivities, each carried out by small groups of design engineers. All designers were located in a large open-plan office space, known as the "bear pit," which was subdivided into a collection of "work pens" in which between four and six designers, who constituted a particular subgroup, would work. These pens were separated from others by low-level partitions. Over time each subgroup had developed a series of collective routines they would use in the completion of the various design activities. For example, all members of each group would use routines relating to the selection of a suitable reference machine as a starting point in the design for any new customer order. This selection would be based on similarities of key design parameters. Other routines might relate to simple calculations carried out in the design process. For example, key design parameters were often calculated based on simple rules of thumb applied to key operational details. These rules of thumb developed over time based on the accumulated wisdom within the groups, and on many occasions were influenced by the experience of individuals on-site during the installation and commissioning of the equipment (discussed later). In the same way, these simple rules of thumb acted to simplify the design process or reduce the risks involved in the process.

The mechanisms of variation, selection and retention might be used to describe the coevolution of these components of knowledge within the design groups at the level of the individual and group. While each design task was clearly unique and specific to the job in hand, when completing a particular task individuals tended to "select" collective routines, which they "shared" with other members of the group. So, for instance, an existing employee in the roll design group *Oldtimer 1* would use a collective routine R_{R1}, which, for example, might relate to the selection of suitable reference machines at the start of the design process, as shown simplistically in Figure 20.1. Once selected by the individual, the routine would become enacted through actions, which would in turn receive feedback from other agents, such as other members of the group, managers and customers. Individuals within groups tended to interpret this feedback in a collective manner. Given the close physical proximity of individuals in work pens, this selection and interpretation process was facilitated by continual communication and dialogue. This continual communication related not only to the use and development of routines, but general "banter" as individuals talked about their personal lives and interests. Indeed the bear pit housed not only a collection of design subgroups, but with it a chorus of separate group conversations and even quartets of whistlers! In one subgroup four individuals whistled songs as they worked, with individuals whistling separate parts of the same group song for long periods throughout the day. Others developed nonverbal group signals, understandable only by members of the group, such as a practice of rattling a spoon against the insides of a mug to signal a group tea break.

In addition to the continual dialogue and interaction between individuals within groups, cognitive frameworks played a key role in the selection of routines and subsequent interpretation of feedback. As with the routines, these frameworks became increasingly collective over time, and in a

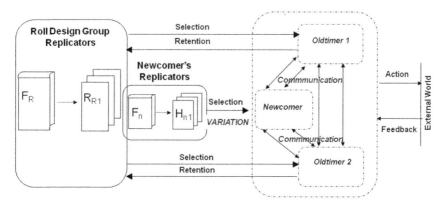

Figure 20.1   Coevolution of practices within the design groups.

sense represented the worldview of the groups. For example, one dominant framework in many of the design groups was the perception that customers preferred "solid," overengineered, "sturdy" machine designs. This view derived from the previous experiences of the organization in the 1970s and 1980s, including occasional equipment failures. In order to address these failures, and produce machine designs that would perform and last in the very demanding environments typical in steel manufacturing, designs became increasingly "heavy" and overengineered. With each successive machine failure, designs became more overengineered with perceived risks of future failures being reduced. This cognitive worldview became known by a number of terms as "it must be built to last," or "if it looks right then it is right." The latter term referred to the view within the design group that the final machine design should be perceived by designer engineers, commissioning engineers and customers as having a certain "sturdy appearance." As a result of the dominance of this perspective, any variation in routines that led to designs being perceived as being "a bit thin" were dismissed. In this sense, the dominant cognitive framework within the design teams severely constrained the degree to which new design practices could be developed.

As routines and frameworks became increasingly collective in nature over time, a sociopolitical status quo became established within the group in which individuals "knew their place." This sociopolitical dimension and the constraining effect of established frameworks and routines acted to suppress variations from incumbent members and new arrivals. On arrival the latter would typically use more individual habits, such as H_{n1} (see Figure 20.1) when completing tasks, as they weren't familiar with the routines used by the group. The enactment of these habits would result in feedback both from other members of the group and other external actors including customers. While the newcomer might interpret this feedback using individual cognitive framework F_n, others within the group would tend to interpret it in a manner that was consistent with the underlying view of the world represented by the collective cognitive framework F_R. As a result of these "biased" interpretations, existing design engineers tended to discount variations on existing routines, as being naïve and ill-suited to the heavy working environment of the steel industry. Through a process of dialogue and negotiation, these new habits would be policed and downplayed by the existing design teams (Cyert & March, 1963; Nelson & Winter, 1982). Existing members of staff used stories of previous attempts to change routines, with a familiar "it'll never work in a million years . . . " anecdote to persuade the new arrivals that the existing practices were more appropriate for the conditions in which the equipment would operate. Ultimately, most new arrivals who remained with the organization eventually adopted the collective framework and routine, and in this manner, the collective pressure acted to maintain, and continue to exploit, existing practices. In this way, the label bear pit acted as a metonym for the battle for dominance that existed in the design area (Price, this volume), and further represented a simplified 'black-and-white' collective understanding (Musson & Tietze, 2004, p. 1317) within the design group itself.

As newcomers adopted collective routines, they also assumed the identity and meaning of the group, which acted to further reinforce the retention of "accepted" collective routines (Lave & Wenger, 1990), and collective cognitive frameworks such as F_R. In this way, a number of dominant collective routines and frameworks became established and retained within the design groups. The dominant bear wins the fight! The close proximity, continual communication and "shared" experiences of the engineers acted to reinforce this process, as the selection and retention of existing collective practices suppressed variations, and with it the engine of future evolution of the group. As noted earlier, the "if it looks right then it is right" framework tended to lead to the selection of routines that resulted in designs being consistent with this worldview, and as a result equipment designs became increasingly heavy and overengineered, with material costs and resultant equipment prices becoming uncompetitive in the marketplace.

Coevolution of Groups and Organization

The Project Teams

As noted earlier, the three key operational activities in Steelco were design, sales and projects. Whilst the design operation dealt with the basic and detailed design of all plant and equipment, the sales teams were responsible for finding and securing new orders throughout the world. The projects group was responsible for fabricating, supplying, installing and commissioning the plant and equipment. It should be noted that whilst many individuals such as project managers, planners and procurement officers worked only in the projects team, many engineers spent periods of time in both design and projects groups. The objective of rotating staff in this manner was to ensure that all design engineers gained vital experience on-site, and as a result would understand the difficulties experienced during the installation and commissioning of the equipment. This rotation would ensure that equipment was designed for the task at hand, thereby reducing the risk of errors being made. As a consequence of this rotation, routines and frameworks were replicated within both groups through learning by doing and working closely together in teams (Lave & Wenger, 1990).

A number of routines used in the design group had been developed from the experiences of individuals on-site. On-site designers worked in small teams together with subcontractors and client engineers and technicians. Most designers socialized together in the evenings, with discussions largely centering on work-related matters. In the same way that routines evolved in the design group, these "site" routines evolved through the mechanisms of variation, selection and retention over time, following direct feedback as represented by, for instance, equipment performance, mechanical failures and customer feedback. As a result of this experience, the site groups had become more risk averse over time, and influenced the development of the "site" routines themselves through feedback between group members. In this sense, some routines developed within the site group, and were then subsequently replicated in the design groups as engineers returned to the office to continue working on the design activity. As a result these simple rules of thumb evolved over time to reduce the perceived risks of mechanical failure of equipment once in operation and resulted in actions and consequent designs being conservative and overengineered. In this same way, the guiding framework used by designers was heavily influenced by the development of frameworks in the site group, which espoused the view that equipment designs should be "sturdy" enough to last in the extreme conditions of the steel plant. As noted earlier, the "appearance" of the final design became the accepted measure of product quality. So in a sense routines and frameworks used by the designers were varied over time by the on-site teams. These practices were then supplanted back to the design office, where they became firmly ingrained within the groups. In this way the bear pit acted as an "incubator" for routines and frameworks which were varied over time based on feedback received on-site.

The Sales Teams

The sales teams comprised a number of individuals from various departments, including design engineers, commercial managers, procurement officers and sales managers. When working in the head office, these teams were located in separate small open-plan offices, located around the "bear pit," and even above the central design space on a mezzanine floor. Individuals within these teams viewed themselves as distinct from the designers, and often referred to "the pit" as a physically and culturally different place. In this regard there was an implicit collective understanding (Musson & Tietze, 2004) that new ideas and change in general was likely to be problematic when dealing with the design group. The sales teams frequently visited different client sites during the sales process, as the process of selling new equipment involved rounds of lengthy and detailed technical discussions with clients. Whilst the sales group would use well-established routines, such as those associated with processing enquiries or putting together proposal documents, the practices adopted in the sales meetings themselves would vary according to the customer grouping. For example, the format and protocol of sales meetings in China differed from those adopted in meetings in Europe. In this way, the sales group developed collective practices with particular customer groups for each setting. Moreover, other competing sales groups from other organizations were included in this interaction process as collective routines for sales meeting coevolved amongst these parties. For instance, routines associated with the assembly of proposal documents for

Chinese customers evolved over time and became adopted by all competing sales groups (at the insistence of the customer). So, unlike the design teams, the sales teams continually varied routines as the composition of the teams themselves (including customer teams) and the environments in which they worked changed.

What is important to note about this coevolution of sales routines is the influence it had on the cognitive frameworks adopted by the sales group. Over time, individuals within the group began to alter previously held frameworks regarding the product designs. As the composition of the group changed with new arrivals and through communication, negotiation and feedback with customers, individuals recognized the inadequacy of previously held frameworks in light of changes in the marketplace. As time progressed, the sales group gradually became the most significant voice of objection to these existing design practices within the organization. So whilst returning design managers and engineers interpreted the failure in securing orders as being due to external factors, such as "the strength of the pound," senior sales managers increasingly identified the designs of the organization as being a key source of uncompetitiveness. In the face of these difficulties, a number of individuals, including some designer engineers, sales engineers and senior sales managers, attempted to address these threats by calling for a variation in the design routines and indeed the guiding frameworks advocated by existing design frameworks. In this manner, individuals within the sales group collectively interpreted feedback from the customer, following failed sales inquiries, through dialogue and communication, as being due to practices used in the design group, which led to uncompetitive designs.

Sales-Design-Projects Team Interaction

This interpretation of customer feedback was not shared by the design group, which continued to interpret poor sales figures as being due to external market factors. As a result, the increasing calls for change by the sales group were continually suppressed by the more dominant design groups and senior design managers within the organization. In this manner, the collective routines and frameworks that had emerged in the project groups and then developed within the design groups continued to act to suppress variation from outside, not only from within the groups themselves (as discussed earlier), but from the sales group in particular. As a result of the political power wielded by the design group and its associated replicators, feedback received from this group became the predominant factor influencing the evolution of the organization, with the strength of the feedback signal from the design groups overpowering other signals from other sources, suppressing any variation away from existing practices. So whilst an individual designer might attempt to vary a replicator, select it for enactment and interpret feedback from the customer as positive, the overwhelming strength of the feedback signal from the existing design group acted to "bring the individual back into line."

As the 1990s progressed and sales orders became increasingly difficult to secure, the number of relevant reference plants, which was a key tool in the sales process, became increasingly outdated. Steelco became trapped in a viscous circle, of designs being overengineered and uncompetitive, and failure to secure new orders became more commonplace as orders became scarcer. Faced with this increasingly poor sales performance, senior design managers could no longer resist growing calls for change from the sales groups. And following repeated attempts by senior sales managers to identify the problems as including equipment designs, senior design managers took action to radically revamp the plant designs and practices. Towards the late 1990s a number of specialized engineers were recruited, with the task of optimizing the designs and minimizing the extent of overengineering using a variety of techniques, including numerical modeling. Whilst the habits and frameworks used by these new arrivals were given full support from the senior management of the organization in an attempt to overcome some of the inertial effects mentioned in the preceding, the move proved to be too little too late. Incorporating the new designs, which were produced as a result of these new habits, proved to be more complex than originally anticipated. The new arrivals enacted radically different practices in order to overhaul the designs of key pieces of equipment at the basic design stage. However, at subsequent design stages incumbent design groups "beefed up" the newer, "thinner-looking" products. After all, it can't be right "if it doesn't look right!" At the same time Steelco continued to struggle financially in the face of difficult market conditions. These difficulties were compounded by losses in other parts of the organization, which led to the acquisition of the company by a key European rival in the late 1990s. So in a sense the dominant frameworks and routines that had developed within the design groups assumed a life of their own, and continued to resist attempts to change and threats to their survival, despite attempts by key senior design managers and newcomers to change them.

DISCUSSION

The entrenchment and dominance of routines and frameworks within the design group acted to suppress any attempts to introduce new replicators from outside and interpret negative feedback in line with existing cognitive frameworks. This resulted in designs becoming increasingly out of touch with changing market expectations in the 1990s, and the collective cognitive framework represented by the expression "if it looks right it is right" became a backward-looking framework that resulted in designs becoming increasingly overengineered. I would argue that the working environment as represented by the bear pit and associated work pens acted to aggravate this process. Existing routines and frameworks found an ecosystem in which they could thrive, and through the socialization of subgroups of designers acted to erect cognitive and sociopolitical barriers to new entrants or threats to their survival. While these same replicators also acted to influence those adopted by the projects and sales team, the groups were separated at both a cognitive and a physical level. As a result the mechanism of variation and strength of the feedback signal from outside the group was weakened and with it the continuing evolution of the group to suit changing customer needs.

On the contrary, the constantly changing physical space in which the sales teams operated acted to prevent routines becoming strongly ingrained. Not only were the sales teams separated (indeed at a higher level) from the bear pit, but they worked within a wide variety of client locations with different operating procedures. In addition, they were made to alter routines and frameworks to suit different sales environments. As a result, the mechanism of variation and the strength of the feedback signal from the customer became more dominant. As the marketplace became increasingly competitive in the late 1990s, the cognitive frameworks adopted by the sales team started to coevolve with those of other competitors and customers. These changes resulted in the senior sales managers identifying links between increasingly commonplace negative feedback from customers and design practices (or replicators). Whilst initial attempts to change practices were met with resistance from the design groups and senior managers, over time these signals became undeniable for all concerned.

What can be seen from this discussion is that replicators evolve at each level within the organization's hierarchy depending upon the strength of the feedback signals from the outside environment. In the case of a newcomer design engineer, the most significant feedback signal was that received from the group. Whilst the newcomer may have interpreted positive customer feedback following the enactment of any variation, through discussion with colleagues this interpretation would be systematically questioned. Over time, the individual concerned would reinterpret feedback, as he also acquired the collective cognitive framework as represented by the metonym of the bear pit. Indeed, this process reflects the difficulty experienced by individuals in interpreting a multitude of customer feedback signals based on a package of services and products delivered. This ambiguity in identifying links between routines and feedback resulted in different interpretations of failures by both senior design and sales managers. The dominance of the design group also strongly influenced the development of other groups within the organization. Whilst the sales group became increasingly aware of changes in the marketplace, senior sales managers failed to trigger variations in the design practices. Again, the strength of the feedback signal received from the design group strongly constrained the path of evolution of other groups within the organization.

CONCLUSION

Ultimately, managers at all levels within the organization must manage the library of replicators through the evolutionary processes of variation, selection and retention. Following the discussion given in the preceding, senior managers must ensure that the selection environment at each level is appropriate for the challenges facing the organization, increasing the strength of competitive selection at lower levels when needed. In addition managers need to be aware of the influence of spaces on this coevolutionary process. Routines and frameworks are selected and retained through continual communication, dialogue and negotiation; the close proximity obtained through open-plan offices, such as the bear pit, can act to reinforce this process. While the external environment is stable, such processes lead to the replication and exploitation of practices within groups. However, when external environmental conditions change, as in the case of the equipment supplier, this same process can act to resist and constrain variation. In the organization examined, competition was downplayed at the level of the individual, as practices in the design group acted to constrain variation and maintain status quo. In particular this involves untapping sources of variation from individuals within the group and exploring different practices used by other groups and individuals both within the organizations and beyond. As senior management strives to manage the evolution of interacting practices at multiple levels throughout the organization, the collective practices (including maladaptive practices) are themselves struggling to survive.

REFERENCES

Aldrich, H. E. (1999). *Organizations evolving.* London: Sage Publishing.

Becker, M. C. (2004). Organizational routines: A review of the literature. *Industrial and Corporate Change, 13*(4), 643–677.

Breslin, D. (2011a). The evolving organizational routine. In F. Belussi & U. Staber (Eds.), *Managing networks of creativity* (pp. 46–62). London: Routledge.

Breslin, D. (2011b). Reviewing a generalized Darwinist approach to studying socio-economic change. *International Journal of Management Reviews, 13*(2), 218–235.

Burgelman, R. A. (1991). Intraorganizational ecology of strategy making and organizational adaptation: Theory and field research. *Organization Science, 2*(3), 239–262.

Cyert, R. M., & March, J. G. (1963). *A behavioral view of the firm* (2nd ed.). Oxford: Blackwell.

Dawkins, R. (1976). *The selfish gene.* Oxford: Oxford University Press.

Hodgson, G. M., & Knudsen, T. (2010). *Darwin's conjecture: The search for general principles of social and economic evolution.* Chicago: University of Chicago Press.

Hull, D. L. (1988). *Science as a process.* Chicago: University of Chicago Press.

Lave, J., & Wenger, E. (1990). *Situated learning: Legitimate peripheral participation.* Cambridge: Cambridge University Press.

Murmann, J. P. (2003). *Knowledge and competitive advantage: The co-evolution of firms, technology and national institutions.* New York: Cambridge University Press.

Musson, G., & Tietze, S. (2004). Places and spaces: The role of metonymy in organizational talk. *Journal of Management Studies, 41*(8), 1301–1323.

Nelson, R. & Winter, S. (1982). *Evolutionary theory of economic change.* Cambridge, MA: Belknap.

Price, I. (2009). Space to adapt: Workplaces, creative behaviour and organizational memetics. In T. Rickards, M. Runce & S. Moger (Eds.), *The Routledge companion to creativity* (pp. 46–57). London: Routledge.

Reflections

Keith Alexander and Ilfryn Price

Various contributors have stressed dialogue and creativity so here is our concluding conversation, as it developed in real time. The book was completed 'in the cloud'; on a Dropbox folder. As the conversation developed, other contributors joined in. That in itself is an indication of technology changing the ecology of work and organization.

Ilfryn: So, Keith, what has bringing the book together achieved?

Keith: The contributions lay out a clear challenge to the business community, across all sectors of the economy. The centers for Facilities Management development that we lead and represent are positioned with strong connections to business school settings, with a mission to influence future business leaders and to persuade them of the opportunities for improving organization effectiveness through the creation of places for innovation and creation.

Kathy Roper's contribution gives us a starting point for rethinking the educational implications of a socially constructed paradigm for FM. Fellow academics internationally should take the lead and develop the curricula and research agenda that carry a momentum for change forward.

And, of course, there is nothing as practical as a good theory. George Cairns has been reminding us of the need to lay a stronger philosophical basis for FM since he joined the Strathclyde team almost 20 years ago. The theoretical contributions in the book, with authors from a wide range of backgrounds, will strengthen our resolve to establish the foundations for an open community of interest.

We have suggested that we are addressing three communities. However, some contributions suggest that we might address a broader audience and develop as social entrepreneurs in recognition of the possibilities for creating shared value with local communities. So, If, what do you see as the implications for *our three communities?*

Ilfryn: Let me start with managers and their FMs. I hope they will appreciate what space can do for organizations by providing opportunities for different groups to reach shared understandings. I first saw this happen across wide cultural divides in Guangzhou, PRC, in 1984. They do not have to go creating and living in workspaces that have floor plans that resemble military encampments. Breslin has shown what happens when they do. I hope management educators and researchers will realize the potential of space as something other than a power symbol. Most of all, I hope more professional space providers will realize they have to engage with the constructs and narratives of users. Looking back, even at the work of pioneers like Becker or Duffy, I see them imbued with the classic architectural professional and functional view: study it hard enough and we can solve your problem. For me, it is debatable if that view made sense even in the ORBIT studies of the 1980s. It cannot prevail today. I dread to think of the money that has actually been wasted, and the value lost, by FMs pursuing the classic approach. If they do not wake up there are HR professionals such as Alan Green or Julie Kortens starting to realize it for them. The 2007 special issue of the *California Management Review* has been cited a few times and I would still say what I tried to say then, different spaces for different results demand different 'conversations.' Don't so many of this book's contributions seem to make the same point?

Keith: For me one powerful message that came through was the real difference between the space created by professional actors in the process and the places created and inhabited by users of the environments and services coproduced through FM.

Ilfryn: I agree. In Chapter 7 I cited an old journalistic piece about who should be running the office, "you or the experts." I'm afraid the 'experts,' despite the best of intentions, have generally let businesses and communities down. Whether it is communities in Cape Town, schools, hospitals, university learning spaces, outsourcing contracts or commercial offices the same message comes through. A big discovery for me has been Markus saying it years ago. What else? In the spirit of dialogue should we offer any contributor who wants to, 20 words (the word budget will take it) for their end thought? It would be different and it would demonstrate the power of the virtual, which is another lesson for me out of the whole process.

I saved that sentence to the cloud at about 8:30 p.m. BST. In the next 24 hours the contributor community joined in (at more than 20 words each). The discussion became nonlinear.

George (Cairns):   I agree with a core message, that FM should be done with users, not to them, with experts demonstrating options, not defining the answer.

Colin (Stuart):   I think the reason is that the "experts" often do not use the space themselves and don't have to live with the results of their creations, whereas the users experience it on a daily basis. Given the right "tools" and some initial guidance the use of the workspace tends to evolve over time as the users adapt their working habits to suit any changes to the environment—it seems to find a natural equilibrium.

Dermot (Breslin):   Following on from Colin and If's comments, spaces might be viewed as coevolving alongside collective behaviors and cognitive frameworks. In a number of different organizations, I have observed groups of individuals modify working spaces to create physical barriers that reflected the behavioral and cognitive barriers that had evolved within the groups (and between them) over time. This process is inherently multilevel, so while spaces might be designed in a top-down fashion, users will self-organize, collective routines and frameworks will evolve and act to alter spaces to ensure their continued survival. From a creativity perspective what is interesting to explore is the extent to which the reverse happens in organizations, with individuals breaking down physical barriers to reach other individuals through communities of practice. In line with Rachel's comment in the following, perhaps FM should take a multilevel coevolutionary perspective in the design and continual adaptation of spaces to support the emergence of present and future behaviors needed to meet the demands of the business.

Rachel (Macdonald):   I worry that FM's focus is on the buildings, not on the people and their business. I would like to see a greater emphasis on the high value skills of facilitation and cooperation rather than the more traditional management skills of 'tell' and 'do to.'

Ian (Ellison):   From my own perspective—part academic, part professional—the challenge is always in the communication. I hope this collaboration has in part helped move some powerful ideas and concepts off the academic shelf and into the hands of capable, inquisitive practitioners, keen to champion the true organizational value the this perspective can bring.

Jenny (Thomas):   One hopes that FMs will realize the importance of their holistic role within an organization and users begin to understand their environment thus demanding more from their facilities.

Kathy (Michell):   I think the book demonstrates the need for FMs, in the creation and management of space, to consider not only profit-related bottom-line objectives, but to include the social and behavioral impact on users in the nature of the said space.

That seems, to us, a good summary to close with.

Contributors

Keith Alexander is qualified in architecture and Facilities Management and has directed the Centre for Facilities Management since its creation in 1990. He has worked in higher education for most his career and has pioneered action research in FM to advance knowledge and its application in education, research and practice, through CFM and the European Facility Management Network, which he cofounded.

Colin Beard originally trained as an ecologist. A professor of experiential learning, he works as an educationalist and learning and development consultant. A Fellow of the Royal Society of Arts, he holds adjunct and faculty chairs in China and has business links with leading corporations in India. Holding a PhD in experiential learning and a National Teaching Fellowship, he is the author of a number of texts on experiential learning.

Dermot Breslin is a lecturer in entrepreneurship at Sheffield University Management School. In his research he is developing an evolutionary approach to study changing behavior in organizations, and has published in a number of international management journals, books and conferences. He is currently developing his research to study growing small businesses with a view towards informing key organizational and strategic choices as companies adapt to suit changing business environments.

Melanie Bull has a master's in communications and is a senior lecturer in the Centre for Facilities Management Development at Sheffield Hallam University. She is currently studying for a DBA, and her doctoral research interest includes the use of reflective practice in Facilities Management. Her general research interests include communication within FM, change communication and the impact of alternative workplace strategies.

George Cairns is professor of management and head of the School of Management at RMIT University, Melbourne, Australia. He has published widely in the field of FM; has been invited to present at academic and professional conferences in the UK, Europe, Asia and Australasia; and he has a particular interest in how the organizational environment is perceived and understood by those that occupy and use it on a day-to-day basis.

Christian Coenen is professor of marketing and services management at the Zurich University of Applied Sciences. His research interests cover topics such as service quality, customer satisfaction and relationship management, as well as employee service behavior. In Facility Management, his current research projects deal with service value management along the service profit chain, industry-wide reputation and salary subjects, user-centered process management tools and the stakeholder's perspective of perceived value within a client-customer-end-user network.

Morten Elle is associate professor in urban management at the Department of Management Engineering, Technical University of Denmark. His research interest is within the field of sustainable transition of the built environment. He is especially interested in the interplay between technical infrastructure, buildings, citizens and other users of the city.

Ian Ellison graduated in geology and psychology at the University of Durham and holds an MBA in FM from Sheffield Business School, where he now lectures. His research interests concern the interplay of space and language.

John Flowers is responsible for the effective management of Eversheds global property portfolio of just under 1 million square feet of grade A office space. Prior to joining Eversheds, he managed facilities services within the NHS, directing a £200 million PFI scheme, and worked at a national level advising on new procurement initiatives including PFI. John is a chartered engineer; he also holds an MBA and a social sciences degree.

Alan Green offers high-level consultancy and executive coaching services that help leaders realize the benefits of personal or organizational development and transformational change. He was for many years a senior manager at GCHQ, a UK security and intelligence organization, and served across many functional specialisms, including engineering, IT, HR and program management. He was the business change manager and latterly the program director for GCHQ's New Accommodation Programme.

Geir Hansen is an associate professor at the Faculty of Architecture and Fine Art, Department of Architectural Design and Management, NTNU. His research interests are in usability of workplaces, programming and evaluation, architectural management and architectural value and quality in the broadest sense. He is head of two master programs in real estate development and Facilities Management and involved in the Centre for Real Estate and Facilities Management at NTNU.

Barry P. Haynes, PhD, MBA, MSc, BSc (Hons), CBIFM, MRICS, is a principal lecturer at Sheffield Hallam University. Barry is the coauthor of the textbook *Corporate Real Estate Asset Management: Strategy and Implementation.* He is a member of the editorial advisory board for the *Journal of Corporate Real Estate.* In addition, he has been a guest editor for the *Journal of Corporate Real Estate* and *Facilities.*

Birgitte Hoffmann is an associate professor at the Technical University of Denmark, Department of Management Engineering, working with strategies for sustainable transition of the built environment. She has a special focus on cross-sector innovation and learning processes involving citizens/users. She is an experienced facilitator of creative and collaborative processes bringing together different groups and perspectives.

John Hudson is a lecturer at the School of the Built Environment at the University of Salford. He is currently pursuing research into the representation of human and organizational interaction with the built environment in popular culture.

Julie Kortens is head of FM at Channel 4 Television, responsible for FM, estates management, refurbishment, space planning, nonprogramming procurement, business continuity and corporate responsibility. She was 2010 BIFM FM of the Year and Deputy Chair of Women in FM. She previously spent 15 years in HR completing an MA in Employment Strategy. She is committed to bridging the gap between HR and FM.

Goran Lindahl is an associate professor at Chalmers and adjunct professor at Tampere University of Technology. As an architect he has carried out both research and practice within the fields of Facilities Management and project management. His work focuses on users and their experiences, roles and action in projects and workspace planning.

Rachel Macdonald's 30 years in FM, starting in food and beverage services, saw her rise to being the facilities director on the board of a large, acute hospital trust. She is now an independent researcher and consultant with wide networks in the UK's National Health Service. She holds an MBA from the Open University and a DBA from Sheffield Business School with whom she is a visiting research fellow.

Kathy Michell is an associate professor in the Department of Construction Economics and Management at the University of Cape Town. Her primary research interests lie in community-based FM, the social reality intrinsic to FM and in the relationships that exist between the facility, the users and the wider urban precinct.

Huw Morris is pro-vice-chancellor (academic) and dean of the College of Arts and Social Science at the University of Salford. Prior to taking up his present appointment he held academic posts at five other UK universities. He is the author of three books and many journal articles, book chapters and conference papers, and he currently chairs the Association of Business Schools, which represents 116 business schools in the UK.

Peter Munthe-Kaas has a master's degree in welfare studies and performance-design from Roskilde University, mainly working with youth culture and citizenship. Currently he is doing a PhD project on user-driven innovation in socio-technical systems, focusing on urban spaces.

Jeremy Myerson is director and chair of the Helen Hamlyn Centre for Design at the Royal College of Art, London. An author, academic and activist in workplace design, he has written, lectured and consulted widely on the subject. He leads the Centre's Work & City Lab at the RCA and chairs the management board of InnovationRCA, the college's innovation network for business. A graduate of the Royal College of Art, he is the author of many books on design, technology and architecture. His latest book, *New Demographics New Workspace*, was published in summer 2010 by Gower.

Ilfryn Price, originally a geologist, became interested in space and conversations while part of the first Western office in Guangzhou in 1983. He moved into research, then change management, then an academic career with FM since 1993. He has been exploring the parallel dynamics of evolution in geological and organizational timescales since 1991.

Wim Pullen has directed the Dutch Centre for People and Buildings since its inception 10 years ago. The Centre's mission is to develop knowledge about people, work and workplaces and to bring this knowledge to corporate real estate end users. Before that Wim was head of research for the Netherlands' Government Building Agency.

Kathy Roper, CFM, MCR, LEED AP, IFMA Fellow, is associate professor and chair of Integrated Facility Management at the Georgia Institute of Technology, School of Building Construction. She edits the new

IFMA-sponsored *International Journal of Facility Management* and currently serves as IFMA's second vice chair.

Colin Stuart graduated in civil engineering at the University of Bristol and is a member of the Association of Project Management and the Workplace Consulting Organisation. Specializing in office fit-out early in his career, Colin became increasingly interested in the impact of good design on an organization's culture and bottom line. Formerly a partner at EC Harris, Colin is now a principal of Fastfwd Limited, specializing in workplace-driven change.

Jenny Thomas received a PhD from the University of Northumbria, the subject of which was holistic building evaluations. She is an associate of the British Council for School Environments and with them developed a model of post-occupancy evaluation for a national government organization. She is founder and director of Performance Consultancy, specializing in evidence-based design.

Jacqueline Vischer is the author of numerous articles and several books about workspace design and Facilities Management. She has degrees in architecture and psychology, and ran an international consulting practice before joining the University of Montreal to head up its new interior design program. She now runs the new Work Environments Research Group (www.gret.umontreal.ca) and continues to lecture and write about her work.

Daniel von Felten is assistant professor of marketing and business administrationat the Zurich University of Applied Sciences. His research interests in Facility Management cover topics such as service value management along the service profit chain, industry-wide reputation and salary subjects, user-centered process management tools and the stakeholder's perspective of perceived value within a client-customer-end-user network.

Index

Printed in Great Britain
by Amazon

42027280R00163